Margaret Owen

A WORLD OF WIDOWS

D1522551

Ⓩ

ZED BOOKS

London & New Jersey

A World of Widows was first published by
Zed Books Ltd, 7 Cynthia Street, London N1 9JF, UK,
and First Avenue, Atlantic Highlands,
New Jersey 07716, USA
in 1996.

Cover design by Andrew Corbett
Typeset by Photosetting and Secretarial Services
Printed and bound at Biddles Ltd, Guildford and Kings Lynn.

This book was researched with support from Planet 21, a British charity which
promotes people-centred options for sustainable development, and funding
from the Swedish International Development Authority (SIDA)

British Library Cataloguing in Publication Data is available
from the British Library.

Library of Congress Cataloguing-in-Publication Data

Owen, Margaret, 1932-
    A world of widows / Margaret Owen. p. cm.
    Includes bibliographical references and index.
    ISBN 1 85649 419 5. -- ISBN 1 85649 420 9 (pbk.)
    1. Widowhood - Developing countries - Psychological aspects. 2.
Widows - Developing countries - Social conditions. 3 - Widows - Developing
countries - Economic conditions. 4. Widows - Developing countries - Public
opinion. 5. Public opinion - Developing countries. I. Title.
HQ1058.5.D4094 1996
305.9'0654'091722 - dc20   96-16270
                                                                          CIP

ISBN 1 85649 419 5 Hb
ISBN 1 85649 420 9 Pb

Contents

	Foreword	vii
	Introduction	1
1	Becoming a Widow	7
2	Poverty, Work and Income Support	23
3	Laws and Customs Concerning Inheritance	51
4	Sex and Sexuality	71
5	Widowhood in the Context of AIDS	81
6	Remarriage	102
7	Child Widows and the Children of Widows	124
8	Older Widows	148
9	Refugee Widows	166
10	Human Rights, Equality and Legal Protection	178
11	Conclusion: Widows Organising for Change	194
	Index	209

To Robert, greatly missed,
without whose death
this book
would not have been written.

Foreword

I had been widowed only a few months and was about to leave for the USA to teach a course on 'Women, Law, Development and Health' when a widowed Malawian friend, Miriam, came to stay with me. Almost the first question she asked as she look round my livingroom, was whether my husband had living brothers. When I told her that he did, her expression changed to astonishment. 'You mean that they let you stay in this house and allowed you to keep all these things?'.

Although I had been vaguely aware, from anthropology texts, that in some cultures widows were taken over by their husband's kin, or sent away to their natal family, I had not realised until that moment how prevalent the practice still was. (Soon I discovered that it affected many widows in different societies, both urban and rural, illiterate and educated, like my friend.) During her visit she told me of the cruelties she had endured from her brothers-in-law, how she had lost her home, and of the struggle she had fought through the courts to regain custody of her children. I learned about other widows in her ethnic group who had been physically assaulted, forced into remarriage to a relative of the dead husband, refused help by officials, accused of witchcraft, and reduced into begging from neighbours in order to survive.

I too had found adjusting to widowhood painful and traumatic, even though I live in the West where there is no legal or institutional discrimination against widows, and where widows are not openly and obviously ostracised. But Miriam's descriptions of the sufferings of some widows in African societies, and the reports I had read of the austerities traditionally prescribed to, and often endured by widows in rural India in some Hindu castes, made me aware of how fortunate I was to have a home, my state and husband's occupational pension and, most important, my education and earning potential. It was imperative to draw attention to such misery and injustice, not only for widows themselves but for society as whole.

All widows suffer some loss of status in society, since even in many developed countries a woman's position is influenced by that of her father or husband, and a woman on her own is an anomaly. We widows all feel loneliness, grief, and fear concerning how we will live the remainder of our lives. But in the West we enjoy our legal rights, whilst in many Third World societies widows enjoy almost none and are among the most marginalised and oppressed people in the community.

In my professional work as a women-and-development lawyer, I confess I had not thought to address the neglected claims of this category of women. Working for the International Planned Parenthood Federation (IPPF), and as a consultant to United Nations and other international agencies, I tended to concentrate in my work on women at certain stages in their life cycle, as infants, adolescents, mothers, wives and workers, ignoring the life cycle as a whole. Yet almost all ever-married women will at some stage become widows. Even though, at the IPPF, we were concerned with how to tackle the conviction, held by so many women, that they must bear many sons in order to be sure of support in old age, not one of us during my years there suggested that one constructive strategy to reduce family size might be to make widowhood itself less wretched.

My library browsing for studies on widows in developing countries proved unrewarding, although there was an abundance of books on widowhood in the West. The anthropological texts on widows in African ethnic groups, with some notable exceptions, appeared to me to be neocolonial, anthropocentric and too theoretical, studying widows in relation to the kinship group, but not in the context of their daily lives as household heads, carers and workers, often performing triple workloads compared to their married sisters. Nor did the literature on human rights, development, poverty or, indeed, women reveal more than passing references to the status of widows. Although at last domestic violence is being addressed by the Committee on the Elimination of Discrimination against Women (CEDAW) and by governments, the mental and physical abuse that widows in many regions endure remains a neglected topic. A significant omission, for example, in the 1995 Global Platform for Action (GPFA), the document agreed by governments at the 1995 Fourth World Conference on Women, is any specific reference to the physical violence that is the common experience of widows in so many traditional cultures, although other forms of abuse such as genital mutilation, dowry-related assault and child sexual abuse are mentioned. As for India, there are many books, historical and sociological, on the origins and practice of *sati*, but literature is sparse on how present-day Indian widows manage their lives. The excellent work of Marty Chen and Jean Dreze which I came to learn of some time later, did not show up on the computer screens of the libraries I worked in during the early 1990s. Their work is essential reading for anyone interested in research on widowhood.

Inspired by my friend Miriam's visit, the purpose of this book is to open up the hitherto neglected subject of Third World widows and to create awareness of the topic's importance. I do this by drawing attention to major policy issues and to some of the creative initiatives taken by widows organising themselves, and by providing case stories to illustrate the kinds of constraints affecting widows in the Third World and their families.

I hope the chapters that follow will encourage further multidisciplinary and detailed studies exploring what happens to women as they move from marriage to widowhood.

In addition, the book is intended to suggest to those researching other topics - for example, refugee women, ageing, violence, conflict resolution, AIDS, rural development, poverty, child labour, street children, prostitution, domestic service, women and the law - that they prioritise widows as a special category in the process of their studies.[1]

It is thanks to the initial enthusiasm and encouragement of Judith Bruce of the Population Council, New York, and Anna Runeborg and Lena Ekroth of the Swedish International Development Agency (SIDA), that I was able to pursue this neglected area of women's rights. Judith arranged for a small group of interested scholars, including Marty Chen and Betty Potash, to meet together periodically to share information and discuss what might be done to get widows on to the international agenda. SIDA gave me a travel grant. John Rowley of People and the Planet made it all possible.

I cannot thank everyone by name in this foreword, but I am especially grateful to Marty Chen for inviting me to participate at her stunning Widows' Conference in Bangalore, India, in 1994, whose proceedings inform so much of this book, and where I met many wonderful widows who have become my friends. Also I want to thank all the many widows and those organisations that work with them in the countries I visited - Bangladesh, India, Malawi, Kenya, Uganda and Zimbabwe - for the time they gave me in their busy days, for their kindness and their frankness. Their voices speak from this book. This is their story.

Finally, no words can really express my appreciation for the help I received from Anna Gourlay and Louise Murray of Zed Books, and their copy editor, Pat Harper. And to Maggie Jones for reading so many of the drafts and making useful suggestions. I apologise for any errors, especially where current customs are discussed. Such errors are inevitable in a book in which a Westerner, from a particular culture and religion, addresses the issues affecting women in the context of other traditions and norms on the basis of disparate sources of information. I have been mindful of the delicate ground I walk on, and hope that my failings in this area will encourage local scholars to put me right by presenting their own studies of the ethnic groups they are familiar with.

See, example, *Zambia Poetry Assessment* (World Bank Report No. 12985-ZA 1994, 46-7, which presents an analysis of the daily workload of married women and widows.

Introduction

Data

Although widows make up a large proportion of the female population in all societies, research concerning their status in developing countries is lacking. [1] More and better data are needed to inform policy formulation and law reform, so that the commitments made at the international and national levels to promote the equality of men and women are sustained.

We do not know exactly how many widows there are in every country because in only a handful of developing countries has the data been collected and tabulated. Widows are often missed out in census data, especially those who are elderly and are shuttled between the homes of their relatives. Not only are they not counted, but their economic contribution and health status are also invisible.

In India, one of the few developing countries for which data are available, the 1981 census showed that there were over 25 million widows, who comprised about 8 per cent of the total population. This extremely large number means that the proportion of widows in the total female population is comparable to that of agricultural labourers in the total male population. Among women over the age of sixty, the proportion of widows in the female population is more than 60 per cent. Similarly, in a number of countries in Southern Africa, where also data has been collected, the great majority of people widowed are women rather than men: in Botswana 87 per cent, Lesotho 82 per cent, Swaziland 91 per cent, Zambia 87 per cent and Zimbabwe 89 per cent at the 1991 census. [2] (In Britain, the 1991 population census showed 3 million widows, comprising about 6 per cent of the total population.)

In countries where there have recently been armed conflicts, such as Mozambique, Cambodia, El Salvador, Rwanda and Bosnia the proportion of widows is likely to be even higher since so many men have died fighting. (Many women do not know if they are widowed or not: they are the wives of the 'disappeared'.) The majority of refugees are women and children, and their numbers include many widows. The AIDS pandemic has widowed millions of women. In addition, girls are still married as children - often to much older men - in many parts of the world, and in consequence may find themselves facing all the disadvantages of widowhood even before they have reached adulthood (see Chapter 7). Such unions are reported to be on the increase in some communities where myths about protection from the AIDS virus have encouraged men to seek school-age brides (see Chapter 5).

Figure 1.1 demonstrates that across the globe widows make up a significant proportion of all women ranging from 8 to 13 per cent of the adult female population. Proportions of widows are generally highest in the developed countries because in them greater longevity and lower fertility levels increase the ratio of old to young in the population, and as women tend to outlive men there are more females among the elderly.

In all regions the proportion of widowers is far lower. The reasons for this include the frequent great age gap at marriage, the longer life expectancy of women, widower remarriage, polygamy, and the high risk of early death among men in consequence of accidents, crimes of violence, war, and AIDS. Although according to the World Health Organisation (WHO) more than half a million Third World women are estimated to die anually from causes relating to childbirth and pregnancy, unsafe abortion and genital mutilation, these early deaths do not significantly change the demographic picture.

The lack of precise demographic data and research concerning widows contributes to the persistence of misconceptions about the prevalence and conditions of widowhood in many countries. Although very few national surveys of widowhood have been conducted in developing countries with the express purpose of revealing the special circumstances of widows' lives, available national census data from a cross-section of these countries calls into question the five most common assumptions about widows: that they are mostly elderly women whose children are fully grown; that they can rely on an extended family network for financial and emotional support; that the joint family system guarantees a woman's access to family resources in widowhood; that offspring, especially sons, provide secure financial support to widowed mothers; and that widows remarry, often into the extended family. Such myths were firmly dispelled when widowhood was discussed by activists and scholars in a series of workshops at the Non-Governmental Organisations Forum in Beijing in September 1995.

The failure to focus on the conditions in which widows live in many different cultures and countries is particularly reprehensible considering the seriousness of the deprivation suffered, how widespread it is, and how badly it affects the welfare of their children. For example, among girl children it is the daughters of widows who are most likely to be deprived of education and thrust into an early marriage to an older man, so that the cycle of deprivation and premature widowhood perpetuates itself.

The two major exceptions to the literature's neglect of widows are the work of Marty Chen and Jean Dreze on north Indian widows and Betty Potash's collection of essays on widows in African societies.[7] However, empirical evidence and anecdotal reports from many regions of the Third World indicate that widows, of all ages and from different backgrounds and cultures, are likely to be subject to multiple forms of discrimination, neglect, oppression and abuse. Throughout history widows have been seen as needing support, but today community and family support systems are frequently no longer capable of providing what is needed.[4] Therefore concerted action has to be taken by governments and NGOs working in tandem at local, national, regional and international levels.

Who is a widow

A major problem for researchers and policy makers in developing countries is how to define widowhood. The way in which a woman who has lost a partner views herself and how she is viewed by her community has a bearing on whether she is a widow or not.

During the course of interviewing widows for this book, I discovered that some women were regarded by their community as widows for the purpose of rituals even though they did not perceive themselves as such. Conversely, many widows, despite considering themselves to be the official wives of the deceased, were rebuffed by their in-laws who refused to accept them as such. Various situations painful to a bereaved woman can arise: for example, it is not uncommon for a widow attending her husband's funeral to find that women are present with their children - of whom she had no previous knowledge - claiming that they are the real widows and that she has no rights. Such confrontations are distressing and difficult to resolve. Confusion can arise when co-widows and co-habitees each compete for the greater share of a deceased man's property. It is not often clear whether co-wives inherit equally or in order of seniority.

A woman might think that she had been married according to custom, only to learn at her partner's death that she had not - because, for example, all or part of the brideprice had not been paid. Such a disavowal has implications for the woman's access to resources, land, home, inheritance, for the custody of children, and indeed for the widow's economic survival.

The extent of cohabitation and the processual nature of customary marriage, as well as the confusion arising from the plurality of legal systems in many developing countries, make basing the definition of

widowhood on marriage alone an unsafe approach. Even if both parties
believed that they were married under the modern law, at death the
widow may still find herself subject to customary law as interpreted by
hostile male elders. This ambiguous and confusing situation compounds
the difficulties of collecting valid data on widowhood.

With few exceptions, loss of status appears to be the common
inheritance of widows everywhere - even in developed countries such
as Britain. But the widow's loss of status in many Third World countries
is such that she is deprived of her fundamental human rights, as are often
her dependent children (see Chapter 1).[5]

Population and sustainable development

Widowhood should be acknowledged not only as a human rights issue
but also as a population issue since it is well documented that a woman's
fear of widowhood without adult sons for support is an important factor
in influencing family size. Childlessness is particularly disadvantageous
for widows, more so than for widowers. Loss of a husband coupled with
childlessness (or in many societies specifically sonlessness) generally
increases dramatically the social and economic burdens imposed on a
woman; moreover, such a situation is regarded as a disgrace and the
woman's fault. A childless or sonless widow is generally more insecure
and vulnerable than one who has male offspring. Women believe they
must bear many sons to ensure their security in old age, as well as to
ensure their husband will remain with them. Although there is substantial
evidence in both Africa and India that sons may abandon their mothers
and that a mother's relationship with her daughter is often closer than
that with her son - many elderly widows are in fact looked after by their
daughters - the girl child continues to suffer neglect and discrimination.
If girls were treated as equals with their brothers, given inheritance rights
and equal access to education and employment, widows would know they
could depend on their daughters when they become old, and fertility
decisions might alter.

Equally important is the need for support for rural widows' claims
to land for subsistence farming. Many widows are forced to migrate to
towns once they lose their rights to cultivate family land. Ensuring that
widows' land rights are protected by the local courts helps to save
widows and their children from destitution. Protection of land rights is
a particularly urgent issue when refugee widows return to their countries
of origin (see Chapter 9).

Human rights, equality and the elimination of discrimination
During the UN Decade for Women, 1975-85, little concern was

expressed about the impact of widowhood on women's lives. Neither the Convention on the Elimination of All Forms of Discrimination against Women (CEDAW) nor the Decade for Women's key document, the Forward-Looking Strategies for the Advancement of Women to the Year 2000 (FLS) addressed in any depth the constraints women face on the death of a spouse.[6] It is remarkable that the only reference to widows in the FLS is in Paragraph 286 concerning elderly women, as if the millions of child and girl widows did not exist.

The 1995 Global Plan for Action does not directly or specifically commit governments to remove discrimination against widows, but its general concern with human rights, family law and violence is most pertinent to their status. The reference to the need to reform inheritance laws is particularly relevant to widowhood.

It seems that at last, the international community is beginning to understand the importance of protecting the rights of this very large category of women: not merely for their own sakes, but for the sakes of their children. The majority of ever-married women are likely to spend some part of their lives as widows. Widowhood is the inevitable destiny of almost every girl child in those developing countries where most women are married when young.

The Global Platform for Action 1995 (GPFA) recognises this fact in Paragraph 274(d), which requires governments to 'eliminate the injustices and obstacles in relation to inheritance faced by the girl child by enacting legislation guaranteeing equal rights to succession and equal rights to inheritance, regardless of the sex of the child'.

The GPFA, the Convention on the Elimination of All Forms of Discrimination against Women, as well as other key international instruments and declarations (see Chapter 10 on Human Rights) do provide strong leverage for ensuring that governments address the inequalities and injustices that victimise and marginalise widows. It is now up to lobbyists and campaigners in national NGOs and in academia to make sure that at least the country plans for implementation of all the important world conferences of the 1990s put widows and widowhood on the agenda.

In some societies of course widows enjoy a respected status, commanding considerable economic resources, and, freed from the restrictions of marriage, possessing far greater independence than their married sisters. In the chapters ahead, however, the focus is on those widows who are the most economically, socially and physically vulnerable group of women within a population.

1.   *The World's Women*, 2nd edition, 1995. United Nations.

2.   *Picking Up the Pieces: Widowhood in Southern Africa*, 1995. Women and Law in Southern Africa Research Trust/Working Paper No. 13, p. 3.

3.   See, in particular, M. Chen and J. Drèze, 1992. 'Widows and Well-being Rural North India', London School of Economics, Development Economics Research Programme; and B. Potash, *Widows in African Societies*, 1986, Stanford Press.

4.   Margaret Owen, 'The World of the Widow', *People and the Planet*, Vol. 3, No. 2, 1994, p. 17.

5.   See, for example, Helen Lopata on Widows in the US, and Peter Townsend in the UK *Widows and their Families*, Routledge and Kegan Paul, 1958.

6.   The Nairobi Forward-Looking Strategies for the Advancement of Women adopted by the Third UN World Conference on Women, Nairobi, to appraise the Achievements of the UN Decade for Women.

CHAPTER 1

Becoming a Widow

'The first time someone called me a widow it was as if my body burst. The pain, the grief. "Keep your eyes downcast. You are a widow now," my mother-in-law ordered me. "You have eaten up my son, so you must suffer".'

This was how a thirty-year-old widow from Bihar, attending a widows' conference in India in 1994,[1] recalled her introduction to widowhood. Later, after she had returned to her village she wrote to the nongovernmental organisation which had arranged the workshop:

'Attending this meeting was the first and only time I had ever left my house or my village since my husband died when I was twenty-two. My neighbours taunted me for going away to the widows' meeting. When I returned they jeered and accused me of having gone off with a man.'

In some traditional societies initiation into widowhood may be violent and cruel. In developed regions of the world too, widows may discover that the change in their marital status is deeply disturbing, and that the alteration in the way the outside world regards them contains elements of callousness and insensitivity.

Death is always shocking to those closely associated with the dead person. Whether it comes after a long illness, or is sudden and violent, it is an awesome event, a challenge to our emotional and spiritual understanding. But for all women, the death of a husband has an extra significance because it represents not simply the departure of a partner, protector, and breadwinner but also heralds a radical change in her social status and lifestyle. The situation is bad enough for many widows in the West. Elderly women living alone with an aged husband may feel redundant once that husband dies and there is no longer a companion to care for. Those who lose their husbands in middle age may feel they have missed out on the delights of growing old together in a planned retirement, sharing the pleasures of grandchildren and recreation.

Suddenly such women are faced with the new responsibility of dealing with matters, such as wills, mortgages, finance and taxation, formerly dealt with by their partners; they can easily be victims of exploitation and sometimes dishonest practices by those representing themselves as competent to administer their affairs for them. All this applies to many Third World widows also. Widows in poorer countries, however, also often endure cruel and institutionalised social ostracisation; their inferior status is underscored by the dictates of traditional mores associated with mourning and funeral rites, by discrimination under both modern, customary and religious laws, and by the engrained attitudes of government officials and community leaders.

Disorientation is felt by almost all widows everywhere. Widowhood tends to impact far more traumatically upon women than men, altering forever the way they are seen by the external society and affecting their self-image. Loneliness, reduced income, loss of status, fear of the future, and depression are the common experiences, whether the women bereaved are mothers encumbered with young children, middle-aged women whose children have flown the nest, or the elderly, and whether they are from the First or the Third World. Feelings of deprivation and isolation are usually more severe and long-lasting than among widowers, since bereaved men are more likely to remarry. As male members of society they have freedom to socialise, and their movements are not restricted by taboos.

Significantly, so common is widowhood to women and so uncommon to men that no word exists in the vernacular languages of Southern Africa to describe a man whose wife has died. 'We looked, we searched, we asked "where are the widowers?" and no one could find us such a man! They remarry so fast or they have several wives and girlfriends", explained a woman lawyer at a Southern African workshop on widows held at the Beijing NGO Forum in 1995.

In Western countries, although no laws or institutionalised traditions exist that seclude a widow in her house and force her to withdraw from the company of men, subtle constraints may still operate to control how she comports herself. She must act discreetly as she explores new relationships, aware that if she is too outgoing she may be regarded as sex-starved and 'searching for a man'. Wealthy widows may be an easy prey for male fortune-seekers. But in some Hindu castes and certain African ethnic groups a widow who manifests interest in a member of the opposite sex is in danger of being regarded as a prostitute, branded as evil because by surviving her husband she is suspected of causing his death. She may be persecuted and accused of witchcraft. (There are frequent reports of widows being murdered in these circumstances.)

Thus the need of many widows for male companionship and a sexual relationship is barely recognised except in negative terms.[2] (See chapters 4 and 8.)

In developing countries extreme poverty afflicts great numbers of widows, especially the elderly or those left with dependent children. (See Chapter 2.) Even in industrialised countries, where national state social security schemes operate, a considerable gap in living standards exists between widows dependent on state handouts and those with private pensions or other private means. One English widow wrote that the derisory amounts of UK state benefit ensured widows' 'virtual imprisonment in their homes because money is so short'.[3] Such relative deprivation can be almost as soul-destroying and humiliating as total destitution in the developing world.

All human societies have sought ways to make death acceptable, less fearful and absolute and to provide opportunities for expressing grief and showing respect for the dead person. These traditions evolved to accommodate the irreconcilable conflicts inherent in death. Where they have died away, the experience of managing bereavement may be, in some ways, harder without family and community support.

In Western countries today, the ceremonies are minimal and once the funeral is over so is the public display of mourning. Fifty years ago in Britain, widows might have worn black for several months and men might have worn black armbands, but since the end of the Second World War such marks of grief are rare. Some European widows admit to longings for the old trappings of widowhood: 'So that the world can witness the great change in my identity and position' as one said. They feel a need for some rite of passage to mark the sudden change in their circumstances, and find the weeks and months after the funeral most difficult to bear and an anticlimax to the drama of the death and funeral ceremony. In traditional societies mourning rites still possess important cultural values, but behaviour surrounding mourning is inherently gendered. Rituals are more to do with exalting the position of the dead man than with allowing a real outlet for the widow's grief, although women are expected to grieve openly and to demonstrate the intensity of their feelings in formalised ways. Far more restrictions are placed on a widow than on a widower. It is widows, not widowers, who must endure the most humiliating rituals - in relation, for example, to dress, food, hygiene, and sexual activity. These rituals were intended as ways of showing public respect for the dead and proof of the inconsolable sadness of the widow. The fundamental social change in her lifestyle is dramatised, emphasising her faithfulness to his memory, and her chastity. Hence, many mourning customs diminish a widow's

attractiveness by desexualising her through dress codes and placing
taboos on her participation in social affairs.

In northern Ghana, where polygamy is common, a man may die
leaving many widows and numerous children.

> 'When a man dies his widow or widows must all stay inside, sitting
> alone, stripped naked with leaves on the private parts. They cannot
> go out of the house unless they carry a calabash which is a symbol
> of the deceased. They are taken out naked, accompanied by an old
> lady, to drink a special brew. After the funeral the widows are asked
> who they wished to marry but they invariably have little choice, for,
> if a man can get to sleep with one of them and can tell a close relative
> of his success he will be given the widow as his wife'. [4]

In the funeral rituals of the matrilineal Akan, of southern Ghana,
widows must remain constantly with the body of their dead husband
until burial: 'their position is one of great danger during this period, for
it is thought that should the *sunsun* or spirit of the dead man return and
have sexual intercourse with them, they will forever be barren[5] (see also
Chapter 4). In Swaziland and the western part of Zambia, the widow is
kept under a blanket until the burial. During this time she will be verbally
abused and accused of killing her husband. Similar customs are followed
in Zambia and Lesotho. [6]

In India, Pakistan and Bangladesh, a widow may face a life of extreme
wretchedness and deprivation from the moment her husband dies (see
Chapter 2). Muslim widows, although they have a right to one eighth
of their husband's wealth (see Chapter 3), can still suffer grave
disadvantages, for they may not necessarily enjoy the rights the Koran
has decreed for them. In purdah and in higher-caste Hindu households
widows are often denied the freedom to remarry or to move freely
outside the home, and are also often resented and regarded as economic
burdens by the relatives they must reside with (see Chapter 6). Far too
little is known about how these women actually fare within a household
headed by male relatives, but it is thought that very many Indian,
Pakistani and Bangladeshi widows endure great hardships at the hands
of their in-laws (and sometimes their brothers) within the confines of
the home, exploited economically as unpaid servants, and also sexually.
Research concerning the situation of such women is difficult to
undertake since they live in virtual seclusion.

Among some ethnic groups in Africa many customs subject the
widow to degrading treatment. When widows' obligations to conform
to tradition were balanced by the reciprocal duties of support from the

husband's family, they may have seemed less inhuman, but today they represent discrimination. Today's reality is that increasingly, in the Third World, as many of the case studies describe, the extended or joint family is fragmenting and in many regions is becoming a myth of the past through the combined pressures of poverty, migration, urbanisation, land shortage and conflict. Studies in some Southern African countries, for example, show that so-called customs are often used as an excuse to gain control over a widow so as to acquire property, and not to protect her. [7]

> Jose, half Yoruba, is more fortunate than many Nigerian widows for she escaped the most extreme treatment in her widowhood. When her Igbo husband was shot by armed robbers the elders took pity on her, coming as she did from the town, and working as a qualified accountant. She was *not* forced to wear black for a year, drink the water used to wash her husband's corpse, maintain a dusk-to-dawn curfew, or submit to other types of degrading and distressing practices inflicted in the name of tradition. Nor was she inherited by her husband's brothers or forced to have sex with one of them. Not one of her in-laws raided her house or seized her possessions.
>
> She did however lose her beautiful waist-long hair within hours of her arrival at her husband's village for the three-day funeral, for Igbo custom insists that a widow must be shaved after the burial of her husband. She returned to Lagos and her job with a scarf round her head, grateful to the old woman barber for having not made her completely bald as was usual. [8]

A widow often suffers from the cruelty and greed of her husband's kin: with no adult male to protect her, she becomes an easy victim of various forms of exploitation, including sexual exploitation.

Studies of aspects of widowhood in some Latin American and Caribbean countries tell the same story of poverty, vulnerability, and loneliness. [9] In Jamaica, a study showed how middle-class widows were as prone to sudden changes in their social status as those in lower classes. Invitations to important social functions for persons who were members of the local economic elite, as their husbands had been, were now withheld from them. Some women noted that in the first year of widowhood these invitations continued to be extended but gradually the numbers diminished until invitations ceased altogether. [10] Such experience is echoed in the social treatment of some British widows. Peter Marris found that in east London widowhood impoverished women's social lives and that some widows were driven to suicide because of loneliness.[11] Similarly, Helen Lopata found extreme deprivation and desolation among widows in the USA.[12] Married women often view the widow as a threat, as an available woman who might steal their husbands, and so tend to isolate her socially. Sisters-in-law, the wives of brothers from whom a widow, with memories of close childhood ties, had anticipated kindness and support, may show a harsh unwillingness to include her in their social life and accept a resurrection of former sibling affection. As families are now smaller and children and other relatives dispersed far away, the widow often lives alone. One English woman wrote, 'Every time I was asked out it was for "supper, just the three of us" in the kitchen, when we had previously enjoyed long evenings of laughter and gossip in the dining room, and the only widow at the feast was Veuve Cliquot'.[13] (This author recalled how, once widowed, invitations to dinner with couples diminished in number significantly. She was, however, summoned to 'test' the recipes for forthcoming dinner parties from which she was excluded, and invited to eat up the 'leftovers' the day after such dinners had occurred.)

In Western societies such alterations in status are not institutionalised in laws and rigid customs and are so subtle as to be barely visible to the outside observer. Probably the sort of discriminating social attitudes described above apply more to an older generation, are possibly class-orientated and, in any case, are now steadily declining as more women move into professional and business life, single motherhood becomes the norm, there is less dependency on couple-oriented recreation, and the independence and sexuality of women of all ages is acknowledged. Western widows, with state or private pensions, legal rights to their husbands' estates, free health care and shelter in old age, will never experience the extreme discrimination and breaches of fundamental human rights that millions of Third World widows endure.

In a small hut made of mud, branches and leaves, in Gujerat, northern India, a Hindu widow described what happened when her young husband died after a bus collided with his rickshaw. A week later she gave birth to her third child alone, except for a kind old widowed neighbour. Her mother-in-law and her sons had visited her just once, the day after the accident, to collect what they considered was their property. The brothers-in-law searched the small shelter for money. Her husband's mother screamed abuse at her: ' You have eaten my son.' They took away her cooking pots, and her store of rice and ghee. By the end of the month they had managed to persuade the local *panchayat* (village council) that they had a right to the small strip of land on which the young mother grew her subsistence crops. They threatened to seize her older children if she made any complaint to the authorities.

Another widow from Maharashtra in India reported how she was blamed for her husband's death: ' My mother-in-law shouted " You are a witch. You ate him up. You brought bad luck on our family. Don't show me your face, you are evil", and her other sons also accused me saying "You ate him up."'

Ritual cleansing

In African societies, the end of mourning is usually marked by some form of cleansing ritual. For example, in Botswana, Lesotho, Swaziland and western Zambia, as in several Francophone countries, shaving the widow's hair and washing her in herbs is believed to wash away the deceased's spirit and the general bad luck associated with the loss of a husband. But in Lesotho and Swaziland in-laws have been known to punish the widow physically and psychologically by delaying the end of the mourning period so that she cannot mix in the normal way in the community.

Because only a husband's family can undertake the cleansing ritual, the widow often finds herself unable to assert herself in relation to other matters arising from the bereavement such as inheritance, access to land, and custody of children. In Zambia an inheritance study revealed that one reason why widows would not permit further interviews with their in-laws for the case studies was that they feared that the cleansing ritual would be extended as a punishment of them for talking to the researchers. One thirty-year-old widow in Zambia said: 'They are a very difficult family. If you talk to them they will think I am complaining how my brother-in-law has taken over our shop completely. I am not yet cleansed and I know they won't bother if you go and interview him.'[14]

Cleansing rituals, which may be degrading and harmful, can be used to instil fear in a widow and to control her. Yet, many conversations with widows in different ethnic groups show that even when the rituals may be humiliating, many widows desire to be 'cleansed' so as to prove their identity as the widow of the dead man. Without the 'cleansing' they may lose whatever rights a widow has under custom to his estate. Also, in some ethnic groups in Zambia, widows are expected to have sexual relations with a male relative as a cleansing ritual. In other groups, the sexual partner may have to be a stranger, or the heir, or even a group of male relatives. Sometimes these activities take place at the time of the funeral ceremonies, or on a journey. Or the widow might be approached very soon after her husband has died. The idea is to cleanse the widow of the evil spirit that could harm her children, but such customs can facilitate the transmission of HIV and other sexually transmitted diseases. Succumbing to pressure from the husband's family, they may be cleansed because they fear ostracism or physical violence.

A Kikuyu widow who had been married to a Luo man recalled such a 'cleansing' ritual:

> 'The day my husband fell down and died in our house, his brothers came to collect his body for burial in his village. There were three of them and they forced themselves on me sexually saying it was their custom. I could not resist although I fought with them. They beat me and pulled out my hair. They said I belonged to them. I pleaded that my husband had never believed in these things, but they were too strong for me. They gave me a special brew to drink so that I felt dizzy. Later when I awoke I found that they had taken away my children and all my household items. They left me only the bed, and one cooking pot. All my husband's clothes had been taken. They had put them in a van with the body.'

Not all widows oppose ritual cleansing by sex with a male relative. One Kenyan widow who now runs a highly successful organisation assisting AIDS widows and their children to become self-supporting spoke candidly of the sexual needs of widows. 'Grief is like passion. Passion can make us full of desire, or greatly needing to find love and intimacy. AIDS widows, expected to sleep with their husband's brothers, have come to me begging me to help them crying " we are full of sexual desire but we do not want to kill our brothers-in-law or harm their wives. What shall we do?' She suggests that they find a man who is, like them, HIV positive, and she provides them with condoms. (Ritual cleansing through sexual intercourse is discussed more fully in chapters 4 and 5.)

Sexual harassment

Outside these customs, there is much anecdotal and cross-cultural evidence that widows without a man to protect them are more open to sexual attack than other women and that this vulnerability extends to their daughters. One of the reasons African widows give for withdrawing fatherless daughters from school attendance, where the distances to school are great, is that they are concerned for their daughters' safety and reputation since predatory men need have no fear of a father's wrath.[15] In addition, worsening economic conditions in some countries affect how women are treated on the death of their husbands.[16] Sexual services may be expected in return for any assistance a man renders a woman on her own. Widows are reluctant, with good reason, to report sexual attacks (see Chapter 4). The rising tide of religious fundamentalism also contributes to how society perceives the woman, extolling female chastity, and encouraging prurience. The slightest wrong move and the widow is branded as immoral.

The levirate
In various ethnic groups in Africa and in some communities and castes in India, the custom of levirate, according to which a widow is remarried to her husband's brother or other male relative, exists to support the widow and to ensure that any future children she has are conceived in the name of the dead man. In Africa, death does not necessarily end a marriage.[17] A fertile wife, for whom *lobola* or brideprice has been paid may continue to belong to her husband's lineage, and his brother will help to honour him by making his widow pregnant. In past times, leviratic union was acknowledged to provide the support a widow needed in order to continue to live in her husband's village: this was neccessary because rarely, in patrilineal kinship systems, would a widow have rights in her natal home.

Today, with increased awareness of women's rights, concerns for sexual health and for existing children, and fear of conflict with co-wives of the *levir*, many widows, especially more educated women, resist this custom. Tragically, this resistance can sow seeds of violent conflict: too frequently widows have been raped by relatives, sometimes in order to acquire control over the dead man's property. In other cases, a widow's refusal to enter into such a union results in her in-laws taking revenge by abandoning her to destitution, evicting her from her house, denying her rights to property, and access to land for subsistence farming. She may lose her children, or find the husband's relatives have taken all the money, collected at the funeral for school fees, for themselves. Sometimes an elderly widow may be given to a very young man without consideration of the problems of sexual incompatibility that might arise.

Chola is a widow in her late forties in a Zambian village. This is her tale:

'They appointed someone in the family to replace my dead husband, but I refused because I was upset that they had accused me of killing the man I had been married to for many years. They threatened me and said if I would not marry the boy in their family it would show I was guilty. There was so much pressure from the village chief, and even my own relatives, that I had to agree. I even got a son after some months. But after that the boy beat me badly and ill-treated my children. He chased me back to my father and took all the property from me'.[18]

A Ugandan widow, Irene, described her experience to a case worker at the Uganda branch of the International Federation of Women Lawyers (FIDA):

'We were living happily in the town with our two children when my husband was killed. His bicycle ran into a pothole in the road and he broke his skull. His brothers came and they beat me up because I am not from his tribe, and they said I had used witchcraft on him. They were very rough with me. They collected his body from the morgue and took my children to their village. When I went for the funeral they had decided I had to marry the youngest brother. He is only fifteen and I am twenty-six, and he was very feeble-minded, and not strong. They tried to make me have sex with him and they locked me in a hut with him all night, but I protected myself and besides he was only a boy. When I refused they sent me away but they kept my children, Elizabeth was three years and Erissa is a boy of five. I was in a torment for I had no money, we had only a rented room in the city and so I could not send the children to school.'

This widow lost both her children to her husband's relatives. Later she discovered that not only had they not been given schooling, as promised, but that they had been so physically abused that the little girl had died, and the boy had been forced to work in a neighbour's field in return for food. (The practice of levirate is further discussed in Chapter 6.)

Clothes, adornment and food

Rituals concerning the physical appearance of widows, and restrictions on their diet and lifestyle exist in many cultures. Orthodox Jewish women still shave their heads on widowhood, and in Mediterranean countries widows traditionally wear black. There appears to be an almost universal wish, patriarchal in origin, to de-sex the widow, to emphasise her celibacy, to make her look undesirable, whereas a widower normally has no such obligations as a way of showing regret for the death of a wife. By insisting that widows are shabbily dressed, unadorned, and sometimes dirty, the codes reinforce the powerful negative images of the widow as a witch, whore, evil sorceress and temptress.

Among the Hausa of northern Nigeria and in some other parts of West Africa a widow is not supposed to decorate her body; she is forbidden to use perfumed soap and must wash ritually each Friday with the traditional black nupe soap usually used to cleanse the newborn. Instead of her normal clothes she must wear an old gown and neither change or launder it until the mourning period of at least a month is over. She cannot eat cola nuts or rub tobacco flowers on her mouth. In some other Nigerian groups, widows must forgo washing altogether for a specified period, drink the water that has been used to wash the husband's corpse, eat only bland food from a broken plate, and lie on the bare earth to sleep. The Luo of Kenya and neighbouring countries require the widow to wear her husband's clothes inside out, or to wrap herself in a special cloth, instead of the type of skirt denoting status as a married woman.

Some widows wish to discontinue such customs which are considered old-fashioned and which interfere with their work. Women who work in the public sector, in schools, hospitals, or government offices, need to be able to dress normally so that they can continue to earn for their families. However, non-compliance with certain customs can provoke disapproval and retaliation from the husband's kin, enabling them to accuse the widow of impropriety or of not being the true wife but a prostitute. On the other hand, one Shona widow in southern Zimbabwe told of her distress when her father-in-law counselled her to discontinue such mourning customs and wear her ordinary clothes. She felt that her husband's memory was dishonoured, and that she was not accorded the dues of a widow by the kin, as if she were an impostor.

A Hindu widow, especially in the higher castes such as Brahmins, must visibly change her appearance upon the death of her husband, so that for the rest of her life she can be seen by the husband's family and the community to be grieving for his death and doing penance for the sin of having outlived him. In families that adhere strictly to custom, a Hindu widow must live the life of an ascetic. Coloured saris, bright bangles, the *kumkum* (the red mark of marriage on her brow), ornaments, flowers, nose rings, perfumes must no longer be worn. She must sleep on the ground, and dress in a simple white or undyed cotton sari, often without a blouse or petticoat. Rules that widows must not oil their hair or wear attractive clothing ensure that women look wretched; yet it is just these images of unkempt women that are associated with prostitutes and witches. (A Bengali film about the tragedy of a widow's life is appropriately titled *White Threads*.)

In earlier times Hindu widows were expected to shave their hair and there are still strict Brahmin families that enforce this degradation on widows. The righteous Hindu widow is expected to live this simple life until she dies, for in higher castes remarriage is not approved of. A Hindu widow, still today, is considered 'inauspicious'. Just to walk in a widow's shadow is to court disaster. Thus, she may not attend weddings: even if her own daughter is to be married, she cannot attend the festivities for she would bring ill-luck on all the guests.

In some Hindu castes, relish, pickles or spices and other rich food are considered to make a woman lustful. Luxuries in food are thought to heat the blood and stimulate the passions. Similar dietary prohibitions are imposed on some African widows. Sometimes the dishes widows eat from must be broken, or left unwashed. Special alcoholic brews are sometimes served to widows to make them dizzy and less resistant to certain sexual rites. (No one has ever suggested that if hot food were denied to men, women might enjoy greater sexual safety.)

Indian widows attending the conference of rural widows in Bangalore in 1994 resolved that, on their return to their villages, they would put on coloured saris and bangles, sing and dance, and invite other widows to their daughters' marriages. These brave women had risked their reputations to leave their villages to attend the workshop, knowing that on their return, adorned with bangles, *kumkum,* and coloured saris, they would have to face gossip and rumour, as indeed they did.[19] 'Cannot! Cannot! Cannot!' thundered one indignant and militant young northern Indian widow at that meeting. 'That is what we are told from the moment we lose our husbands. We cannot show our faces early in the morning. We cannot attend public functions or celebrations. We cannot wear flowers, or jewellery.'

Health and mortality

In societies where the status of women is low, the sufferings of widows are particularly acute. In northern India research has uncovered a high mortality of widows compared with currently married women of the same age. In southern India where remarrying castes are more prevalent and where women tend to be less restricted, womens' health and mortality appear less affected by widowhood (see Chapter 8).

Little research has been undertaken on the health and mortality consequences of widowhood except in India. But it is known that unsupported widows generally, in particular elderly women abandoned in rural areas, are often left without any access to health services just at the time in their lives when they most need medical care (see chapters 6 and 7).

Suicide

No one knows precisely how many Third World widows commit suicide to escape the horrors of their lives, but suicide among widows certainly occurs in all countries where the status of women is low and where widows face extreme degradation and neglect.[20]

The most extreme manifestation of cruelty toward widows is the Hindu custom of *sati*, the ritual immolation of a Hindu widow on her husband's funeral pyre. [21] Here her life is seen to be so worthless that she is considered to be better off dead. *Sati* was made a criminal offence in 1859, after years of campaigning by Indian activists, scholars and the British administration. [22] In the twentieth century there has been additional penal legislation, but the practice still occurs in the more backward states of northern India. Draconian laws introduced in 1988 have sought to punish those involved in this hideous rite, and prohibit any celebration at *sati* shrines. But like Indian laws to reduce bride harassment and dowry murder, or to reduce female foeticide or infanticide, they have only a limited effect. Every act of *sati* in India immediately attracts a vast amount of media attention, but no corresponding concern is shown for the daily sufferings experienced by millions of Hindu widows that drive some to the extremity of ending their lives. The following case was widely reported in the Indian press.

Roop Kanwar was an educated eighteen-year-old woman from a modern village in the state of Rajasthan who became a *sati* in 1987 and was elevated to a mystical level throughout the country. Hundreds of pilgrims made their way to the glorified shrine, considerably enriching local traders. To be promised '30,000 years of paradise - as many years as the hairs on a human body' can be seen as an understandable inducement to such suicide, when the alternative is a life of suffering and shame. The case of Roop Kanwar made headlines in both the Indian and the international press, but the people involved, the girl's father and brothers, were never imprisoned.

The following case story from a northern Indian village illustrates the harsh predicament of a widow trying desperately to protect herself. Kodiben had three children when her husband died. Soon afterwards her married brother-in-law, living with her in the joint family, tried to rape her. His wife knew of the incident and was jealous. The second time he caught Kodiben when she was collecting firewood and she was badly hurt. Bravely she appealed to the *panchayat* (village council) for justice and protection. Its members decided that she should live separately but that her widowed father-in-law should live with her to protect her. The jointly owned land was divided and she, her children and the old man began to live in another house. At first everything was all right, but then the father-in-law began to harass her sexually. Desperate, she appealed again to the *panchayat* but its members refused to believe her this time. They accepted the father-in-law's version and condemned Kodiben for her loose ways. Kodiben was distraught with shame and felt she could no longer hold her head up in the village. She drowned herself in the pond the next night.

Unhappy marriages

Whether the marriage was arranged by parents and kin as in traditional societies, or occurred following a Western pattern of dating or cohabitation, relations between a husband and wife can be fraught with conflict. At the widows' conference held in Bangalore in 1994, many Indian women spoke of their relief at their husband's death: something they could never admit to anyone before they met together. It was suggested by one woman that emphasis on the problems of widowhood often submerges those of marriage. Yet the death of a husband may still be a tragedy for the survivor; guilt as well as resentment can make recovery from the shock of bereavement more difficult.

In societies where marriages are arranged by the family and women have little independence or equality, as in India, Pakistan and Bangladesh, for very poor women marriage can be a torment. The Anti-slavery Society calls some unions 'servile marriages'. Childless or child widows are likely to be given as brides to much older, often widowed, men. Very poor girls without dowry find themselves wedded to men whose physical, mental, social or economic attributes make them the least attractive of possible partners. When these women's husbands die, they may feel nothing but relief, but this sentiment must never be divulged. They must still go through the motions of mourning and obey the customs.

A Nigerian Hausa widow remembered: 'When your husband dies, you must wail. If you loved him you are sad at heart also; if you didn't particularly like him, you wail because of compassion and you had got used to him and he isn't there.' Hiraben, a Hindu widow from Uttar Pradesh said, ' I could never admit this to anyone before, but I was relieved when my husband died. My life has been living hell. He drank so much and he beat me. I could never give him a son. I gave birth to eight children and all the boys - there were three - died within a few days of their birth. He has poured boiling water over me; he has hit me with a stick. I am glad he is dead. No more drunken beatings. No more forced sex. No more torture. Now, even so, I have to show respect, live now with this white sari, eat the dull food.' She told of how much she had cried on becoming a widow; but one day her tears suddenly dried because she realised she wasn't really sad. At last she could enjoy a day without a beating.

Abusive names

Indicative of the disfavour in which widows are held, the words used to denote bereaved women often have obscene meanings. It is significant that similar language is used in many different regions - usually to do with witchcraft and lasciviousness.

Rand, randi, raki are vulgar names for widows in Bangladesh and in India. They mean 'prostitute', 'harlot', and 'whore', someone who is easily available. Widows are also named *daken* which means 'witch' or 'sorceress'. In one northern Indian state a widow is called a *'ghoomane phirnavvalli'*, or one who moves around. Describing a woman as being mobile is tantamount to calling her loose. To name her as 'one who laughs loudly', another much used form of abuse, is also to imply that she is unchaste.

To be called by their own personal names and not by any of the pejorative words used to describe their marital status was one of the principal demands made by a group of widows who came together for a workshop in southern India.

In English- and French-speaking African countries, widows are frequently called witches, especially those who are old or without sons to protect them. When something very bad happens - a fatal illness, a lethal snakebite, a house falls down, cattle die or are stolen - old widows living alone are often suspected of being witches.

Notes

1.   The conference, 'Widows in India', was held at the Indian Institute of Management, Bangalore, 23–25 March 1994. The organiser was Dr Marty Chen of the Harvard Institute of International Development.

2.   Jean-Claude Muller, 'Widows' Choices among the Rukuba', in Betty Potash, *Widows in African Societies*, Stanford Press, 1986, pp. 182–3.

3.   Nonie Niesewand, 'After the Mourning', *She*, September 1994.

4.   Report from the NGO Widows Ministries – Northern Sector, based in the Bolga Region of northern Ghana.

5.   Betty Potash, 'The Widow among the Matrilineal Akan', in Potash, ed., p. 225.

6.   Doo Aphane *et al.*, *Picking Up the Pieces: Widowhood in Southern Africa*, Women and Law in Southern Africa Research Trust Working Paper No. 13, 1995.

7.   Ibid.

8.   Personal communication.

9.   See, for example, *Mid-Life and Older Women*, Pan American Health Organisation, 1989, in particular Carmen Delia Sanchez, 'Informal Support Systems of Widows over Sixty in Puerto Rico', and, on Jamaica, Joan Rawlings, 'Widowhood: the Social and Economic Consequences'.

10.   Rawlings, p. 324.

11.   Peter Marris, *Widows and Their Families*, Routledge and Kegan Paul, 1958.

12.   Helena Lopata, *Women as Widows: Support Systems*, New York, 1979.

13.   Niesewand.

14.   *Picking Up the Pieces*, p. 46.

15.   World Bank, *Letting Girls Learn: Promising Approaches in Primary and Secondary Education*, World Bank Discussion Paper No. 133, 1991, p. 29.

16.   L. Heise, 'Violence against Widows'. World Bank Discussion Paper 255, 1994.

17.   Potash, ed.

18.   According to Bemba tradition, if a man returns his wife to her father he has divorced her.

19.   Widows' Workshop Report, Network Co-ordinator, Udaipur.

20.   The report by Widows Ministries – Northern Sector refers to suicides.

21.   See Neerja Mishra, 'The Murder of Roop Kanwar', in Pramila Dandvate, ed., *Widows, Abandoned and Destitute Women in India*, Radiant Publishers, New Delhi, 1986, pp. 49-53.

22.   A. K. Ray, *Widows Are Not for Burning*, ABC Publishing House, New Delhi, 1985.

Poverty, Work and Income Support

Crucial to the quality of life of most widows is the degree to which they can at least maintain a standard of living for themselves, and any dependent children who live with them, that is not too drastically below the one they enjoyed during marriage. Many widows are reduced to poverty as a result of being evicted from their homes and losing their property to acquisitive and often ruthless in-laws. Local traditions and religion may debar them from engaging in paid labour, so that they are left without any resources. Few will have had any education or training equipping them for a livelihood, if such opportunities were available locally. Restrictions on women's activities that often result from widowhood (for example, mourning rites that prohibit a widow from free movement outside the home until she has been cleansed (see Chapter 1) and from the gender division of labour and related social norms, alongside the other disadvantages of widowhood, frequently have a severe adverse effect on women's possibilities of employment.

Elderly widows and widows with children too young to work are likely to be the most vulnerable people in the community. The correlations of extreme poverty gathered from local definitions, in many different developing countries, invariably include widowhood, along with age and disability. [1]

In many parts of the Third World, widows are often debarred from enjoying any inheritance rights in property owned by their husbands; a widow can thus lose her home, the land she has worked for subsistence as well as her household possessions.(see Chapter 3). Modern, traditional and religious laws all frequently discriminate against widows; in some cultures a widow may lose even her children to her husband's relatives. Because local custom, as interpreted by male patriarchy, usually takes precedence over any statutory laws aimed to protect women's rights, widows are often unable to seek legal remedies. Traditional courts and local officials perpetuate the discrimination against widows, and widows risk incurring the wrath of male relatives if they seek to establish their rights. Millions of widows in the least developed countries eke out precarious existences working in the most exploited and degrading occupations of the informal sector: as domestic servants, or, in situations of extreme desperation, , reduced to begging or prostitution.

Few developing countries possess any system of national pensions, nor are their economies likely to be able to support such schemes in the foreseeable future. Where some form of pension or social security scheme exists on paper for destitute widows and their children, corruption and bureaucracy frequently block access to them. Besides, the amounts available are so low that they usually fail to provide sufficient funds to support the bare essentials of life.

For example, the Pakistan government has a system for collecting *zakat,* a religious tax intended primarily for the support of poor widows and their children. Considerable amounts are collected but little of this money ever reaches the destitute widows; instead it enriches corrupt government officials and local *zakat* officials. The few widows who manage to obtain some of this money find that in any case it is not enough to support them for more than a few days. The *zakat* committees consist of men, whereas the money is intended to be dispensed to widows from orthodox Muslim backgrounds observing purdah. Their very seclusion prevents male officials from visiting them to make any adequate assessment of their needs. It is acknowledged that women too are involved in the corrupt system: women from powerful families are encouraged to misrepresent the facts, so depriving poor widows of some assistance. [2]

In the majority of developing countries, the reality for any widow is that a whole lifetime of inequality and the general devaluation of women's contribution via the process of reproduction and production exacerbate the economic disasters of widowhood. Deprived of education and training, women work mainly in the informal and subsistence sectors; their efforts are poorly remunerated, minimum wages legislation does not apply, and so inevitably they are less able than men to accumulate savings or to have access to private pension schemes of their own.

Across cultures, older women share a common bond of being more likely to be living in poverty than older men. In the least developed countries millions of young widows find themselves destitute and with the heavy responsibilities of supporting dependent children or older relatives. They are often totally unprepared for living on their own. On their husband's death, not only are they faced with having to come to terms both with grief and with a total change in their status, and often the hostility of their relatives, but almost overnight they have to adjust to the fact that they alone have the responsibility of securing their livelihood. The husband's death will make them think of their own future as old women, and they will live in fear unless, through their own efforts, they can find paid work and save for the future, or know that they will be accorded inheritance rights and acknowledgement that they have contributed to the family resources.

The following views are typical of the hopes expressed by widows encountered in my research:

> 'My greatest wish is to be able to work for my children.'
> ' I want to get a loan so that I can start a business.'
> ' I want to be able to earn money so that I can send my daughter to school so she will not be like me when she becomes a widow.'
> ' I want to work for cash not just to be given the crumbs from someone else's table.'
> ' Why cannot we be paid the same as men, or more? We do the same work and we must feed our children.'
> ' How can I get a loan if I have no land?'

In many developing countries poor widows worry most of all about their children's future: how to feed and clothe them; pay school fees, or find the dowry to marry off a daughter (see Chapter 7). Medicines, special food for a sick husband, and funeral expenses may have depleted the usually available resources leaving many widows in debt or forcing them into increased dependence on exploiting moneylenders.

> 'When my husband became ill I borrowed from the moneylender. I used his land as collateral. When I could not pay back, the moneylender took all the land, although it was worth more than the value of the loan. Later, I offered him the interest and the return of the loan but he would not accept it. Now I am landless, and I cannot find work so I beg,'

explains a widow in rural Bangladesh. This particular widow had become a member of Proshiko,[3] a Bangladesh women's non-governmental organisation that had offered her the means to pay back the loan; even they were unable to persuade the moneylender to return the land. Many cases have been reported, in many areras of the Third World, of widows who have lost their land and home to moneylenders, even when the value of the property far exceeded the original loan. A 1991 study by Chen found that households headed by widows in northern Indian villages had, over a period of fifteen to twenty years, sold or mortgaged a disproportionate share of the land.[4]

In some communities, children are forced into debt bondage for years as a consequence of the father's death, or are sent to work as cheap labour when they should be enjoying the benefits of education and the experience of childhood happiness, security and play.

As pointed out earlier the common assumption that Third World widows are usually looked after by their extended families, or remarry, is dispelled by current research and anecdotal material. Nor are widows always able to enjoy rights they might have to their husband's property under modern or customary law. To what extent they can rely on other forms of support - from their neighbours, their community, and non-governmental organisations (NGOs) - is also problematic. Widows are often unable to participate in existing income-generating and training schemes because of the pressures of maintaining the family single-handed. Such initiatives often fail to target widows as a specific group, to take into account the obstacles to their involvement and to explore ways in which projects can be made more accessible to them.[5]

But widows are working hard, and in many cases harder than married women, even though they may not be as involved in NGO work projects and programmes as other women are. Their economic contribution often remains invisible. Rural women involved in a World Bank poverty assessment study in Zambia in 1994 suggested to its organisers that there were major differences between the daily workloads of widows and the workloads of married women. Widows started the day one or two hours earlier than married women; rising at 4 a.m. in the dry season and 3 a.m. in the rainy season. They worked far longer hours during the day and went to sleep much later than women with husbands to support them, because they had to undertake, in addition to their normal work, tasks usually done by men.[6] Similar differences in workloads and activities were noted among widows in rural Gujerat, north India.[7]

Although in recent years women's credit needs have received increasing attention and a number of interesting women's banking programmes, such as the Grameen Bank in Bangladesh and the SEWA schemes in India have been successfully developed[8] still many widows are unaware of what might be available, or are unable to take advantage of the schemes because they own no collateral, such as land. The very uncertainty of their rights to house and land makes their eligibility for loans more difficult to prove. In rural Bangladesh, every village seems to have its moneylending 'touts' who are known to prey on defenceless women desperate to find money to pay for expenses during their husband's last illness, or for the funeral which is often costly (the degree of hospitality offered on such occasions is seen as a mark of respect to the dead man).

Housing and land

Many widows lose their home and access to land because in-laws assert what they insist are their traditional rights over the deceased's property. In such situations, the widow and her children have not even the recourse that was available traditionally, namely the support and care of the children in the extended family. The relatives will have their own problems, aggravated by poverty, unemployment, land scarcity and the consequences of structural adjustment programmes. Such economic hardships make it increasingly difficult for a widow to access housing and land, or income and material and other support from either her natal family or that of her husband (see Chapter 3). She may be forced to reside in the home of a relative, an unwanted burden, resented and badly treated. For rural widows with children to look after, loss of land is loss of food security. Since land allocation schemes for poor people are often targeted at men, widows, if they lose their land, are often unable henceforth to use their skills as subsistence farmers.

The impact of the denial of widows' claims to remain in their homes and on the land differs according to their age, socio-economic and educational status, and whether they are from rural or from urban areas. An economically strong widow is more likely to succeed in retaining her home and land than a weaker widow. She is, moreover, better equipped to find and afford competent legal representation in disputes relating to house and land, and to employ expensive safeguards to resist eviction. One Zimbabwean widow, for example, installed electric gates around her Harare house to keep out her 'greedy, amorous and aggressive brother-in-law'.

Institutions play a role in the widow's ability to retain house and land. In Zimbabwe, the municipal and resettlement authorities automatically transfer the lease and permit relating to a leased municipal house and resettlement land to the widow. This is possible because both the house and land were only rented to the deceased, ownership remaining with the municipality and the state which have discretion to transfer these assets to whoever they find is legally entitled. The Harare Municipality has decided that municipal housing is awarded to a man and woman on the basis of their marriage and is 'family' property; it can only be transferred to a third party when both have died. Urban widows living in municipal housing in Harare are therefore in a better position than women whose husbands owned the matrimonial home; under customary law, these widows are disinherited.[9]

If the house was 'tied' to the husband's job, as is common in Indian villages, the widow must find money to rent alternative shelter. In some Indian states, however, moves are being made to allow widows to 'inherit' the husband's job, thus qualifying them to remain as tenants in the matrimonial home. Moves are also being made to allow the title deeds and land registration documents to be transferred automatically to the widow's name on production of the death certificate.

Widows in Gujerat, northern India, voiced their priorities in this way:

' I must get work so that I can have my own house. I will not stay at my in-laws or my parent's house.'
'I want the government to give me a house or at least a loan so that I can rent or build one.'
'I have no land. I should be allotted fertile land so that I can cultivate that and be self dependant.'
'There should be a law that automatically transfers land into my name when my husband dies. Marriage should automatically transfer all the husband's assets into our joint names'.[10]

At an Indian workshop on widowhood, widows were asked to draw pictures to describe their hopes: most of these pictures were of themselves imagined in their own houses and vegetable gardens.[11]

Health and nutrition
Nutrition is an important indicator of poverty. How much has the family's diet changed on widowhood? Widows interviewed from many different backgrounds and countries invariably reported that, since their bereavement, their family's diet had changed. Many widows have to forgo all but the most basic foods, often doing without meats and relishes because these items are too expensive). The children of widows are more likely to suffer from malnutrition and the maladies that accompany malnutrition, than those with a working male head of household. Girl children are known to be more neglected in terms of food, health care and education than their brothers.

A young widow in Malawi explained:

'We used to eat meat two or three times a week. My husband would buy the foods we did not produce ourselves when he was in the town. We have not eaten meat since he died six months ago. We just eat maize and some vegetables I grow. I should like to own a cow - then the children would be healthier, and I could sell the surplus, but I cannot get a loan.'

Widows in many different cultures and countries tell similar tales. Widows living within the household of other family members, such as that of the brother-in-law, may be discriminated against in the allocation of food. Indian and Bangladeshi widows have recounted how, in a relative's house, they are left to eat what remains after the host family has had its meal. Living as virtual prisoners, working as household slaves, their poor nutrition, along with other deprivations, causes morbidity and mortality rates that are significantly higher than those for married women of the same age. (In India it is estimated that widows have a 85% higher mortality rate than married women.[12] Paradoxically, widows in higher castes in India may be in greater poverty than those in lower castes who are able to remarry and have more freedom to work on their own account. These factors underlie the frequently greater relative deprivation experienced by many north Indian women upon widowhood; whereas widows in southern India generally face fewer limitations on their freedom to move outside the home and take paid work.

Often, the only work that destitute women can find puts their health at risk. Unhygienic and dangerous sweatshops and factories in the informal sector and domestic service are examples. Casual agricultural work may expose widows to noxious pesticides and risk of accidents from machinery. Public works programmes, for example in roadbuilding and brick carrying, may be too physically taxing for malnourished women, and lead to permanent disability.

Education and child labour
Finding money to pay their children's school fees is one of the principal worries confronting widows. This chronic problem is discussed more fully in Chapter 7. Sometimes primary school education is free, but not secondary school. However, even if education is supposedly free, the high opportunity costs must be considered: chore time, sibling care, children's foregone earnings, and, especially for girls - mothers' foregone earnings. If choices must be made, sacrifices are more likely to be made in favour of sons. In general girls do more chores than boys. They care for siblings, fetch wood and water, and in other ways ease their widowed mothers' drudgery. Time allocation studies in Nepal and Kenya show that girls gets involved in household production tasks at a much younger age and work longer hours than boys, so the opportunity costs of their education are considered higher. Widows' daughters are less likely to continue in school than their brothers. Uneducated and impoverished, they are often doomed to perpetuate the cycle of female disadvantage in their own early marriages and widowhood. Often widows' daughters are required to stay at home to look after younger siblings so that their

mothers can go out to work. Some widows feel that governments should provide free schooling and hostels for their children.

SAP (structural adjustment programmes) have led many governments to reduce the amount of the state budget spent on education. Very poor children, both male and female, are often reluctant to attend school, even when free education is offered, because they are ill equipped, lack adequate clothing or the money to purchase schoolbooks and other essentials, and fear the taunts of more advantaged children.[13]

Nevertheless, in recent years, women everywhere have become increasingly aware of the substantial economic and social returns of education. Men are less conscious of the trade-offs in improved status of women, better health, delayed marriage, reduced fertility, and improved productivity, so many countries continue to invest less in the education of girls than of boys. Help with school fees offered by male relatives may be restricted to sons. On the other hand, women's heightened awareness of the benefits of education may make some widows more determined to make sacrifices to provide their daughters with advantages they have been deprived of.

The family backgrounds of children who either do not attend school, or who work as cheap child labour, or in debt bondage (for example, as domestic servants, or in carpet factories), or are living as 'street children', or are involved in child prostitution need to be studied to identify to what extent widowhood is the determining factor.

Equal pay

In a public works programme in the state of Mysore, southern India, widows working on road building were paid less an hour than men doing similar work; in Gujerat, women vegetable and tobacco pickers were paid three-quarters the hourly rate of men, although the widows among them had to support several children and elderly dependants with their earnings. Often the only work that illiterate and inexperienced widows can find to do - domestic service, seasonal field work, child care - may be remunerated not by cash but by food, either eaten on the premises or given to them to take home. But it is cash that widows need to buy essential commodities and send children to school.

Inadequacy of socio-economic surveys

Unfortunately, as Jean Drèze has commented, there is very little empirical evidence on the link between widowhood and poverty.[14] Most socio-economic surveys take the household rather than the individual as the basic unit of observation, with only a few individual characteristics such as marital status being recorded. This approach precludes any analysis of intra-household inequalities, so that the poverty of a widow within the household of a brother-in-law or son remains hidden..

Most national labour statistics do not describe the economic contribution that women, married or widowed, make to the gross national product as unpaid family workers. Given that women do two-thirds of the world's work for less than 5 per cent of the income, the measurement and valuation of unwaged work are fundamental to the human, economic and legal rights of women, particularly to widows who are among the poorest and work the hardest. Over 470 NGOs representing millions of women worldwide have urged governments to value unwaged work. Macroeconomic policy decisions in relation to employment, industry, and the family, Third World debt, structural adjustment or aid programmes cannot be accurately evaluated unless the implications of such policies on widows and their children's unwaged workloads is considered.[15]

Informal-sector work is not counted, nor is home work (both paid), and nor are activities such as unwaged housework, the servicing of male workers, and the reproductive work.[16] Because the informal sector is a shifting and fluid entity, with women moving in and out of it, it is often difficult to know how much of the labour force is employed in it, and what proportion are women. It is thought that one in two economically active women in sub-Saharan Africa and South Asia and close to one third in the rest of Asia and North Africa are self-employed.[17] The entire process of collecting information for census and household surveys needs to be rethought, on the lines suggested by the UN Statistical Office (UNSTAT) and the International Research and Training Institute for the Advancement of Women (INSTRAW).[18] Interviewing arrangements and the collection of statistical data on women's economic activity need to be reviewed so that the true contribution women make is made visible. Using specific questions it should be possible to get a better idea of how widows in particular earn their living, and how this compares with the economic activity they were involved with before widowhood. The Indian surveys conducted by Chen and Dreze provide useful examples of approaches that can be taken to illuminate the question of how widows earn their living.[19]

Africa

Betty Potash, in her foreword to *Widows in African Societies*, a selection of essays published in 1986, makes the point that in sharp contrast to widows on the Indian sub-continent, African widows are surprisingly self-reliant in economic terms.[20] She notes that this is because generally in marriage these women made a substantial contribution to the household and provided most of the support for the children. However, various contributors to the book, which is based on field work undertaken in the 1970s, emphasise the difficulties faced by widows without sons. More than a decade after the book's publication, much has changed, and these changes overall have not been beneficial to widows. Nevertheless, widows who are resourceful and tough can certainly take charge of situations, use the law to their advantage and become successful market and business women.[21] Many African widows are very powerful and control businesses. In some ethnic groups such as the Nandi and the Luo, the widow acquires effective managerial control over the husband's estate. In many ethnic groups in Africa a widowed woman is free to engage in economic activity which is denied to a married woman living under the rule of her husband. Such independence among West African widows is evidenced by the numbers of them that become successful traders and entrepreneurs.[22] Nevertheless, for every one successful African widow there are thousands who are made destitute by their bereavement and who desperately need income-generating work to add dignity and meaning to their lives.

Widow-headed households
In Botswana and Zimbabwe, over 60 per cent of widows with dependent children are household heads.[23] Female-headed households are generally considered to be poorer than male-headed households, but this is not always the case. In India, where a considerable amount of work has been done on analysing the National Sample Survey (NSS) data, it has been found that female-headed households are often smaller than male-headed households, and therefore do appear to be consistently poorer if total household expenditure is taken as a criterion of poverty.

But the larger the household, the greater may be the economies of scale. Research done in India suggests that widows living alone, or heading households where there is no adult male, are likely to be poorer than, for example, widows heading households where there are adult sons.[24] Similar studies are needed in many other countries of the South.

Paid and unpaid work
Widows have of course always worked, but not necessarily, when their husbands were still living, for a cash income. Men might have sent remittances back if they were working away from the home, or would have used some of their wages to buy certain essential commodities such as oil, salt, soap, fertiliser. They might also have paid school fees for their

children. Many widows thus need for the first time to engage in activities that earn income (in cash or in kind) that gives them an independent command over commodities through market exchange. These activities allow them to enhance their economic independence and bargaining power in a way that child-minding, cooking, and fetching water and firewood do not, even though these tasks are equally productive to the household economy.

Cultural restrictions on taking paid work
Religion or tradition may require a widow to wear 'widows' weeds,' some special costume for such an extended period of mourning, that it is impossible for her to work in the modern sector. A Zambian widow complained that she had to give up her job in a modern hospital because her father-in-law insisted that she wear the obligatory widow's black dress with black head-dress for a whole year. In both Francophone and Anglophone Africa, a widow in some other groups must wear rags, or her husband's clothes for an allotted time, or be scarified and have her head shaved. Sometimes widows are forbidden to leave the house.

In India, in the higher castes, including the Brahmins, widows are not expected to work outside among strangers. By contrast tribal widows, women from the scheduled castes, are allowed to go for *nata* (marry outside the family) and they can do whatever work they can find. However, in some parts of India steps are being taken to allow widows to 'inherit' their husbands' jobs.

In Muslim communities, where purdah is observed, a woman is not expected to work outside the home; to do so is to lay herself open to malicious gossip and to abuse. Bangladeshi widows working on a fishpond project in the Manikganj district were criticised by male elders in the village as 'loose' women. The men said they would never allow their wives to work. Homeworking is a form of informal-sector work seen as suited to women living in seclusion (see below). This type of work is unregulated and Bangladeshi widowed homeworkers in the Brick Lane area of London are engaged in similar work, toiling long hours in unhealthy and sometimes dangerous environments, without any protection from employment laws.

Informal-sector work
There are few openings for uneducated untrained women in the formal sector, and therefore it is predominantly in the informal sector that the majority of women work. Here they are not protected by labour and health-and-safety legislation, and have none of the benefits of formal-sector work such as paid leave, sick pay, maternity benefits, and the right

to trade union membership, and collective bargaining. For many years, the International Labour Organisation (ILO), which represents governments, industry, and the trade unions, did not consider that informal sector workers - so many of whom are women - were its responsibility. Governments ignored them, unions rejected them, and industry was able to exploit them. However, in the last few years, due, in the main, to the efforts of some notable NGOs and independent scholars and their submissions of draft codes of practice for employers, the ILO is now showing a more active concern in the conditions of work for millions of women which falls outside the remit of the law. For example, at a1994 ILO conference on women, work and poverty held in Harare, it confirmed its commitment to assessing the wide-ranging implications of the multiple roles of women as workers for their vulnerability and marginalisation. Far more, however, needs to be done by governments to protect the most vulnerable women, many of whom are widows, from gross exploitation for profit.[25]

Homeworking and piecework

Much has already been written about the evils of homeworking.[26] For widows who are confined to home because of the demands of child care or for cultural reasons, homeworking may be the only option for income generation. In Maria Mies's classic *The Lace Makers of Narsapur,* which she wrote in 1982 originally for the ILO, a high percentage of the lace-making women from a purdah community who were widowed were forced to go on working on lace until they died because their sons and other relatives had migrated far away. (Mies's work shows that already, two decades ago, prevailing social norms in rural India were breaking down, and that widows were no longer neccessarily living with their married sons but having to work on their own account to survive). Often children are co-opted to assist with the work. A significant proportion of homeworkers in both rural and urban regions of the Third World and among immigrant ethnic communities in the West are widows. Whatever the region, they receive almost no protection from the law. A Bangladeshi widow speaks of her situation in London's Brick Lane:

'Sister, I am a widow and I do not really know what my legal status is. If I apply for insurance cards and things I may be asked to leave the country. My uncle brings me garments to sew at home and I am paid 50p an hour. But I earn to feed my children and I do not have to deal with strange men or face the racial abuse of the outside world'.

Widows who are homeworkers dare not complain for fear they will lose their jobs.

A study showed that women rolling 'beedis' in Pakistan and India knew they were being cheated when the middleman underpaid them but it was the only work available for widows who could not work outside.[27]

Prostitution

Prostitution may be the only strategy open to women without employment opportunities who are left destitute when their husband dies. The red-light areas of Bombay, Dacca, Nairobi, Llilongwe, Blantyre, Kampala, and so on, offer at least a precarious livelihood to the destitute widows who come from the rural areas seeing prostitution as the only way they and their children can survive. (See also Chapters 4 and 5 on sexuality and AIDS respectively.) Defining prostitution is not easy since the context of the provision of a widow's sexual services in exchange for male assistance, food, shelter, goods, or cash varies widely between different cultures and countries.

Widows are visible as prostitutes and beggars on the streets of many Third World towns and cities. Prostitution also occurs in the villages (and widows are often accused of being prostitutes whether they give sexual services for money or not), but the town provides greater financial rewards. There are obvious reasons, too, why a widow would not choose to live as a prostitute in her small community.

Prostitution may start in the village when a widow, desperate for assistance with tasks that can only be performed by men, or in need of food and shelter, gives in to the sexual demands of a man in the belief that he is offering 'friendship'. She becomes marked as a prostitute when she is abandoned by this man and taken up by another. There are many stories of widows who, deserted by a series of men, eventually migrate to the cities and become real prostitutes, either on their own account or working for a pimp. Others become prostitutes after having been taken in as domestic servants, sexually abused by the men in the household, and then thrown out because they have become pregnant.

Begging and prostitution are often the end of the line for widows. The alternative is dying on the streets unless they are taken in by a shelter such as Mother Theresa's refuges in Calcutta, other ashrams in India, or the few widows' refuges gradually being set up in some African countries. The rewards of prostitution may not be monetary but simply food and somewhere to shelter. Empirical research into why widows turn to prostitution would provide a compelling argument for targeting widows for training in income generation and self-employment.

Food-for-work and public works programmes

'It was much better during the drought, for then we could join the
Food for Work programme, and so we could always depend on
having some maize to eat, and milk for the children.'

- a widow in eastern Zimbabwe

Food-for-work and public works programmes often provide a lifeline
to poor widows. In many parts of the South, poor women, many of
them widows, are employed in such activities as road construction, earth
digging, and brick breaking, often for less pay than men doing the same
work. However, women engaged in public work programmes often argue
that they work as well as men and should be paid the same. More militant
women have demanded that they should be paid more than a man, since
if they are mothers of minor children, all their earnings go straight into
food for the family, whereas men do not always provide for their
dependants and spend money on drink and tobacco and other women.

These schemes, whilst they are very important to destitute women can
also be a distressing experience since the women involved are on public
view as having fallen into poverty, and are often seen as being without
shame, having to endure community insult. More important might be to
give destitute widows first priority in rural public works programmes and
to explore how they might best be employed in such statutory areas as
nutrition programmes and health centres, and schools.

Rural widows
Most of the work available to widows in rural areas is in the informal
sector, where there is little security of employment, no bargaining power,
and no minimum wage legislation. A recent study of some northern
Indian villages found that not a single widow was engaged in wage
labour outside the village.[28] This was particularly remarkable since a large
number of men and children commuted daily to the nearest town for
wage employment in the formal and informal sector. More generally,
the rapid expansion of urban employment of men appears to have
actually widened gender inequality, and might be said to have worsened
the relative economic position of widows, who 'suffer from the
progressive extinction of traditional occupations within the village
without gaining, as many men do, from the increasing availability of
outside employment'.[29]

'I don't know any work' lamented Chobi Prodhan, a widow in a
Gujerat village who was left with half an acre of land on which to
support herself and four young daughters. This pattern reflects the sexual

division of labour as it affects all women in rural India and is in sharp contrast to the situation in Africa where women generally play a major role in agricultural work.

Because of the many cultural obstacles to cultivating any land they may have, many Indian widows resolve the problem by leasing the land out. The vulnerability of these female 'landlords' creates problems for those who advocate giving greater rights to tenants. The story is told of how one helpless old widow in an Indian village succumbed to the demands of her tenant for a larger share of the crop; she would almost certainly have been left without her traditional share had not the local Communist Party branch come to her rescue and beat up the members of the political party that supported her aggressor.

Agricultural work
Where widows have inherited land, or have usufructuary rights to land, they are able to continue with subsistence agriculture to support their families and to sell surplus.

But often problems arise when, either on account of taboos concerning certain tasks, or because of physical incapacity, women are unable to cultivate without some male assistance. In Muslim Bangladesh and in purdah communities women who work in the fields or in outside jobs are frowned upon. In India, whilst women of lower castes are generally allowed to work, tasks such as ploughing may, in some cultural settings, only be performed by men. Widows may have no money to hire male labour for this work. In parts of Africa, women are not supposed to build or repair buildings, or to graze cattle.

An African widow may have access to land but be prohibited by her relatives from using the well or farm implements. She is often bypassed by extension services, which provide male farmers with assistance such as agricultural loans, subsidised fertiliser, seeds, and training. In Uganda, many widows living in areas where coffee was the main cash crop found themselves unable to manage the cultivation on their own, and had been forced to abandon the plantations since there were no men to assist them.

As the mechanisation of agriculture proceeds, many of the technologies so far developed are more appropriate to men than to women. High-yielding crops may impose too heavy a strain on widow farmers used to seasonal hoeing and harvesting. Women often do not drive tractors or grow cash crops such as coffee. Without a husband to transport produce to market, widows may be at a commercial disadvantage. As the usual tasks involving women, such as planting, hoeing, weeding and harvesting, are taken over by men or machines, it becomes harder for women with no access to land of their own to find agricultural work. This is one of the factors influencing husbandless women to migrate to the towns.

'It is very difficult suddenly to take on the man's role in the village' says Kamla, a twice-widowed woman from rural Bihar 'If a woman wants to cultivate her land, get a loan, wants wages to be increased, or needs to get some official information, she has to talk to men, which she has never done before. She must not contradict them. She cannot argue or bargain. All these days you have never come out into the open to talk to any man but your father, brother or husband, and that only occasionally. How can you suddenly lift your eyes and start a conversation with a man?'

Widows who try to keep on their husbands' small businesses easily run into problems because of their illiteracy and total lack of experience in management and dealing with finance.

Kundania's husband had a successful village shop in Gujerat before he died. He was literate and could make a good bargain with wholesale traders in the nearest town, and he had enough clout to obtain loans from the bank and refuse credit to his customers. Kundania, whose only child, a daughter, had gone away in marriage, tried to continue the business but soon ran into trouble. Illiterate, she could not bargain with the traders, or get loans. She did not dare refuse demands for credit from customers, nor did she know how to ward off the bank's demands for payments on her husband's debts. The banks refused her new loans because she had no son, suspecting that she might have no title to any property worth confiscating. Eventually she lost everything; the shop was empty, and she was too weak to work as a wage labourer. Her neighbours and her three brothers kept well away from her to avoid having to help her. 'These days no one wants to help anyone' she sobbed. 'If I get ill, no one will even give me a glass of water'.[30]

This story illustrates well some of the causes of poverty and underemployment of rural widows in India and Bangladesh. First, their low educational level; second, their poor health (widows in India in their forties or fifties often look as if they are in their seventies, and their poor health is often the reason for their inability to work); third, their powerlessness and inability to 'bargain' and argue with a man; fourth,, their ineligibility for credit (rural banks and credit co-operatives are still resisting the Indian government guidelines urging them to lend to women). This north Indian widow decided to migrate to the city rather than continue to struggle to survive in the village.

Widows are to be found working long hours in the fields as seasonal paid labourers. Their pay is lower than a man's doing similar work, but since they are seasonal workers minimum wages legislation does not apply. The survey of Gujerati women tobacco pickers referred to above found that widows who were heads of households with dependent children rose at 3 a.m. in order to prepare food for the family, clean the house, collect water, and look after the domestic animals before starting work at 7a.m. Married women in the group rose at 5a.m. They all worked till noon. Then they returned home to prepare a meal for the family, returning to the fields for another five hours. The women finally arrived home for the evening meal at 7p.m. For this long day of ten hours they earned only 24 taka a week. (A 12kg bag of rice which would last a family of six no more than two days cost 12 taka.)

Rural self-employment
In the rural setting, opportunities for gainful self-employment are severely limited since the success of any venture must depend on the demand in the community and the competition of others engaged in similar activities. In villages in Bangladesh, widows spoke of selling rice, making rice cakes, collecting cowdung and selling it for fuel. In Malawian villages, widows make little cakes and set them outside their huts in the hope they will be sold. But since other destitute women are doing the same thing the rewards are small. Few illiterate widows work out what is their profit after they have spent time or cash acquiring the raw ingredients, which include expensive ingredients such as oil for frying. To sell well, the price must be lower than someone else's. And if prepared food is not sold on the day, it is wasted. Some widows travel to towns on buses to buy commodities and sell them in the village, but they are often in competition with men who have access to transport and can buy in bulk, making greater profits and selling at a discount.

In the lake area of Malawi, widows selling fish bought from the fisherman along the main road spoke of unfair competition from married women whose husbands had access to transport to carry large consignments of fish to the towns. The widows had to rely on hot slow journeys in crowded buses, so the quality of their stock was poor. Often they were unable to sell the fish, and lost their original outlay. Sometimes there was conflict between poorer widows and richer ones who could hire transport of their own or had managed to obtain loans to set up stalls where the fish could be kept in cool storage.

Crafts such as embroidery, crocheting, weaving and hand-block printing are also options for widows. But even when women work together in NGO-supported co-operatives and income-generating projects, they are frequently at the mercy of middlemen who pay them barely enough to cover the costs of material; the profits from selling in capital-city tourist shops or overseas at a huge multiplier rarely are returned to the grassroots worker.

Urban and rural-to-urban widows

Many widows migrate to towns to seek work because life in the village has become too difficult. Not only may they have lost all rights to their home, and have to bear community neglect and abuse, but there are no opportunities for paid work. Widows may also feel that in the towns there will be more support for their children, and organisations that can assist them with paying school fees. If they have well-disposed relatives already established who can house them and get them started in some economic activity, they may be better off than if they had stayed in the village. For many, however, urban life is a rude shock, for everything costs money and they must rent a shelter. Hawking, marketing, and trading require some capital outlay, and widows who are new migrants to towns lack savings to invest in goods to sell. Widows, along with other unattached women, the divorced and deserted, tend to gravitate to the most menial jobs, including prostitution and begging.[31]

In northern Indian towns, widows predominate among the exhausted thin women who work as hand-cart pushers and head-loaders in the cloth markets; as waste-paper pickers, rubbish collectors and beedi-sellers (hand-rolled cigarettes made with leaves and shredded tobacco). In Dacca, Bangladesh, widows who have been chased out of the village get work as part-time workers in the garment sweatshops, working long hours in dangerous conditions, paid well below the minimum wage, and liable to be laid off at any time.

Domestic service

In contrast to the beggars and prostitutes, domestic servants are hidden from the outside world. Domestic service can be, and often is, a form of abject slavery and degradation, unless the woman happens to find a caring and sensitive employer. It is an obvious solution for a destitute widow for it provides her with the essentials of shelter and some food. It is in the town that widows are most likely to find work, and they retreat into anonymity once they are engaged in it.

> A Bangladeshi village widow worked as a domestic servant for some richer relatives in the village after her husband died. She was paid no money but they gave her leftover rice, and some vegetables if she hoed for them. They were not kind and often spoke to her roughly. Sometimes the grown-up daughters hit her if she was too slow. 'But I would rather work for a family I know, though they ill-treat me, than have the shame of working for strangers and be treated like a prostitute,' she explained.

Sometimes a poor widow may be fortunate in finding a kind employer who will let the youngest children accompany her, and employ the older ones as well. The children may then find secondary employment hawking, as messenger boys, or working in sweatshops or factories. But many widows must lose their children to the streets when they take a live-in job.[32]

Domestic service is unregulated. Women's lawyers groups in Dacca have been made aware of many cases of severe abuse including sexual harassment and rape. Often domestic servants are paid no money, only given food. They may have no proper place to sleep in and they may work eighteen hours a day. Without any bargaining power, and with the streets as their only escape, women frequently put up with violence. The victims of harsh treatment at the hands of employers, women as well as men are usually reluctant to complain; when they do, police frequently take little action.[33] The cases seen by the few organisations in Dacca addressing the problem are only the tip of the iceberg.

> A Bangladeshi widow rescued with appalling injuries from a police inspector's home in Dacca, after having been locked up for three days in a bathroom whilst the family went to their village, told this story: 'I worked all hours. If the master came home late at night I had to stay up to serve him food. If I was late in the morning the mistress pulled my hair, threw ashtrays at me. He, the master, stubbed cigarettes on my chest when I broke a plate in the kitchen. They called me 'donkey' and 'dog'. When they went out they locked the door. I have not been outside the house since I came here seven months ago. They had promised to pay me, but I never got my wages as they said it was to cover the breakages.'

Nor does this type of servitude only happen in Third World countries. Rich families are able to bring their servants with them when visiting

Europe. A new organisation, Kalaayan, opened in London in the early 1990s to provide refuge and assistance to foreign domestic servants maltreated in the UK. Among the women it helped were many widows, from the Philippines, from Sri Lanka, from Bangladesh, who had suffered terrible exploitation and cruelty at the hands of their employers. In 1993 out of a total of 229 women working as maids in Britain who sought help from Kalaayan, only 90 were paid regularly, and then only about £20 a week. The UK Home Office allows foreign visitors to bring their servants into the country, but these servants have no independent status as worker and risk deportation if they leave their employers.

NGO income-generating projects

The best option for widows wanting work is to join an income-generating group and receive training in production and marketing through one of the rural development or women's organisations, or through co-operatives supported by women's bureaux or by international NGOs such as Oxfam. Training in a craft and in management and marketing, and in addition support for setting up co-operatives, or provision of loans to set up small businesses have helped many widows not only to earn an income but to experience the benefits of working alongside other women and enjoying solidarity. (Some of the schemes that have targeted widows are more fully described in Chapter 11.)

A particularly innovative initiative is being tried out in Bangladesh where, instead of the conventional charity-aided NGO project, poor widows are invited to become shareholders in a profit-making company alongside the richer men who have surrendered their uncultivated land to be developed for fish ponds. The poorest women in the village, of whom half were widows, were invited to become shareholders in the company's fish farming industry through their work contribution in digging the ponds. A small sum was deducted from their wages and they were able to understand perfectly well the value of the share as an asset.[34] When I visited the project in 1994, the women's leader, a vigorous widow of thirty, encouraged her team to keep at the digging inspired by the knowledge that every ton of earth they moved added to their investment in the company and to their share of the profits once the fish-farming enterprise was on its feet. In spite of the obvious disapproval of the men - and of some of their wives - at the sight of women working in public view, dishevelled, muddy, and showing their ankles and bare feet in the mud, the women not only looked strong physically but had obviously gained in confidence because they were involved together in something they believed in and that held out long-term benefits.

Pension schemes

In the West, most widows receive statutory pensions automatically on the death of their husband, and many also enjoy private pensions accumulated through their husband's work. Also, many more widows today than in the past will have worked in formal sector work and contributed to their own company pension schemes. Although many Western widows live in relative poverty, they are unlikely to be living in total destitution. When they are old, if they have no resources of their own, the state will provide for their needs in residential care.

In Third World countries, only a small minority of privileged women are provided with pensions from the husband's employment. In Bangladesh, for example, a retired man's company pension ceases on his death. The contribution the widow made to his working life is ignored. Elsewhere, a dead husband's pension or accident compensation is often seized by the in-laws, and the widow receives nothing (see Chapter 3). Few Third World countries can afford, or will be able to afford in the foreseeable future, a system of national pensions for widows, those living in poverty, or the aged. Since governments cannot be relied on to address the special circumstances of widows and their children, some NGOs have developed uniquely impressive self-help and welfare schemes for women. The exception is India, where, at least on paper, most states have some pension schemes for destitute widows; nevertheless. the cash benefits are not only very small but the administration of schemes is often so bureaucratic and corrupt that many widows do not receive what in theory they are entitled to.

In India, almost all states and union territories have some old age pension arrangements. The amount of pension provided and the criteria for establishing eligibility vary from state to state. In Kerala, for example, old and destitute widows receive 65 rupees a month, former agricultural workers 70 rupees and disabled people 85 rupees. Destitute widows with one or more children receive 5 rupees extra per month. These payments are equal to no more than two days' wages for men and two and a half days' wages for women. Judged by the criteria of the going wage rate for the unskilled labourer, pension entitlements are grossly inadequate. Overall, Indian states spend roughly only 1.2 per cent of their budgets on pensions. Government pensions (paid to retired government employees) are thirteen times higher in Kerala than the general pension.

In the state of Karnataka also in southern India, destitute widows without adult sons supporting them are eligible for pensions. This proviso, as critics have observed, has possibly encouraged sons to abandon widowed mothers.

One way of assessing the adequacy of social support is to examine how far it can meet basic food needs and other requirements. In some states, for example Kerala, the public food distribution system for the poor is fairly comprehensive in its coverage of rural as well as urban households. Eligible recipients can obtain quantities of oil, grain, sugar and kerosene at discount prices. Older non-working people have a lower calorie requirement so that the pension plus subsidised food might well meet food needs. However, the level of pensions in Kerala can never be adequate for a young widow or one with one or more dependent children.

A pension paid to an old widow living with her family makes her less of a burden to them and might enhance her acceptability and status in the household. Widows who live alone may have to find rented accommodation; for them the pension is never enough. If the pension remains fixed but prices rise, its value declines. Rather than being revised periodically, the pension should be incrementally increased automatically reflecting rising cost of living expenditure.

There are huge difficulties in organising social security for illiterate rural populations whose members live below the poverty line and work in the disorganised informal sector without job security. A few Indian states such as Andhra Pradesh, Gujerat, Kerala and Tamil Nadu have special pension schemes for agricultural labourers of whom a high percentage are landless women, including widows. Slightly more than half of all the widows claiming pensions in Kerala claimed from the agricultural pensions scheme. But the sum provided monthly amounts to the wages for only two days work and is not enough for a widow with children. Service pensions are four times as much.

Tamil Nadu, Kerala, Gujerat and Orissa have special pension arrangements for destitute widows and the physically handicapped. In Kerala there is no age limit for a destitute widow's pension, and financial incentives are provided to encourage widow remarriage. In Tamil Nadu since 1992, destitute widows have been included in the old age pension scheme providing they are unemployed, over the age of forty, have no jewellery worth more than 500 rupees, or living relatives owning a house or land worth more than 1,000 rupees (£100).The benefit paid per month is very small - 75 rupees - and is certainly not sufficient to provide more than a week's basic food supplies. In addition, the widows are given two saris every year and free meals or rice rations (10kg). Local officials are supposed to vet all applications and search out any male relatives who might provide support. The existence of grandsons and more distant male relatives can invalidate a widow's claim.

A destitute and desperate illiterate widow usually needs assistance to process a claim. Anybody prepared to help will want to claim his share of the final payment. The complex bureaucratic procedures cause delay as well as corruption. Implementation at the village level is so poor that only a small percentage of widows entitled to pensions ever receive them. Application forms have to obtained from *taluk* offices, offices of the *panchayat* (local council), or village elders. When researchers visited such offices, they found that the forms were usually not available or had to be purchased from vendors. No one seemed to think it was their responsibility to stock the forms.

If widows managed to overcome this preliminary obstacle, they still had to grapple with the problem of how to get proof of their birth, marriage, and husband's death. In the absence of certificates, either a doctor's certificate proving her age, and an authentication from a government servant or member of council or parliament on other matters, is essential. Such people are difficult to locate, and are not easily available. The required documentation, together with such evidence as photographs, is not easy for an average destitute widow to obtain. Widows often have to travel long distances to reach the specified office, and transport is expensive and time-consuming.. The widow may have to pay a private doctor to obtain an age certificate, and other intermediaries to corroborate her claim that she has no relatives to support her. Thereafter she may have to repeat the journey to check on the process of her application because no aknowledgements are sent out.

If a poor widow is found to have a son or grandson over the age of twenty, her case is usually summarily rejected, even if the men in question live far away, have no regular contact with her, and can be of no help. Local government officers may arbitrarily value the widow's dwelling to her disadvantage, since no measurable criteria exist. If widows have been granted housing under a poverty alleviation programme, such a grant may make them ineligible for a pension. Similarly, no one assesses the productivity of any land a widow might own (irrigated or unirrigated, accessible or remote). Yet it is possible for a widow to remain destitute even though she is the owner of a small plot.

In this bureaucratic nightmare land, a widow must be living alone, without a suitable dwelling, unable to work, without relatives, yet at the same time capable of negotiating the minefield of pension application - visiting offices, travelling to see officials, obtaining documents, waiting for long periods, and willing to pay bribes and costs along the way.

Geetha is a 35-year-old widow in a village in Tamil Nadu. She had no children but her deceased husband had had five children outside the marriage. Geetha had no contact with this family, but her application for the small pension was rejected because of the existence of her husband's sons.

The village administrative officer (VAO) said he might change his mind if Geetha was able to pay him. But Geetha had no money for such bribes. One frank VAO admitted that few of them really wanted to help the needy, 'although each of us has the power to make a positive recommendation if it is worth out while'.

Even if a widow is successful, the pension is small, and it will have taken several months, sometimes a year, for her to get; furthermore, some months can elapse before the pension order can be cashed, or for it to be the turn of her village to be visited by the paying official. More applications for destitute widows' pensions came from women whose villages were nearer the central *taluk* office. Widows living in remote villages were discouraged from seeking assistance. At 75 rupees a month the pension works out at less than 10 per cent of the poverty-line income, so eligible widows still found they had to find paid work round the year. If they were caught earning small amounts, they risked losing their pension.

Widows in this scheme have now been ordered to visit the *taluk* office twice a year on a regular basis to prove they are still alive and have not changed address; more recently, they have been asked to provide yearly photographs on pain of losing their small pension. Often the postman fails to locate the address, the order is returned and the poor widow may have to spend months pleading with officials to renew it.[35] The system needs to be changed.

All over India, officialdom and bureaucracy decide on arbitrary grounds whether a widow is eligible or not, and set up almost impossible hurdles in her way. The village authorities, the *panchayats,* have not shown they can be trusted to identify the beneficiaries and ensure the latter obtain their pensions without delay. NGOs could play a major part in improving the process, yet they seem reluctant to challenge the local political institutions, treating them as if they were government ministries with whom all conflict should be avoided.

The provision of pensions to widows, however small, represents a basic means of action. Governments, NGOs, and donor agencies can show their commitment to raise the living standards of widows by co-operating in the development of a pensions policy. Methods of identifying destitute widows should accommodate the fact that widows might be destitute although living within a household that receives some income. It is important to address the problem of intra-household neglect. More generally, proposals must address the reality that policies based on criteria for establishing eligibility have always been dogged by bureaucratic obstacles, corruption, and arbitrariness. [In Britain, studies have showed that more potentially eligible beneficiaries were passed over than there were false claimants.] The Conference of Rural Widows in Bangalore in 1994 endorsed the recommendation that widows' pensions should be universal - paid even into rich households - and should not be selective as such a policy would be likely to destroy family support. The pension should be legislated so that widows receive it as of right, and not as charity. Policies that centre on the existence of adult sons to avoid pension eligibility are sex-discriminatory for they underscore traditional attitudes of son preference which the Convention on the Elimination of All Forms of Discrimination against Women (CEDAW) attempts to remove. Nor would the addition of adult daughters to the criteria improve the situation, for daughters are likely to have married and moved far away.

A universal, non-selective, legally established pension system, although expensive, could tackle the problem of intra-household neglect and protect the fragile family dynamics; the pension itself should be protected from expenditure cuts. With the pension put on a legal footing, widows would have a statutory basis for making a claim through the courts or the *panchayat*. NGOs could work with the *panchayats*. Because of the debate it would attract, a universal pension system, however small the sum - 100 rupees a month would be 4,000 cherea a year - would raise awareness about the neglect of poor widows and why the issue is a crucially important one for the whole country.

Professor Richard Titmuss remarked on the benefits of food rationing for all in wartime Britain, because 'even the rich had a vested interest in how it worked'. The same could be said of the proposed Indian state pension scheme. If it is a universal system, then better-off widows will take an interest in how it works, and some of the more caring members of the privileged classes will be made aware of how inadequate the benefit is, and wish to see it increased.

Widows' organisations could work with NGOs and the *panchayats* to educate all women on their pension rights and prepare them for widowhood and the matters they will have to deal with: documentation, authentication, and certification. After all, most girls will become widows at some stage in their lives. They are taught about family planning and nutrition, so they should be instructed about aspects of widowhood and how to act independently of male relatives, officials and middlemen.

Conclusion
Most of what has been said here about the economic activity of widows applies to all women on their own, the deserted and the divorced and the unmarried. Discrimination operates to restrict the employment of

the unmarried. Discrimination operates to restrict the employment of widows, through direct restriction on the activities that women can perform (such as common taboos on ploughing by women), and also through indirect economic processes. For example, gender biases in the allocation of credit prevent women from taking up self-employment as shop-keepers; the interventions of middlemen deprive women craft producers of a proper price for their skills; women on their own also suffer disproportionately through unfair discrimination in wages and denial of a minimum wage in the informal sector; through the invisibility of women in such activities as domestic service and through the general social stigma attached to women working in the public works sector. Informal sector workers need better protection from the law and the benefits that formal-sector workers enjoy such as trade union representation, bargaining power, welfare provision and pensions. Ideas such as a widow's right to inherit her husband's job, now an option in some Indian states, might be introduced in other countries.

Much more effort needs to go into projects to encourage women to remain in rural areas rather than to become economic refugees adding to the numbers of destitute women begging their living in towns. Legal protection of widows' rights to land, and improving and extending government extension training specifically to widowed cultivators might help to stem this migration tide.

In both urban and rural areas widowed mothers must be provided with childcare facilities. Since almost all married women will at some time in their lives become widows, they should be prepared for this state by being assured education and training when they are young so that when bereavement occurs they have work experience to enable them to remake their lives.

Clearly, a universal pension for widows is not a realistic proposition for most developing countries at the present time, and there is no easy solution to the problem of how to support widows who can no longer work. Initiatives such as SEWA in India, the brainchild of Ila Bhatt (see Chapter 11) which, in addition to organising informal sector women into a union with bargaining power, and developing banking and credit training and services, also has developed a scheme whereby women can insure against their husbands' death, might be adapted or copied in other countries.There is much that can be done to alleviate the poverty of widows by at least providing such social benefits as free access to health care and special nutrition programmes.

Notes

1.   For example, in 1994 an unpublished World Bank appraisal of rural poverty in Zambia ('Zambia Poverty Assessment', report no. 12985-ZA) showed that widows were generally regarded as 'very poor' by their local communities.

2.   Communication from Advocate Shereen Masoud, Lahore, Pakistan.

3.   Proshika can be contacted at I/1-9A, Section 2, Mirpw.2, Dacca-1216, Bangladesh.

4.   Marty Chen and Jean Drèze, *Widows and Well-being in Rural North India*, Development Economics Research Programme, London School of Economics, 1992, p. 6.

5.   In Malawi, the community development office supervising a training programme for women marketing fish products in the Lake region admitted that widows with young children were unlikely to participate, since their children were no longer attending school and the project took place in school hours. Widows interviewed in villages in the area were unaware that such programmes existed.

6.   World Bank, pp. 46–7.

7.   Jean Drèze, *Widows in Rural India*, Development Economics Research Programme Paper No. 26, London School of Economics, 1990, pp. 79–81.

8.   For more on the activities of SEWA (Self-employed Women's Association), see pages 000–0.

9.   Doo Aphane *et al.*, *Picking Up the Pieces: Widowhood in Southern Africa*, Women and Law in Southern Africa Research Trust Working Paper No. 13, 1995, p. 32.

10.   Report of a workshop held at the Bangalore Widows' Conference, 1994, compiled by Lakshmi Murthy.

11.   Widows' Lives, December 1994. Widows' Lives is a quarterly newsletter co-ordinated by Lakshmi Murthy (215 Pancharatna Complex, Beala Road, Udaipur 313001).

12.   P. N. Bhat, 'Widows and Widowhood Mortality in India'. Paper presented at the Bangalore Widows' Conference, 23–25 March 1994.

13.   World Bank, *Letting Girls Learn: Promising Approaches in Primary and Secondary Education*, World Bank Discussion Paper No. 133, 1991, p. 27.

14.   Drèze, p. 34.

15.   Focus on Women, March 1995. Published by the International Women Count Network.

16.   Esther Boserup, *Women's Role in Economic Development*, Earthscan, 1989; see also B. Rodgers, *The Domestication of Women*, Routledge, 1981, in particular p. 96 on the exploitation of widows in craft projects in Bangladesh.

17.   *ILO Year Book of Labour Statistics*, Edition 51, 1992, ILO.

18.   UN Statistical Office, *Methods of Measuring Women's Participation and Production in the Informal Sector*, UN, 1994.

19.   Drèze; Chen and Drèze.

20.   Betty Potash, ed., *Widows in African Society*, Stanford Press, 1986.

21.   Christine Obbo, 'Some East African Widows', in Potash, ed., p. 105.

22.   Potash, ed.

23.   Anastasia Gage, 'Widows in Southern Africa'. Paper commissioned by

the Population Council, 10 August 1993.

24.   P. Visaria and Pal Visaria, 'Poverty and Living Standards in Asia', *Population and Development Review*, Vol. 6, No. 2, 1980, pp. 189–223. Drèze (pp. 39–42) points out that research findings on poverty and female-headed households in India are ambiguous: some researchers found greater poverty among female-headed than male-headed households, and others found the opposite. Many factors intervene to make generalisations impossible.

25.   SEWA has participated in the production of a Draft Convention on the Protection of Women in the Informal Sector, 1994. Personal communication from Renana Jhabwala, SEWA.

26.   Swasti Mitter and Anneke van Luijken, *Unseen Phenomenon: The Rise of Homeworking*, Change, London, 1988; also Maria Mies, *The Lace Makers of Narsapur*, Zed Books, London, 1981; Menefee Singh, *Invisible Hands*, Sage Publications, London, 1987.

27.   Zaria Bhatty, *The Beedi-makers*, ILO Working Paper, 1981.

28.   Drèze, p. 80.

29.   Ibid., p. 83.

30.   Ibid., p. 89.

31.   See SEWA, *We the Unemployed*, SEWA, Ahmedabad, 1985. Also CHANGE country reports; Niki Nielson, *Women in Informal Sector Employment*, Longmans, 1987.

32.   The five-year-old daughter of the widowed servant working for friends of mine in Dacca was recently kidnapped whilst begging in the street. A year later, she has never been found, and it is believed that she may have been snatched for eventual work in a brothel in some other country.

33.   Report by GSS, Dacca, Bangladesh.

34.   Prism runs projects in agriculture, rural industry, science and medicine in Bangladesh (see Chapter 6, note 20).

35.   K. V. Eswara Prasad, 'Social Security for Destitute Widows in Tamil Nadu'. Paper presented to the Bangalore Widows' Conference, 1994.

CHAPTER 3

Laws and Customs Concerning Inheritance

In 1993 A Kenyan lawyer (a man) asked the rhetorical question 'How can a chattel inherit a chattel?' In 1994 President Robert Mugabe rebuked Zimbabwian women who sought joint property rights with their husbands: 'If these are ideas brought by whites amongst you as they came from Europe, they are bringing terrible ideas. I cannot have it that property that is family property should be in two names. If the woman wants property in her own name, why did she get married in the first place?'.

Inequality in inheritance laws based on sex and marital status is widespread in many developing countries. Influential men in local communities argue strongly that giving property rights to widows and daughters as well as sons would increase land shortage, and make families poorer. Commonly, in many parts of Africa, a widow forms part of the inheritance that goes to her husband's heir, either in a levirate, or as a wife. (See Chapter 6.) They cannot inherit. Similarly, in practice Indian and Bangladeshi widows, irrespective of modern laws, have very limited rights to their dead husband's share of the family assets. [1]

There is a long tradition of discrimination against women in inheritance and succession practices in all cultures and religions. In the Bible, Mosaic law dictates that daughters can only inherit if there are no sons, and that they must marry into their tribe (Numbers 27 and 26). Salic law (the mediaeval Frankish law) contains rules on succession to private property barring daughters from inheriting land. The Koran, far in advance of other legal systems of the time, while giving widows and daughters a portion of the dead man's estate allowed them only half that allotted to his male heirs.

Most ancient systems of law that have in whole or in part descended to us treated women as minors or chattels, dependent on their fathers or husbands, or treated them unequally in the exceptional cases where they have been given some qualified legal capacity. Women are still classed as legal minors in several developing countries (Zimbabwe legislated to change this status on independence in 1982).Women have had to - and do still today in many regions - depend upon the fragile good will of male relatives, fathers, husbands, fathers-in-law, brothers-in-law, blood brothers and sons, for access to production and resources; they have no equal right to share in the property of a deceased father or husband. Their relationship with property as owners or as users is for the most part dependent on their connection with male kin (even in matrilineal groups) - for example, in Malawi and Mozambique - it is the male relatives on the maternal side who benefit and not the female). Women were discriminated against in relation to ownership, management and disposal of property even in England until 1888, when the Married Womens' Property Act gave women the right to control their own assets. Previously, under common law, sons took preference over widows and daughters in intestate succession, and women could not make wills. The struggle to introduce this reform coincided with and gathered its momentum from the gains made by women in other fields, such as education and employment.

The study of evolving rules on succession and inheritance in different countries is an arduous task for the most diligent of scholars whether their field is jurisprudence, law, anthropology or sociology, since the subject is vast and complex and conflicting systems of law often operate. This chapter does not pretend to be an authoritative treatise on different types of succession law; readers must consult specialist and comparative law books for in-depth analysis. It does, however, try to identify some of the main issues regarding inheritance that present considerable problems for widows today in many traditional communities, and describes some of the responses to the problem by governments, NGOs and legal activists.

In developed countries, matters of inheritance are governed by statute laws that, with some rare exceptions, no longer discriminate on the grounds of sex or marital status. By contrast in Africa and Asia, where a plurality of legal systems coexist (for example, colonial, modern, religious and traditional), women do not have equality in respect of the ownership, administration and disposition of property. This is so despite the provisions the Convention on the Elimination of All Forms of Discrimination against Women (CEDAW), see Article 16(h)), Paragraph 74 of the Forward-Looking Strategies (FLS), and now Paragraph 274(d) of the Global Plan for Action (GPFA) 1995. This states that governments should 'eliminate the injustices and obstacles in relation to inheritance faced by the girl child so that all children may enjoy their rights without discrimination, by, inter alia, enacting, as appropriate, and enforcing legislation that guarantees equal right to succession and ensures equal right to inherit, regardless of the sex of the child'. The paragraph, although placed in the section concerned with girl children, has direct relevance for widows. It equips campaigning groups to lobby with more effectiveness than previously to ensure that national plans for GPFA implementation include legal and administrative action to protect widows from property-grabbing relatives.

Most of the discussion that follows assumes that the dead husband owned land or other property that the widow might inherit, but of course there are many landless poor whose widows may have little to claim on bereavement except cooking pots or other household items, or the most tenuous of rights to squatter land or rented shelter. Sometimes such widows are even denied those meagre possessions. After the floods in Bangladesh in 1991, destitute widows and their children had to fight to reclaim *char* land, for without a tiny strip of recovered planting ground they would have died of starvation. [2]

Patrilineality and patrilocality

Women's lack of equality in the inheritance of land and property is historically associated with patrilineality and patrilocal residence, the custom according to which when a woman marries she goes away to her husband's lands and family to produce children for his lineage. In many African societies, bridewealth or brideprice (sometimes called *lobola*) is effectively the purchase price of her productivity, and her fertility. It is key to the marriage which is a merger between two families and not, as in the West, a union of two individuals. Among some peoples, the family of a wife who dies without having produced children is expected to provide a sister as a substitute: this is *sororate* marriage. The bridewealth given to the wife's family, sometimes divided between uncles and father, will be used to buy wives for the sons of the lineage,

Patrilocal residence appears to be the most widespread of kinship patterns. In the precolonial era, although wives did not inherit when their husbands died, since the land was communal, it was customary for them to be given access to a plot of land for their subsistence. Individual plots could be inherited only by members of the group: sons or brothers in patrilineal systems; sisters' sons or, in rarer cases, a woman's daughters in a matrilineal system. Until relatively recently, most widows could rely on sons or other male relations for assistance and security, and as these men took seriously their obligations and duties to mothers and sisters, widows were compliant with arrangements for property disposal. As explained in the earlier chapters, changes brought about by development, the cash economy, urbanisation, migration, and poverty have greatly overstrained the limited resources of kin, with the result that the traditional support systems are disappearing, leaving increasing numbers of widows without any maintenance and, under the guise of custom, deprived of even their limited use of or access to the deceased's property.

For women in developing countries, widowhood is probably the most significant lifecycle event in terms of security and property rights. Mainly, but not always, women are totally dependent on marriage for access to land, and they only gain access to productive resources through some kinship relationship. Islamic societies are the exception since, at least in theory, wives and daughters are entitled to some share of inheritance. In some caste systems in India daughters may have rights to inherit land until they marry, but local practice and family tension tend to threaten even this limited enjoyment of title. In patrilineal groups in Africa, widows enjoy no rights at all in their natal family's land. In matrilineal groups a widow has the right to return to her father's village, but in practice her brothers may refuse to recognise her claim to family land. Some ethnic groups accept that widows continue to live in their husband's family either through a levirate arrangement (widow inheritance), or remarriage, but not all. Older widows might not be inherited in marriage, but be allowed to continue on the land. Or they might live alone, or reside with adult sons, taking the management of the husband's estate if their sons are too young.

The variables are so numerous within and between each specific ethnic group in Africa that it would be spurious to provide examples. Betty Potash's collection of essays on widows in African societies provides an excellent source of information on several ethnic groups in West, Southern and East Africa, as do Chen and Drèze for Northern India.[3]

Systems of law: diversity and conflict
Although many Third World governments have passed legislation, agreed constitutions, ratified international treaties such as CEDAW, and added their consensus to documents such as the Forward-looking Strategies (FLS) and the Global Plan for Action (GPFA) in order to demonstrate their commitment to the improvement of women's rights, specifically in the area of inheritance laws, the majority of widows, especially in rural areas where most people live, are unaware of these reforms.

Rapid changes that have affected traditional ways of life, such as the growth in inter-ethnic marriage and in nuclear marriages in the towns, as well as education, migration, and the accumulation of new forms of private property after marriage, have often mutated ethnic and local

customs, with negative implications for widows.[4] The customary ways
of dealing with the property of a deceased husband fall into disarray as
new developments in individual ownership require different solutions;
for example, where a couple have accumulated such modern assets as
bank accounts, insurance and accident policies, shares, pensions, cars
and Western consumer goods. When one family member has 'done
well', acquired an education and migrated to a city job, bought a house,
furniture, consumer durables, married out of his natal group, family
members left behind are likely to feel envious. Even when a Westernised
husband has willed his property to his wife and children, his poorer kin
may believe that they have a right, under customary law, to move in, seize
the property and evict the wife from her home, ignoring the provisions
of the will.[5]

Since there is no written 'living custom' (to be distinguished from
codified customary law), there is no clear means of judging the degree
of partriarchal bias in a (male) elder, village chief, traditional court judge,
or local official who determines the outcome of an inheritance dispute.
Local courts often take no notice of new inheritance legislation and
continue to apply so-called customary law (even when it has been re-
interpreted at a higher court level), so denying widows the right to a
share in the deceased's estate. Furthermore, social and economic change
threatens the traditional ways of solving disruptions in community life;
in relation to 'property grabbing', the interpretation of so-called customs
or religious codes by male leaders often becomes distorted and
manipulated, more chauvinistic, more fanatical, and more oppressive to
women. 'Who really knows what tradition and culture is really all about?'
asks Judith Chikore, who directs the Zimbabwe Women's Resource
Centre in Harare. 'What is considered to be tradition is often what
supports men's superior position'.

Research in southern African countries revealed two categories of
'customary law': that of the courts, and that of people's day-to-day
practices.[6] The courts (traditional as well as civic) tended to be more
rigid in interpretation and application than the local practice. Rather than
protecting widows, both types of court had contributed to their
problems. A perusal of widows' cases in Zambia, Zimbabwe and
Botswana showed that often the outcome was worse if widows appealed
to the courts. At the highest level, appeal courts were found to have
interpreted custom in a more oppressive manner - vis-à-vis the widows
- than the local traditional court. A 1994 High Court judgement in a
Zimbabwe inheritance dispute emphasized the gap between the elite
judiciary in the capital and the majority of the population.[7] Courts, then,
instead of taking the lead in applying progressive laws, may do the

opposite by attempting to reconcile the irreconcilable.

New modern laws of succession giving rights of inheritance to daughters and to widows make little impact where women's status is low, and legal education is lacking. The majority of cases handled by women's legal aid clinics and branches of FIDA, the Africa-based branches of Federation of Women Lawyers in all the countries visited for this book involved widows' inheritance disputes. Most wills and inheritance laws that attempt to clarify the position regarding the disposition of property on a husband's death, have failed to help widows because so few widows are aware of the legal provisions or dare to use them to challenge customary law. Where the law is invoked, it is often too late because of the usually long delays until the hearing: property will have already been seized by relatives, sold, disposed of or ruined. One Malawian widow eventually got a court order for the return of the furniture stolen from her house in the town, only to find that sofas and armchairs had been left to rot in the rain in her husband's village. In Uganda, the 1972 Succession Act has been less than effective for similar reasons.

Until quite recently Zimbabwean laws relating to marriage and inheritance were based on a racial classification, with civil law applying to whites and customary law to blacks. According to the African Marriages Act, the estate of any black African who died without making a will was subject to customary law, which meant that no widow could inherit. But in 1992 Zimbabwe courts ruled that all citizens, black or white, who married under civil law should be treated the same on death. Most people are unaware of this change, and many problems arise where a man has married several wives under different marriage laws. Few black people are accustomed to writing wills, and such wills are often ignored by local officials used to applying the customary law. Consequently, both rural illiterate widows and educated urban widows may find themselves dispossessed. In 1993 the Zimbabwe government issued a white paper suggesting ways to reform inheritance law and soliciting public comment. The responses, although they came only from a tiny percentage of the population, reflected a wide range of views. Some support the old law, the institution of the 'heir' and the continuing practice of polygamy.

The civil courts have legitimised the status of the heir through a rigid clause that states that whenever a man subject to customary law dies, his eldest son becomes the heir to take over the estate. If there are no children, the estate goes to his 'heirs' and not to his widow. Although Zimbabwe law specifically provides that it is an offence for anyone to remove a deceased person's property from his home without a court order, a number of factors prevent widows from making use of this provision, in particular fear of witchcraft and the accusation of witchcraft and fear of ostracisation by family members because they have involved the civil authorities. (In any case, who decides whether a man is or is not subject to customary law? Is a man able to renounce his identity as a member of his kinship group so that his relatives have no claim to bury him according to tradition and inherit his estate? And who decides who decides?)

In Zambia the 1989 Intestate Succession Act was intended to supersede customary law; it made formally 'illegal' those inheritance customs that deprived widows of rights to a husband's estate. However, researchers found that the local courts had no knowledge of its existence and commonly appointed administrators from amongst the husband's relatives; this usually led to the widows being robbed of their rightful inheritance. [8] The continuing mistreatment of Zambian widows by their husbands' relatives and in local courts was dramatically highlighted after the entire Zambian football team were killed in an air crash in Gabon in 1993; their young widows' experiences of embezzlement and property-grabbing were the subject of much media reporting and a case study. [9]

In India, although modern law gives daughters and sons equal inheritance rights, and some castes provide limited property rights for certain widows, in practice the land is divided between each son. If the sons are young, however, a widow may be considered the temporary owner of the land as their guardian, and if she has no sons and continues to live in her husband's village, she should normally inherit his land. When they become adults, sons may partition the land among themselves, even while their mother is alive. In such situations, a widow's relations with her sons (and daughters-in-law) will determine whether or not she is permitted to exercise a use right over some part of the patrimony.

In India, obstacles have arisen in implementing new legislation. The 1956 Hindu Succession Act placed widows in the Class 1 category of heir, but the law had little effect in rural and backward communities where local practices prevail that block widows' rights; nor does it cover the rights of Hindu widows living in other jurisdictions, for example in Bangladesh. Since the act only applies to intestate succession, a man may dispose of his property without making provision for his widow.

Under section14(1) of the 1956 Act an inheriting widow or daughter has an absolute right to dispose of the inherited property as she wishes, but in practice rural illiterate widows are under pressure to hand it over to their husband's relatives. Land ownership and registration still is managed according to local custom and no local official would like to be seen giving in to a woman's demands for parity.

Widows in north Indian villages are often persuaded to sign legal documents renouncing their claim to their husband's land.[10] One survey reported that only 20 per cent of them reported serious conflicts over their claims to officials.[11]

If, exceptionally, daughters succeed to land in India they are usually coerced to give away their share to their brothers, and they do this in order to keep on good terms with them should their support and protection be needed at a later time, in the event of divorce or widowhood. The fact that theoretically a widow has an inheritance through her father may increase her bargaining power and status within the family and community. Widows who control some resources are more likely to receive respect, so daughter inheritance is important to them.

Marriage and other Conjugal relations

The succession rights of a widow often depend upon the type of marriage she contracted. If it was a modern marriage, then inheritance is governed by modern laws of succession whereby a spouse usually inherits intestate with or without reserved portions for children. If the marriage was a customary one, then customary law is applied. Inevitably, definitions are most difficult to arrive at. It often happens that although the modern law should, in many circumstances, be applied, pressure from relatives is so great that property is distributed according to customary law.

Other forms of relationship such as customary law unions, concubinage, polygamy and casual sexual liaisons complicate the question of who exactly is a wife or a widow under any of the legal systems invoked in the context of succession (see Chapter 1). To formulate a law that will determine how property is shared between a number of co-widows and their children is a challenge to the most agile legal mind. Whether the shares should be equal, or give preference to the oldest widow, the youngest, or the one with most children is a question that ultimately the people must decide, for without popular support, there can be no practical change. Given the diversity of ethnic group, caste, religion, class, income and geographical region within any one developing country, unanimity on such issues is unlikely.

Jane, a Luyia, and her husband, a Luo, were an educated professional couple living in Nairobi where her husband worked for the UN. Just three days before they and their three children were due to leave for a posting in Cyprus, her husband suddenly died from poisoning. He had left a will leaving all his estate to Jane and the children. Before Jane could recover from her shock and grief her brothers had "taken control" over her affairs. They had found and destroyed the will, declaring it was against Luo traditions, 'taken control' of his bank account, and life insurance policy, and, through a fraud, obtained his UN salary and pension payments. They ransacked the house and took away Jane's marriage certificate. They accused Jane of not being his proper wife, and of having affairs with other men. At the funeral, relatives and friends donated gifts of money intended for the children's education but the in-laws kept the money for themselves.

Grabbing property or 'chasing off'

'Chasing off' or 'grabbing property', the experience of widows losing their property to relatives in inheritance disputes, is now so common in Africa and in some parts of rural India and Bangladesh that the terms have become incorporated in the vernacular languages. Some legislatures that have attempted to eradicate the practice use these words to specify that it is a crime.

In most cases, it is the brothers of the dead man who seize the property or evict the widow from her home on the pretext that they are the rightful 'heirs'. under customary law. Widows may also be victims of their own brothers, or of other women relatives such as mothers-in-law, daughters-in-law, sisters-in-law, or co-widows. As mentioned above widows' complaints about relatives robbing them of their husband's estate make up the major part of the caseloads in women's legal aid clinics in Africa.

The problem is so severe in Malawi that the National Commission on Women and Development's 1994 law reform proposals boldly referred to the existing legislation's failure to protect widows and children from the 'rampaging relatives of the deceased'. The commission reminded the Minister of Justice that 'in practice, as soon as a husband dies, the relatives of the man descend on his home and forcibly help themselves to any of his assets on the pretext that they are his rightful heirs. By the time the provisions of the Act have to be applied to the estate substantial diversion of property will have occurred to the detriment of the widow and children. These customary heirs, after the plunder, will rarely be seen thereafter to provide for the needs of the bereaved widow and children.'

Miriam is a Yao married to a Ngoni man in Malawi. When her husband died, her parents-in-law, uncharacteristically for Ngoni people, seized Miriam's house whilst it was empty, and put in a tenant who pays rent to them. But their son had declared often in his lifetime that the house was for his wife and children. Her young brother, Fred, now supports his sister totally and pays the school fees for two of the children, as well as supporting his elderly parents in the village. Since the in-laws managed to seize control of the pension Miriam would be destitute if not for Fred. She is reluctant to take legal action through the courts for she fears that just approaching a lawyer to challenge her husband's kinship group would bring about some witchcraft to harm her children. Besides, there is no legal aid, and Fred is resigned to the superiority of the claim of people who are powerful in their local community.

Property-grabbing occurs across the whole spectrum of ethnic, social and economic groups. In 1993 one of Malawi's senior ministers was charged with seizing his sister-in-law's land after his brother died. The national newspapers ran the story for weeks; it carried a cartoon of the minister kicking the widow out the house with his boot, and an interview with the minister's mother who confessed that she too had been 'chased away' by her dead husband's relatives.

The wealthy deceased husband of Lily Kapanda, now one of Malawi's few members of parliament and a campaigner for women's rights, was himself a respected MP. She is a college-educated accountant. Their privileged position did not protect her from her property-grabbing brothers-in-law. Her story illustrates the helplessness of many widows, whatever their social class, education or income.

Instead of a will, her husband left a letter stating that he wished his estate - farm, house, and possessions - to go to his wife and eldest son, and his body to be buried by his home. He often checked with Lily that this letter was in a safe place, as if he feared that something bad would happen. Within a few hours of his dying at home, his three brothers arrived to take his body and possessions away to their village. When Lily showed them the letter, they spat at her. In spite of her appeals over a period of many months to the village chief, the brothers continually harassed her and demanded not only the property, but also his bank deposit, life insurance policy and shares.

She begged 'Go away, I am in mourning, my eyes are blind with tears and I cannot find anything.' They ransacked the house, humiliating her, trying on her husband's clothes and turning out all her cupboards and drawers searching for money. They shouted, 'We are not so stupid as to leave you our brother's property. He left you lots of money which is ours to share, not you.' Eventually they beat her. One night they took off the roof and doors of the house, and stole the sacks of maize. They threatened Lily and her children with violence and informed the district commissioner that Lily had never been legally married and therefore had no rights. Eventually she managed to get police protection, but by then all her furniture, including bed, bedding, radio and fridge, had gone. Three years later she was elected to her husband's old seat in parliament and she now helps other widows to regain their property and is vocal in parliament on this issue. The brothers, however, still make occasional attempts to get a share of the sale price of her crops.

Similar stories can be heard in every part of Southern, Central, West and East Africa[12] National newspapers in some of these regions are at last beginning to understand that such cases are serious front-page news. Elsewhere, the robbing of widows, although widespread, is not considered an issue of importance unless the individuals concerned are public figures.[13]

In northern India, widows tell similar tales of greed, dishonesty and violence. Rampuni Devi, who attended the 1994 Widows' Conference in Bangalore, is one such victim.

Rampuni was a Bhumihar Brahmin who was widowed, still a child of seven, just eight days after her marriage. She had never seen her husband. Her father-in-law had left land in her name, but on his death her brother-in-law and his wife coerced her to transfer the land to his son. When she refused, they began to harass her; they even tried to kill her by pouring boiling water mixed with chillies on her and beating her unconscious. After she had recovered in hospital, she found that they had taken possession of all her property: her land, house and personal possessions. The village council, the *panchayat*, did not help Rampunita Devi.

Muslim widows in India and Bangladesh are subject to the same kind of harassment and evictions as Hindu widows despite the laws that give them inheritance rights. Local officials, ignorant and confused by the mix of customary and formal law, rarely help them. Should officials know the modern statutory provisions they are often reluctant to apply them since these officials must work in an environment where customary and local rules prevail; their principal objective is to maintain the status quo in a village, and avoid upsetting powerful village (male) elders.

In Bangladesh, the slums of Dacca provide refuge for Muslim

widows expelled from their homes and land in the rural areas by land-hungry and impoverished in-laws. The protagonists are often the mothers-in-law, who encourage their sons to carry out the evictions. These are cases where women are against women. In Pakistan, similarly, the inheritance rights of widows under Muslim law are widely and on occasions violently ignored[14]

Some widows faced with property grabbing make no attempt to obtain a remedy through the law, either out of well-founded scepticism or out of fear of violent retaliation. One strategy adopted by Zambian widows is to hide property before the relatives come to take away the body for burial. This ruse is generally only possible if death is anticipated because the man has been ill for some time. Other widows manage to assemble a strong group of friends to fend off the invaders. Sometimes a widow allows everything to be taken in order both to avoid antagonism and to safeguard the possibility of help from the relatives with her children's future - school fees, clothing, and their major ceremonies and rituals. Support groups may be instrumental not only in protecting widows from harassment but also by collecting funds to pay for legal assistance, and giving practical help (see Chapter 11).

Conflicts between different systems of law

The legal difficulties women face are far more complex than a simple conflict between 'modern' and 'customary' laws. Complications result from the coexistence of received colonial law, modern statute and case law, the religious and codified 'customary' law of the traditional courts, and the actual 'living custom' rules as applied by local communities. The issues of family matters and land are precisely the matters that are usually left to the traditional, religious or local authorities who administer 'customary' law and 'living custom'.

Codified customary law was the work of colonial administrators, taken note of in the modern courts and relied on in the traditional courts. But it does not represent the actual 'living custom', applied locally, which adapts to each new conflict situation, seeking solutions to problems through conciliation and diplomacy.[15] Rules governing the settlement of disputes in traditional communities never possess the features of a Western jurisprudence. Under customary law, decisions are made 'ad hoc', there is no court of record or development of case law. Precedence carries no weight. It is 'living custom' rather than codified 'customary law' that defines women's lives in the areas of family and land. Unfortunately for women, the arbiters and interpreters of customs are male and likely to defer to the dominant male opinion, irrespective of any modern law. The interest of local officials is to uphold the status quo and not to offend powerful interests, which means that widows' battles against greedy relatives are rarely won here. Women's international human rights conventions carry little weight in traditional or religious courts. Besides, several states parties to the CEDAW 'reserved' on those articles which, they claimed, are culturally unacceptable.[16]

In those communities in Africa where widows cannot inherit, the customary law has been interpreted (or distorted) to include property acquired during the marriage by the joint endeavours of a husband and wife. Cars, television sets, and microwaves come to be regarded, under patriarchal interpretations of customary law, as the inheritance of the husband's family. Arguments that the widow used her own earnings to purchase the items, or that the husband left a will, appear to carry little weight at the local level..

In Malawi all disputes about land are devolved to the traditional courts, so that even if the marriage is a registered civil one the decision on inheritance of land will be decided according to customary law. In Botswana also, inheritance matters fall under customary law whatever the type of marriage. In Lesotho, the system of law chosen to govern distribution of an estate depends on whether the deceased's life-style was traditional or Western.

Hindu law in India

In India, the 'living customs' that inform the resolution of inheritance disputes before the village councils (*panchayats*) include caste norms, local traditions, and religious law. Although increasing numbers of women are beginning to be elected to *panchayats*, in general the composition of these councils is predominantly male, representing the more powerful families in the community. Considerable differences occur in the extent to which a widow can inherit, even between villages. Some village councils may lean towards a view which incorporates the modern law, and in other possibly more socially backward regions, the traditional view prevails. [17] In West Bengal, for instance, women are more emancipated; women's land rights have become a political issue and the 1956 Hindu Succession Act has helped widows, whereas in Gujerat and Uttar Pradesh there is little awareness that women have any inheritance rights at all, either as daughters or wives. [18] The implementation of the modern law and state statutes may be more advanced in southern India where the status of women is generally higher, than in northern India.

Only a male descendant can ask for partition of the property. It is almost impossible for a rural illiterate widow to fight for her inheritance since she comes up against male bureaucracy at all levels from the village to the city. Often a widow is not used to dealing with officials. In addition there are bureaucratic obstacles and superfluous requirements such as birth, marriage, and death certificates, photographs and legal documents, which are costly to acquire or are not available.

A survey in rural northern India showed that widows' rights to their husbands' property are only upheld by the community on the basis that they maintain the land for their patriarchal lineage, that is, their sons and future generations. Widows can sell inherited land provided the proceeds are for family needs such as dowry, a wedding or a funeral, and not for her own personal wants. Where a widow has only daughters and no sons, the husband's brothers may take all the property, occasionally allowing her a small share in order to provide dowry for them. There are, sadly, numerous reports of sons, who on reaching adulthood refuse to support their mothers and send them away. But some widows are very strong. Drèze refers to a widow in a Gujerat village who claimed to have disinherited one of her sons because he did not provide for her. The determining factor may often be the relationship the widow has with her brothers-in-law and the attitude of the local elders: where this is good it may be that a young widow with dependent children may be able to succeed in her claim to property on the understanding that she has it on trust for her sons, but such cases are rare.

Prabha Devi comes from a Brahmin family, a non-marrying high caste. She had three dependent sons when her husband died. Before he died his brothers had asked for partition in order to get his land. Prabha had already sold some land during her husband's illness in order to pay the medical expenses. She had mortgaged another piece. When her husband died she got no help from his brothers, but the village council upheld her petition and she was allowed to manage the land herself.

Siyapati Devi was widowed at twenty-three. She worked the land herself to feed and support her three small children. A year after her husband's death she asked for partition but the brothers refused and there were violent fights. Finally the caste *panchayat* allowed it and gave her a share equal to theirs. But the land is still in the name of her father-in-law. She too had to mortgage some land to pay for the medical care and funeral of her little son who died. But because she had control (*kabza*) of the land and showed strength, the community and the *panchayat* supported her. Siyapati thinks women are fools if they live by the land and cannot control it. But her neighbour, another widow, could not get her father-in-law to give her any share of her husband's property, and she and her small children had to earn their living by wage labour.

If a widow leaves her husband's village with her children in order to remarry, she forfeits her rights to her husband's land, and so do her children. If she leaves her children with the joint family, they may retain their inheritance rights. The links between residence and inheritance are significant. In this situation, widows complain that pressure is sometimes put on them to go for '*nata*', that is, to marry outside the village, so that the husband's close relatives can take over the property.

Muslim law

In most countries Islamic law, as it applies to women, is enforced in modified form, taking into account modern social conditions. In a few countries, for example, Pakistan, Saudi Arabia, Iraq and Iran, the *sharia* law is interpreted very strictly, and women are in danger of losing all their rights.

Islamic law requires a man to provide each of his wives with a household of her own, so usually only rich men can afford more than one wife. When he dies each of his widows inherit equally, but there is some confusion about whether the legal one-eighth portion of the dead husband's estate must be divided among all the co-widows, or whether each is entitled to this fraction, leaving less for the remaining heirs. In any case, the claims of the 'heirs' have some priority, equal to that of widows, and none of them may be excluded by a will. Nor is a testator allowed to will away more than one quarter of his estate to non-heirs. In her position as wife, mother, or daughter a woman may not be excluded. In essence, a woman only receives half of what her brother would receive from their father, and half of what her son would get from her husband. This distribution is considered unjust by some radical Islamic writers, who argue that a woman has a right to be maintained for the rest of her life, notwithstanding her share, while men have an obligation to maintain women with their inheritance.

In practice Muslim women, although accorded rights in law, are frequently deprived of their entitlement unless there are no close male relatives. This seems to be common among Muslim widows in India, and widows in Bangladesh and Pakistan. A few men have insisted that their sisters take their share, but most women get nothing. A sister may be persuaded to waive her rights or 'forgive' her brother; she is expected to do this out of affection and not through coercion. But the duress is there anyway.

'I felt I must never quarrel with my brother. Perhaps I might need him one day if anything happened to end my marriage. If I gave him my share, then he surely would feel bound to support me in case of bad times'. Thus explained a widow in a village in Managanj district who was forced to abandon her late husband's village when the in-laws were abusive to her. When she tried to obtain support from her brother she was rudely sent away, and his wife hurled insults at her: 'We have no time for you, you are always asking for something'. Now she has had to take work as a domestic servant with other relatives. 'Better to work for people you know a little, of the family, than to toil for strangers'. She is able to get food in return for her household labour, but she has not been able to get her legal share of her father's land.

Men defend the way inheritance is managed, dwelling on the practical problems in dividing up property equitably when most of it is in the form of buildings or household items rather than cash; explaining that a good woman should think of the welfare of her brother, his wife and children before herself; suggesting that if a sister might hope for a brother to house her after divorce or widowhood she should be careful not to press her claim with too much avarice.

So, while widows under Islamic law fare better than widows under customary or Hindu law, there is still a huge gap between what the law says and what happens in practice.

Taking action
The best outcome for a widow is likely when the husband has left a will, and she is prepared to go to court to defend it. Although, as noted above and as the following case from Uganda shows, a widow may still not be successful.

A Buganda (Uganda) widow's husband stipulated before his death that his wife and daughters should have for their own use six acres of the fifteen acres he owned. But shortly after her husband died, the tenants of bordering land began to encroach on her land. Because N had no man to defend her interests, not even any brothers, they thought they could browbeat her. Over the years N was in and out of court. Then when her son reached adulthood he demanded the land, and having got a portion of it he proceeded to sell it and use the proceeds for drinking with his friends. His wife resented N because she was always reproaching her wasteful son, and when she gave birth to a deformed baby and was left slightly crippled she blamed N, although the widow's midwifery skills and herbal knowledge were unsurpassed in the subcounty. When N took the tenants to court for the remaining acres they called her a witch, and mothers warned their children not to pick any fruit in her garden.

When she became old, she was known as a witch although she was also respected as a wise woman and traditional birth attendant of note. One day she was attacked when she was hoeing her garden and died before anyone could take her to hospital.

Even when a widow manages to gain access to legal advice and representation her lawyer may be caught in the trap of male bias in interpreting current 'living custom'.

The FIDA legal aid clinic in Kampala, Uganda, was approached by Elizabeth, a widow who, on the death of her husband, was evicted from her house, lost all her household property and, in addition, was forced to surrender custody of her children to the relatives who pointed out that as she had no income she would be unable to support and educate her two children, a boy of seven and a girl of three. The brothers-in-law took the children back to the village, and Elizabeth found work as a domestic servant. A few months later she got a message that her little son was desperate to see her and was very unhappy. She borrowed money and travelled to her husband's village, where she discovered that the children, far from being supported, were being abused. The boy was hoeing in the gardens of neighbours to obtain food for himself and his sister. The little girl was so malnourished that she died within a few days of her mother's arrival. The widow had come finally to the FIDA office because the family was claiming 500 Ugandan shillings from her to pay for the child's funeral. All that FIDA could do was to arrive at a 'conciliation' by which, rather than pay the whole sum immediately, Elizabeth could pay in instalments. As for the household property taken, it had all been distributed among the family, or been destroyed.

Governmental intervention

Governments, made mindful of their obligations under CEDAW, the FLS, the Beijing Global Platform for Action, and constitutional guarantees of equality, are beginning to address the issues of discrimination in inheritance laws as they affect widows. For example, in 1994 the state government of Maharashtra in Bombay strengthened the 1956 Hindu Succession Act, arguing that such a measure would help to combat sex discrimination and reduce the worst excesses of the dowry system. In a landmark decision in 1995, the Supreme Court of Nepal ordered the government to draft a new inheritance code to give women equal rights to ancestral property, prohibited in the current law. Lawyers argued that the existing legislation was in breach of CEDAW, which

Nepal had ratified. But the court determined that, in such a patriarchal and traditional society as Nepal a dramatic change in the law would be extremely disruptive unless it was thoroughly discussed within the society, including the women's organisations.

In Zimbabwe, Malawi, Kenya, Uganda, and other African countries teams of women lawyers are working closely with governments to develop proposals for the harmonisation and reform of inheritance laws. Action is needed to remove the reservations on equality in constitutions and the ratification treaties of the CEDAW which exempt customary law provisions.

How effective such law reforms will be will depend on the extent to which women are empowered - psychologically, socially and economically - to go to the courts on the issues; the success of legal education campaigns; and the integrity of the local courts to administer objectively new laws on inheritance, however powerful the opposition. In Bangladesh, in 1994 , NGO activities to assist women to fight for their rights aroused the ire of mullahs and conservative groups who threatened both the women and the NGO staff. (The harassment of Taslin Nasreen, the Bangladeshi feminist, in 1994, because she dared to criticise Muslim fundamentalists' attitude to women was an extreme illustration of the fury that can be whipped up when women's rights are discussed in an Islamic context.)

Patrilineality and patrilocality are at the heart of the resistance to implementing changes in traditional systems of inheritance. Without secure inheritance rights, widows will continue to be made destitute on their husband's death, and subject to violence and theft. Allowing daughters to inherit along with sons will upgrade the status of woman, demonstrating that girls should be valued equally with boys.

If daughters and sons inherited equally, the size of the average landholding would remain unchanged but the number of places over which it is dispersed would double in the course of each generation. If daughters and widows inherit, marriage and remarriage may be a problem. If co-widows share an inheritance, the land shares may be too small for subsistence. Law reform and harmonisation of different legal systems is a worthy objective, but most difficult to achieve.

One egalitarian solution put forward by Drèze in the context of rural India is of village 'endogamy' or 'homoparental' inheritance, in which daughters inherit from mothers and sons from fathers. [19] A less radical solution is to retain the existing systems of patrilineal inheritance, supported by local custom and traditions, with the amendment that husbands and wives have joint ownership rights over the land inherited by either spouse. However, as far as widows are concerned, the issue of inheritance from parents is less important than that of inheritance from husbands. This therefore should be the first priority.

The media can help by ensuring that violations of widows' inheritance rights are given full publicity. Existing laws should be strengthened so that those who interfere with the property of a dead person are punished. Educating men and women about the laws of succession, and about the benefits of writing a will is essential. People need to know how and where they can make arrangements for the disposal of their property on death. Women must learn the essential procedures to follow in the event of their bereavement.

Inheritance law as it affects women is a rich area for research. A useful model for analysing the subject is the study, by WiLDAF, which looked at the legal, economic and social issues in six countries in southern Africa [20] Such a multidisciplinary approach is imperative before any blue-print for a new law is drafted.

Notes

1.   For a discussion of inheritance rights of daughters and widows see Marty Chen and Jean Drèze, *Widows and Well-being in Rural North India*, Development Economics Research Programme Paper No. 40, London School of Economics.

2.   Paul Harrison, 'Living Dangerously', *People*, Vol. 18, No. 3, 1991; also *Women in Disaster Areas: Bangladesh Report*, Shamim, 1992.

3.   See Betty Potash, ed., *Widows in African Society*, Stanford Press, 1986; and Jean Drèze, *Widows in Rural India*, Development Economics Research Programme Paper No. 26, London School of Economics, 1990.

4.   Perpetua Karanja, 'Women's Land Ownership Rights in Kenya', pp. 109–35, and Jane Knowles, 'Women's Access to Land in Africa', pp. 1–14, both in *Third World Legal Studies*, International Third World Legal Studies Association and Valparaiso School of Law, 1991.

5.   See D. W. Cohen and E. S. Atieno Odhiambo, *Burying SM: The Politics of Knowledge and the Sociology of Power in Africa*, Heinemann, 1992. S. M. Otieno, a distinguished Luo lawyer in Nairobi, left a will which was challenged by his relatives on the grounds that it breached Luo custom.

6.   See in particular *Women and Law in Southern Africa Project (WLSA)*, Harare, 1994; *Inheritance in Zambia: Law and Practice*, Lusaka; also *Uncovering Reality: Excavating Women's Rights in African Family Law* (WLSA Working Paper No. 7). Also the work of ZARD (Zambia Association for Research and Development).

7.   *Murisa* v. *Murisa* (1994) heard in the Zimbabwe High Court and reported in *Picking up the Pieces*, WLSA, 1995.

8.   *Picking up the Pieces.*

9.   *Gabon Aftermath: The Mistreatment of Widows*, ZARD, 1994.

10.   Drèze, *Widows in Rural India*, p. 63. Sometimes even this formality is

unnecessary, as local lawyers may refuse to acknowledge that the widow has any rights to renounce.

11. Chen and Drèze, *Widows and Well-being in Rural North India*, pp. 15-17.

12. See Tassoum Douai, 'Les Veuves en développement' (unpublished paper): 'Widows are always exposed to maltreatment by their in-laws. Many women find themselves deprived of their assets after the death of their busbands. This situation in widowhood is, with few exceptions, a common phenomenon in much of Africa' (my translation).

13. Reports of the Kenyan court case in which the influential Kikuyu widow of distinguished Luo lawyer S. M. Otieno fought his relatives over his will (see note 5) reached the columns of the *Washington Post*, and millions of Kenyans followed the court proceedings for months. Also, the harassment of the widows of the Zambian football team who lost their lives in a plane crash in 1991 – and their eventual protection by the Zambian government – became a lead story at the time, and is still remembered today.

14. Personal communication from a Pakistani woman advocate, who asked for anonymity.

15. E. Cotran and N. Rubin, eds., *Readings in African Law* (2 vols.), Cass Library of African Law, London, 1970. Also J. Max Gluckman, *Custom and Conflict in Africa*, Blackwell, Oxford, 1993.

16. For example, regarding Article 5 (on customary practices) and Article 16 (on the family), states parties (including the UK) have set down so many reservations that in many cases the convention's spirit and objective were contradicted.

17. See Drèze, *Widows in Rural India*, pp. 62–70 for further discussion of these points.

18. Ibid.

19. As was the custom with the Dimasa Kachari.

20. Botswana, Swaziland, Zambia, Zimbabwe, Lesotho and Mozambique.

CHAPTER 4

Sex and Sexuality

The sexuality of widows in developing countries is an all but taboo subject. It is barely mentioned in the literature on women, poverty, health or ageing. This chapter attempts to bring this hidden subject out into the open and highlight some of the issues.

Studies into the sexuality of widows are needed because if this aspect of their lives is ignored, widows will not be treated as whole human beings. The sexual aspects of losing a partner have begun to be studied in the West but have barely been addressed in Third World studies on women, health and development. [1] (When the topic was first introduced at the Rural Widows' Conference in Bangalore, India in 1994, there was initial shock at the mention of such a hidden and intimate issue, and reluctance to discuss it, followed by eagerness to lift off the covers of silence and get to grips with the nature of associated taboos. The codes concerning widows' sexual expression were acknowledged as being one of the principal obstacles to removing discrimination.)

As a wife, a woman has a place in society; her relationships with other members of the family group are defined and certain. Although many marriages are unhappy and violent and women risk desertion and divorce, it is respectable to have a husband - even if he is absent - and a social disaster to have lost one. Women are expected to be faithful to their spouses; a wife's adultery is frequently regarded as a crime while men's adultery or promiscuity less often causes such opprobrium.

Discrimination in social attitudes to the sexuality of men and women is prevalent almost everywhere. A man's sexuality is usually accepted as his right throughout his life.. His fertility continues into old age; it is accepted that a man whose wife dies has a need to remarry. He can marry many times, and continue to father children for many years. Women's sexuality is linked to their fertility, so an older, post-menopausal widow is in an ambiguous situation. Older women are usually seen as asexual (this 'death' of their sexual identity is perceptively described by Germaine Greer in her book *The Change*)[2], but their asexuality does not protect them from becoming victims of rape linked with other violent crimes. The codes and attitudes governing the sexual behaviour of widows demonstrate more than any other set of rules the vast gap between the social treatment of men and of women. It is important to focus on as attitudes to the sexuality of widows are at the very heart of their low status and marginalisation.

In India, traditional responses to widowhood are intended to draw a curtain over her sexuality and make her into a non-sexual being. In some African cultures, her sexuality tends to be allocated to a substitute husband, usually a kinsman. A widow may be forced into sexual union or marriage with a kin member in order to bear children for the dead husband. This subject is dealt with more fully in Chapter 6.

The taboo on discussing the sexuality of widows appears to evolve from religious and cultural inhibitions which hold either that widows should have no sexual desires or needs whatsoever, or that their sexuality is so rapacious that it must be stringently controlled lest it ensnare susceptible men. Widows thus must be forcibly incarcerated in institutionalised celibacy, or be taken over in remarriage or other sexual union by the dead husband's kin. More generally, outside these specific cultural responses widows become sexually vulnerable and liable to be dragged down into casual liaisons and prostitution. Even in the West, young and middle-aged widows risk being regarded as easily available, sex-starved and anxiously seeking some new relationship. In the West the term 'merry widow', used to describe widows past their prime who enjoy themselves, has a sexual connotation. Such attitudes account for why many married women regard widows and divorced women as a threat and are unwilling to include them in social gatherings. Widows in developed countries can find themselves in humiliating and distressing situations like their Third World sisters.

Patriarchal society holds that for women, sexual activity is only permitted in marriage, whilst there is far less condemnation of men's pre-marital and extra-marital sexual activity. There are many examples of such traditions all over the world.[3] Widows must be seen as celibates and ascetics in continual mourning for their husbands, or safely remarried or living within the protection of the family. A widow living without a male head of household is an easy target for sexual innuendo and sexual assault. In many cultures, the names for widows are synonymous with those used for sex workers.[4]

Societal attitudes

The denial of widows' sexuality can have appalling consequences. Unable to admit that they are having any kind of sexual relationship, those who do may be forced into clandestine liaisons which can leave them vulnerable. Frequently such encounters lead to unwanted pregnancies because the widows will not seek family planning services. (Family planning associations [FPAs] in several developing countries have a policy of not seeing unmarried women. Staff of the Kenyan FPA, asked if it provided services for widows, were astonished at such an enquiry and said they had never considered this category of women as potential clients.) However, like other women, widows of all ages have a right to health services relating to their reproductive health: not simply contraception and abortion information and services, but rape counselling, diagnostic procedures concerning sexually transmitted diseases and HIV, pap tests, smears, and therapies to lessen the problems of menopause. The International Planned Parenthood Federation's 1995 Vision Statement commits member FPAs to 'strive, in particular, to advance the family planning movement among the under-served by addressing their unmet need and demand for sexual and reproductive health; and to work co-operatively in this endeavour with all interested governmental and non-governmental parties'[5] The right of all women to receive health care services including family planning is also endorsed by Article 12 of the UN Women's Convention (CEDAW), and women's right to control their fertility is echoed in the 1993 Vienna Declaration of Human Rights, Article 14. This right was given explicit coverage in the Plan of Action of the Beijing Fourth World Women's Conference of 1995.

In areas of civil war and conflict, in flight and in refugee camps, traumatised widows who have seen their husbands murdered, women who do not know whether they are widowed or not, are often victims of rape. These women require particularly sensitive counselling and family planning and gynaecological services (see Chapter 9). They are amongst the most hard-to-reach women because of the dishonour attached to them. The concept of 'honour', especially in Muslim communities, puts them at risk from violence by their own relations if they have been defiled, made pregnant, or have contracted the HIV virus.

Pregnancy, childbirth and abortion

Neglect of the reproductive health of widows is an infringement of their human right to appropriate medical services. Younger widows are at as much risk in pregnancy and childbirth as married or unmarried women, but a pregnancy can be culturally disastrous for them. Antenatal care, or abortion services, if legally available, may not be accessible to frightened widows terrified of owning up to their predicament. Shame, vilification, and an unattended and life-threatening confinement with eventual destitution may be the consequences of an unwanted conception.

Evidence from various countries - Ghana, Nigeria Uganda, Chad and Kenya - reveals that even in leviratic arrangements, the anticipated male support can disintegrate, concluding with the eviction of the widow following the birth of a child. On the other hand, in several traditional communities a child born to a widow through a casual affair is adopted into the kinship group. [6]

> An old Masai widow of a polygamous marriage accepted with equanimity the two babies born to her young co-widow long after their husband had died, explaining that the 'seed was good', for the young father was also Masai. 'But now it is not so safe. For the seed can come from anywhere, with other young men travelling around, and you no longer know if it is good'.

Living without sex

The received opinion in the West now is that older women are entitled to be sexually active because it is good for them. The logic is that everyone has a right to sexual expression. However, the right of a widow to sexual self-expression is not one she can exercise in the absence of an interested partner. And once she is over forty there is an ever-decreasing chance that she will meet someone she wants to have a sexual relationship with. It becomes all the more important that she does not allow herself to become, in Germaine Greer's words, a "frustrated and bitter old crone".

Some African widows have spoken frankly of how extreme grief and emotion heightened their sexual desire. In a crowded Nairobi hotel lobby, a middle-aged widow working to rehabilitate and assist AIDS widows and orphans related how grateful she was that her husband's brother had been there to 'take her over'. 'In the extremes of my lamentation, I was full of passion. I was happy to be comforted by his brother else I would have gone with *him*, and *him* and *him* and *him*!' And she indicated with her fingers the various guests seated at the adjoining tables. The problem lies in the powerlessness of many widows to exercise real choice in any subsequent relationship, and their vulnerability to male deception.

In some cases, widows may have the opportunity for sexual relationships with men but decide that they no longer want them. Young, still fertile widows are assumed to desire a sexual partner, but their options may be limited if they have children, if they are HIV-infected or have AIDS, and if they are very poor. They are likely to fear further pregnancies, ostracisation by their relatives, and the gossip of their neighbours. Traditions concerning remarriage and widow inheritance are no longer always acceptable options for the young widow; th0se with young children may fear for their welfare in a new union, and young widows must strive to be 'careful, shrewd and resourceful' in accepting a new sexual partner.

In developed countries, where the subject of female sexuality is more openly discussed, it is acknowledged that women who are able to continue to live fulfilled sexual lives in a stable union well into their later years often manage to look younger, and are less likely to suffer from frustration leading to mental imbalance, as well as maintaining their physical well-being.

In Uganda, some young HIV-infected AIDS widows declared that they were so occupied in training, income-generating, helping other widows, childcare and AIDS prevention activities that they had no time for men and were determined never again to get involved in a sexual relationship. Solidarity with other widows had given them a new confidence and strength, They said they felt more able to repel unwanted sexual overtures, and were helped in this by having other women to confide in. Words speak louder than deeds when women are in a group, and in the artificial situation of talking to outsiders; it is harder to resist, alone, the advances of a strong and determined man, especially when a widow is hungry, poor or needs assistance with a specifically 'male' task. 'A man never offers you help without expecting some return. He knows we are poor, so what have we got *to give* him but sex. We have to learn to do jobs on our own. We do not want any men. We have learned to repair our own houses and to build a store for the grain'. Thus lectured another widow in the same group when some of the younger women described negative sexual experiences after their husbands died.

Studies of Latin American widows have revealed that while older widows did occasionally admit to desire, the weight of their religious upbringing, which equates sexual desire with temptation and sin, and the designation of the older women as asexual are so strong that the older woman will almost always find an excuse to refuse new sexual relations or to stop being sexually active during her later years.[7] The widows studied feared the mockery of their children if they entered into a new union, so they viewed themselves as having little freedom to make choices about their bodies and their sexuality.

It is clear that many widows feel nothing but relief that sex is no longer required from them. 'I am grateful that there is no more forced sex, no more pain, no more beating and no more pregnancy,' confessed a north Indian widow in an unusually frank discussion on this subject in company with other widows. Young widows who have been married as young brides to much older men who already have other wives and children, or who are widowers, have possibly never found the sexual act pleasurable. 'I was terrified when they showed my husband-to-be to me. He had one tooth, was a hunchback, and very old. I was so frightened when I was left in his house that I would crawl under his mother's bed and try to escape him. He hurt me. I was glad that he died.' This was how a young Bangladeshi woman summed up her few months of marriage.

In parts of the world where female genital mutilation is still practised, sexual intercourse has with few exceptions been an intensely painful experience for women; indeed, one of the many explanations for the procedure is that it ensures the chastity of a woman by depriving her of the experience of sexual pleasure. Women who have been circumcised in their childhood or youth, often in primitive conditions, may continue to suffer the effects of inept surgery for the rest of their lives. As they get older, and are widowed, their gynaecological health needs may not be met by existing services which are concentrated in Mother and Child Health facilities (MCH) and in family planning. Older widows may need investigation and treatment, but once they are past childbearing the conditions associated with female circumcision in the context of the ageing of reproductive organs are often not detected.

All widows, whatever their age, may admit to feelings of frustration, low self-esteem, and in many cases depression as the important sexual component of their lives is eliminated. It is hard to lose this intimate manifestation of closeness, affection and love, which can reinforce self-esteem and provide an outlet for emotion. Health practitioners and FPAs need to become aware of the psychosomatic effects of this deprivation, and allow widows opportunities to discuss this loss. It is part of the grieving and a fundamental but unrecognised aspect of the change of status that accompanies widowhood.

On health grounds alone, to preserve the mental and physical well-being of widows there is all the more reason to intensify efforts to help them discover alternative fulfilment in living - through community participation, work, and economic and social independence. Although not taking the place of sex, involvement in social life and the restoring of self-esteem through work can compensate for the loss of a partner.

In most peasant societies, there have always been very clear ideas about the stage in life when a woman should cease sexual activity: when the first daughter reaches the age of marriage even if this occurs long before menopause; or the onset of the menopause itself. These older women then took on other roles in the family, managing the households containing younger co-wives or their daughters-in-law and grandchildren; or working in the community as traditional birth attendants and childcarers; or imparting to the new generation the history of the family and the village, and educating them in moral codes and religion. Sadly, these roles seem to be in danger of fading out, with negative implications for women's psychological health and social status, for they gave widows status although their sexual lives were considered to be over.

Widows who have sex

It is not always true that widows have to do without sex. In some African ethnic groups it is quite acceptable for widows of all ages to take lovers who may or may not contribute to household expenses. But these examples seem to be the exception rather than the rule today, where the fear of AIDS has changed some behaviours.[8]

Among the Rukuba of Plateau province, Nigeria, a widow can entertain a lover so long as she remains in her late husband's compound. The choice rests with the woman, who may choose one or more lovers from the men who approach her, who must be relatives of the dead husband. A lover comes in the evening to spend the night and the widow can cook for him if she wishes, but there are no obligations; similarly the lover may help her with agricultural tasks or house repairs but again without obligation. However, no matter how close the relationship may be, a lover is never expected to live permanently with a widow. Any children born of the union of widow and lover become the posthumous children of the late father.

In some cases, widows are forced to have sex against their will. This can happen as part of the rituals of various ethnic groups in parts of Africa and Asia where young and fertile widows must be quickly placed under the control of a substitute husband, whether through the levirate, widow inheritance, remarriage or other conjugal arrangements. Some sexual practices associated with mourning rites, such as ritual cleansing, also involve the widow in having sex with a designated man or group whether she wants it or not (see Chapter 1). Most extreme, however, are situations in which widows, unprotected by a man, find themselves vulnerable to rape.

The experience of rape is horrific for all women. The relating of its details to family, friends, but especially to male officials such at police or judges is doubly humiliating. Even in Western countries, women need considerable courage to face cross-examination in public, which often includes distressing enquiries about their private lives and allegations that they consented to the assault. Widows may be particularly fearful of describing the event and of naming their aggressor, given the public attitudes to their sexuality. On a Christmas Eve night in 1993 an English widow in her seventies was raped as she returned home after church. Showing extraordinary bravery, she insisted on going public about the attack and appeared on television and radio to implore her community to report any suspect. She wanted the rapist apprehended so that other women would feel safe, and she hoped that her openness would encourage more women to report actions of sexual violence without fear. This is not an isolated case, but many widows in this position are reluctant to make a complaint, although public attitudes are beginning to change.

In other cultures, the position is far worse. In Muslim countries, a widow who has disgraced her family by becoming pregnant is seen as beyond redemption. Adultery and sex before marriage are grave sins. Under extreme interpretations of Islamic law a widow who has committed the sin of adultery might be stoned to death. In Islamic countries to be raped is a *zina*, a dishonour for the woman.[9] If she is pregnant or has given birth a prison may be her destination. Somali and Afghan widows pregnant as the result of rape have been executed by their brothers-in-law or brothers. Afghan as well as Kurdish widowed refugees who were raped found that they were not welcomed back to their villages because their children were the issue of the enemy. They had become 'unclean'. The sin of the rapist was transferred to them. (See Chapter 9.) There is a need for more research on the treatment of widows under the sexual codes of religious laws. International human rights law requires governments to eliminate discrimination of this nature.

> In the Somali refugee camps in northern Kenya, the United Nations High Commission for Refugees (UNHCR), alerted to the problems of unaccompanied women, mainly widows, becoming rape victims recently appointed a special women's rape counsellor. Many of the widows, raped by bandits, had contracted HIV, and were pregnant. There were several cases of widows being so rejected by their own blood brothers that they had become deranged, or tried to kill themselves and their babies.[10]

Stories of mothers killing babies conceived after widowhood abound in many countries. Others resort to illegal and clandestine abortion, with its high risks of morbidity and mortality, or to infanticide.

The lack of information on the reproductive health of widows is another illustration of the secrecy surrounding the subject. There are no disaggregated statistics on the numbers of widows who are seduced, raped, aborted, or who become unsupported mothers. Only when the rape and pregnancies of hundreds of Bosnian women, including many widows, in the former Yugoslavia were brought to the attention of the international community did the sexual torture and victimisation of women begin to be discussed as a human rights issue. (The perpetrators of war crimes, such as murder, torture and rape, against civilians now face trial - in 1996, those from the former Yugoslavia at the UN War Crimes Tribunal at The Hague, and, in 1997, those from Rwanda at the International Criminal Tribunal in Arusha, Tanzania.) Not only feminists but Western women in general were appalled that women made pregnant through rape were refused terminations in the former Yugoslavia. It is to be hoped that this concern for white European widows who were victims of rape in war will now extend itself to all the millions of women in Third World countries who are trapped in civil insurrections and violence.

Widows in traditional communities are often forced, because of the extreme social stigma attached to any extra-marital pregnancy and the even greater dishonour when the child is conceived through a rape, to abandon their illegitimate babies, who may die unattended, in some hidden place, unless rescued. An orphanage outside Nairobi cares for sero-positive babies abandoned by their raped mothers in the Somali refugee camps.[11] Some widows commit suicide as the only way out of the terrible situation in which they find themselves. Yet some of these babies, if rescued in time and given essential care, can thrive; they will not necessarily die and may even sero-revert. Traumatised widows have a right to better information. It could save their children's lives.

In India, so intense is the fear of the widow's unbridled sexual appetites that there are widows' ashrams where women from non-remarrying-castes can be put away from society for ever, dedicating themselves to religious duties, receiving alms, and being careful to remove any adornments that might make them attractive and feminine. After the riots in India that followed Indira Ghandi's assassination, and the storming of the mosque at Amritsar, newly widowed Sikh women had to be taken to places of refuge to escape assault and rape. In Poona, an ashram was founded to prevent the suicide of pregnant widows. In rural Maharashtra, an ashram was created to protect widows from the attentions of men who provided social services in the temples (see Chapter 8 for more about ashrams.)

Conclusion

Sex is part of life; sexuality is part of the make-up of every man and woman. Many of the traditions, customs and attitudes to do with widows are linked to a patriarchal view of a woman's sexuality as being either the property of a man, or else to be ignored. From these attitudes has arisen a whole culture of discrimination and a suppression of woman's creative potential throughout her life.

If widows are to be helped to be less dependent on others, to be strong, shrewd and resourceful in order to protect their rights, analysis is required of the many sexual injustices to which they are subject. Widows themselves need to be encouraged to talk about how they feel, and what they want. Working together they can free themselves from the trap of images of widowhood that limit their autonomy.

Notes

1.   For Western studies, see, for example, Peter Marris, *Widows and Their Families*, Routledge and Kegan Paul, 1958; Helena Lopata, *Women as Widows: Support Systems*, New York, 1979.

2.   Germaine Greer, *The Change: Women, Ageing and the Menopause*, Hamish Hamilton, 1991, pp. 319–47.

3.   Kate Millett, *Sexual Politics*, Hart-Davis, 1969.

4.   Bernadette Olowo-Freers and Thomas Barton, *In Pursuit of Fulfilment: Studies of Cultural Diversity and Sexual Behaviour in Uganda*, UNICEF Kampala, 1992, p. 7.

5.   International Planned Parenthood Federation Vision Statement 1995.

6.   Ibid.

7.   Argelia Londono Velez, 'Female Sexuality and Ageing in Colombia', in *Mid-life and Older Women in Latin America and the Caribbean*, Pan American Health Organisation and American Association of Retired Persons, 1989, p. 289.

8.   Betty Potash, ed., *Widows in African Society*, Stanford Press, 1986.

9.   For more on this see CHANGE reports on women in Iraq and papers by the Association of Women for the Reform of Muslim Laws, France.

10.   Personal communication, UNHCR Nairobi, 1993.

11.   Information obtained during a visit to the Father Agostino orphanage in Karen, Nairobi, Kenya.

CHAPTER 5

Widowhood in the Context of AIDS

The scourge of AIDS, sweeping through the world, has created a new generation of widows. In several countries in Africa and Southeast Asia, HIV/AIDS is currently one of the leading causes of death among adults. In the epidemic's initial stages, in the 1980s, more men were infected and died than women, but since the start of the 1990s the epidemiological gender pattern has been changing.

According to a conservative estimate by the World Health Organisation (WHO) in 1994 over 18 million men and women had already been infected with HIV, the virus that causes AIDS. To these must be added 1 million children. Every day, approximately 6000 additional persons - nearly half of them women - are infected with HIV. Some 5 million persons with HIV have progressed to AIDS. In the last one and a half years almost as many persons have progressed to AIDS as did over the first thirteen years of the epidemic. [1] The World Health Organisation estimates that 7 to 8 million women of child-bearing age have been infected, with women in developing countries having by far the highest rates of infection. Southeast Asia, where infection was not reported until the early 1990s, is fast catching up with sub-Saharan Africa. In 1994, 1 million cases of HIV infection were reported in Bombay alone. [2] The WHO reported in 1994 that 100,000 people in that region have AIDS. [3] On the eve of the 1994 Tenth International AIDS Conference in Japan, a WHO spokesman said, 'The end of the epidemic is nowhere in sight.'

In sub-Saharan Africa, the effects of the epidemic on the families of the (mostly male) victims have been catastrophic. Millions of widows, often HIV-infected themselves, have been left as the sole supporters of their families, including sick and dying children and other dependent relatives.

According to the 1995 WHO report, worldwide up to 50 per cent (and in some places more) of all new HIV infections are in women - mainly adolescents and young women; in 1994, women represented 40 per cent of all new AIDS cases - a dramatic fourfold increase in the short space of a decade. [4] In the next decades the World Health Organisation predicts that the numbers of women infected by AIDS and dying as a result will increase, reversing the earlier male–female ratios. Many of these women will be widows whose husbands have already died; others may predecease their partners, leaving orphaned children. There will be increasing numbers of very young widows as men search for partners who they believe will be 'safe'.

One factor making women more vulnerable than men, according to the WHO, is the higher prevalence of sexually transmitted diseases (STDs) among women, ten times greater than in men. Such infection makes women more predisposed to HIV infection. In addition, female circumcision has been linked to the AIDS epidemic in Africa, since sexual relations can involve laceration of tissue. The poor health status of many HIV-infected widows makes them susceptible to opportunistic illnesses and there is evidence that they enjoy a shorter latency period between infection and the onset of AIDS, with death occurring earlier than in the case of men. In addition, poor social and economic circumstances may expose the widow to unsafe sexual relations, whether consensually or under duress.

But this epidemiological gender comparison masks the true significance of AIDS for widows and their families. There are few disaggregated statistics to show how many women have been widowed through AIDS, or who among them are HIV-positive; or the numbers and ages of children left fatherless. Moreover, whilst widowhood generally may carry many disadvantages, when it occurs as a consequence of AIDS, the disadvantages are compounded, intensifying the marginalisation of widows in many ethnic groups. And wherever AIDS strikes it ravages the lives of children left behind, placing huge demands on governments to care for and educate the next generation, for widowed mothers often find it impossible to pay the costs of schooling. (See chapters 1 and 2.)

Resources have, in the main, been directed to study of the clinical and epidemiological aspects of the disease and towards research to find a vaccine or cure. Social science studies have focused on the life styles of gay men, prostitutes, and drug addicts, but less attention has been devoted to the social and economic consequences for widows whose husbands have died from AIDS.

Insufficient information exists on how widows support themselves; how AIDS has impacted on their social and economic status; who cares for them when they eventually become ill with AIDS themselves; what support exists for them as carers. Nor is enough known about the spread of the disease among different categories of women. Censuses and the

Fertility and Health Surveys (FHS) do not disaggregate the statistics, so that there is no information on how many times a 'currently married' woman has been married. The numbers of women widowed through AIDS and infected by the husband, or through other sexual liaisons after his death, are not known. What about the new implications and new exploitative aspects of traditional customs such as widow inheritance, the levirate and ritual cleansing? [5]

Very little research has been undertaken on how AIDS has really impacted on widows' day-to-day lives, and what are their special needs as they struggle to support themselves and their dependants, which may include old, sick and disabled people as well as the very young. A neglected area of study is the impact of AIDS death among men on agriculture, cash-cropping and subsistence farming. For example, what happens to such coffee production where there are no able-bodied men to manage cultivation? Widows' economic needs, including the effect on food security, agriculture, sustainable development and the environment, have all been neglected. Data are lacking on all these question yet an understanding of the relationship between women's status and HIV/AIDS is critical to the future spread of the disease, and to the welfare of widows and their dependants. And a country's future depends on the good management of land, and the education and welfare of its women and children.

Women's unequal access to education, health services, training, income-generating activities and property and their lack of legal rights affect both their access to knowledge about AIDS and the measures they might take to prevent its transmission. The low status of many widows may be exacerbated by the stigma of AIDS, as the following pages describe. One consequence of women's generally low status is that in areas such as sub-Saharan Africa far fewer women with HIV or AIDS have access to appropriate health care, and so they are likely to progress more rapidly from HIV infection to full-blown AIDS and death than men. In Uganda, far fewer women than men die in hospital. The costs of using the formal health care system may be too high, and the distances too great, for women, but many widows have recounted how they sacrificed to send their husbands to hospital. [6]

Much of the material and case stories in this chapter are taken from Uganda because, of all the countries in Africa affected by the epidemic, it has been the most open about the prevalence of HIV/AIDS; it has been in the forefront of efforts to collect and publish data, and it has supported some of the most creative and innovative projects in Africa to support AIDS widows. In Uganda there seems hardly a family, whatever the ethnic group, educational level or income, which has not lost some close relative to AIDS. In the villages, behind the huts, among the banana trees, a visitor is likely to come across some freshly dug graves. In Malawi, Zimbabwe, Kenya and Zambia, and in the Francophone region of Africa, the same situation prevails.

In 1994 the Ugandan AIDS control programme (ACP) reported that almost 10 per cent of the population - about 1.5 million Ugandans - were HIV positive. In that year 43,000 cases of AIDS had been reported to the WHO, although experts say that the figure is a gross underestimate. Between 20 and 30 per cent of pregnant women tested HIV positive. In some districts, such as Rakai in southwest Uganda, the percentage was even higher. The ACP has also reported that the number of persons with AIDS in Uganda is doubling every 8 to 12 months. The numbers of AIDS widows are increasing, as well as the numbers of widows dying from the disease.

Uganda was the first African country to introduce an AIDS control programme (ACP), sponsored by WHO, and the only one, in 1996, to have an independent AIDS commission. Strenuous efforts made since 1987 by government and NGOs to change attitudes through enlightened education programmes appeared, in 1994, to be paying off as the infection rate slowed down. [7] The First Lady (the wife of President Museveni), Mrs. Janet Museveni, has played an important role in helping to change social attitudes, and is closely involved with one of the AIDS NGOs that assists orphans. [8]

Governments in some other countries have been reluctant to make so public the prevalence of AIDS, fearing that publicity would have negative effects on investment and tourism. [9] Kenya saw its tourist revenue severely reduced when the world's news media began to report the high incidence of HIV/AIDS among prostitutes working in the coastal resorts around Mombasa. [10] In Zimbabwe, where the spread of infection among widows and women generally is likely to outnumber the spread among men by the end of the century, there is a similar disinclination to collect and publish information. Dr Robert Choto, a Zimbabwean public health doctor, says, 'We must be open. Without having facts we cannot make effective public health policies, educate populations, or protect our women.' [11] In Malawi, where, at the time of my 1994 visit, there was a similar lack of openness and awareness, a 1994 UNICEF report revealed that 35 per cent of all women attending antenatal clinics in Lilongwe and in Blantyre (some of whose husbands had AIDS or had already died), tested sero-positive. [12]

In Bangladesh where the status of women is low and where public health messages about safe sex are unacceptable in a Muslim culture increasingly influenced by fundamentalists, a WHO spokesman in Dacca reported that in February 1994 there were fewer than ten reported cases of AIDS in the whole country.[13] However, the existence of flourishing red-light districts in Dacca and Chittagong, and the trafficking in women, suggests a considerable under-reporting of cases.[14] The clients of brothels are usually married men. But widowhood in the context of AIDS in South Asia has not yet been a subject for public concern nor research.

The unwillingness to collect data and report on the spread of the disease, the denial factor, impedes the success of health education programmes, and keeps women in ignorance of facts which, if known, might help to protect them from infection. Many widows in sub-Saharan Africa are never told the true cause of their husband's death. Because of the general scarcity of resources to undertake post-mortems, which would identify AIDS cases, other conditions such as heart attack, cancer, pneumonia, or an opportunistic illness are often cited as the cause of death; moreover there is little follow-up in the rural areas to educate and inform widows of the facts, and counsel them in health prevention strategies.

No cure for AIDS is in sight for the millions of people already infected or for the 30-40 million people the World Health Organisation expects will be HIV positive by the end of the millennium. But the preventive measures - such as safe sex - suggested by the World Health Organisation, governments and NGOs are often not available to women because of cultural, economic and legal restraints.

As pointed out above, the issue of widows in the context of AIDS and economic security, in both the rural and the urban setting, has not been sufficiently addressed by the international community or by governments. The bulk of resources have gone to medical research. And while social science studies have investigated the sexual lives of prostitutes, they have generally avoided, possibly for political reasons, issues of the cultural attitudes to sexuality, marriage, women and widowhood. Indeed, with the exception of Uganda, inadequate attention generally has been given to the behavioural aspects of the HIV/AIDS epidemic such as the prevalence of various 'traditional' practices which carry a high risk of transmitting the virus. Research is desperately needed to identify social and cultural practices that may promote or inhibit the spread of HIV in order for effective preventive strategies to be devised. Women alone cannot challenge traditions; they need a commitment from governments to support them and the NGOs who work with them.

Thee traditional support systems provided by kinship groups for their weaker members, which was anyway stretched to breaking point by economic and environmental factors, has, in many families and many societies, been dealt a death blow by the scourge of AIDS.

Stigma and blame lead to violence and rejection. Age-old traditions whereby the widow was accommodated and her needs were satisfied within the family or kin group are being cast aside - by the widows themselves as much as by their kin. Widows of men who died of AIDS, questioned on the point, say they do not wish to remarry when, in addition to other pressures, there is a risk of transmitting infection or being infected. Conflicting views were expressed by widows in a group outside Kampala:

'I do not wish to kill anyone. But I want to have a man'.
'We widows do not want another husband. He will give us the illness. He will go with other women. We want to stay away with out children, have our own house, our own work.'

Studies on cultural and sexual diversity in Uganda, such as In Pursuit of Fulfillment, a UNICEF publication, have been useful in helping health planners, policy makers, health workers and educators to tailor HIV/AIDS prevention efforts to local patterns, rather than oversimplifying the information for a single national message.[15] However, customs as they are interpreted and constantly evolving (through the influence of men, not women) can prove resistant to conventional health messages. For instance, criticisms of practices such as ritual cleansing, the levirate, widow inheritance, scarification, and sexual behaviour during funeral ceremonies may be rejected as being too 'Western'.

Whenever a woman finds out her husband has AIDS it is a shock. In developing countries, because many women have no access to diagnostic procedures such as AIDS tests, and since death certificates may cite the symptom of AIDS rather than AIDS itself as the cause of death, widows might discover the truth only when they begin to fall ill. A doctor at a hospital in Zimbabwe explained that only 1 per cent of widows of men who died from AIDS in his hospital return afterwards for checks.

Bereaved, traumatised, impoverished through the expense of nursing the sick man, rejected and attacked by his family, widows in this situation have almost impossible burdens to carry: becoming main breadwinner, nurse, carer and manager of the family, whilst still expected to participate in traditional customs associated with mourning. Some of the rituals described in this chapter and elsewhere increase the risks of spreading HIV infection. Resisting participating in them may result in further accusations of evil practices and eventual rejection by the kin.

Widows of men who have died of AIDS, knowingly or unknowingly infected themselves, may pass this infection on to children in the womb or through breastfeeding. In polygamous marriages, co-wives are at high risk. After a man's death there may be other co-widows requiring support in their illness. Always there are the babies and children to be cared for. At the burial ceremonies, widows are often horrified to meet previously unknown women and children, claiming the rights of widows and orphans. Who is a wife, and who is a widow in such circumstances is a matter for the local community administering customary law, or for the courts.

Shock and sadness at the death of the breadwinner and protector are experienced at the same time as fear about the fate of the children.[16] Babies born with HIV infection are sometimes abandoned by their mothers, although it is now known that provided they are not breast-fed by sero-positive mothers, sero reversion can occur.[17] Widowed mothers, aware of their own illness, suffer the anxiety of wondering who will care for their surviving young when they are dead. The shock widows experience can cause mental breakdown, severe depression and suicide. 'What about my children? What will happen to them in the event that I go?' is a question that often confronts those counselling AIDS widows[18]

AIDS further creates a stigma for the widows which makes society cruel and unhelpful. 'Why are you looking so fat? What did you do to him for him to get so thin?' In Uganda, widows have told how their in-laws accused them of using witchcraft to kill their husbands, and 'chased' them away from their homes.. Others told of being evicted by landlords who learned of their association with AIDS. In addition to suffering all the disadvantages and discrimination attached to widowhood in general, AIDS widows are often stigmatised as a result of ignorance and misinformation about the pandemic. It is commonly believed that it is the woman's fault if her man gets ill.

Widows of men who have died of AIDS are frequently rejected by their families. Their association with the disease is fearful to communities fed on myth and rumour. At the same time, the threat of stigmatisation inhibits openness in discussion and causes sero-positive people to deny they are carriers, and widows to admit the cause of their husband's death, should they know it.

Widows without a male protector easily become victims of sexual harassment or rape.. Forced widow inheritance, and ritual cleansing of widows after bereavemeent or in association with funeral ceremonies can often take the form of rape, or be accompanied by other forms of violence. Unprotected widows may be the victims of rape by family members as well as by strangers, and the shame associated with such an attack inhibits them from complaining. Rapists carrying HIV are more likely to infect their victims as rape carries greater risks of passing on HIV infection than consensual sex; first, because contraceptive protection is unlikely to be used; second, because the violence of the act makes it likely that the woman will suffer lacerations and internal bruising which may make it easier for the HIV virus to enter the bloodstream. (See Chapter 9.)

There are no precise figures on the numbers of women or widows who have contracted AIDS or HIV infection as a result of rape, but it should clearly be a matter of concern. Widows need to work together and explore how they can collectively find the strength and means to resist harmful and degrading traditional sexual practices; for those widows without a strong network behind them, who try to protect themselves from an unwanted sexual liaison, may risk attracting to themselves more violence.

The double standards which allow husbands to be unfaithful creates further problems for women when their partner contracts AIDS. It is hard for widows to accept the fact that their husbands have not only betrayed them sexually (a not uncommon occurrence in most patriarchal societies), but have also infected them with a deadly disease. If the men had divulged the truth, the women could have protected themselves, for example, by using a condom.

When women are informed of the dangers of unprotected sex with partners whom they have reason to believe engage in extra-marital affairs, their low status and lack of equality with men often preclude them from questioning the men about their sexual activities; neither are they able to discuss the use of condoms. Introducing this sort of topic into a conversation can lead to the woman herself being accused of promiscuity, and to incidents of violence. Women need help to find ways to talk about sex and sexual health with their partners.

'I knew about AIDS. A health visitor had talked to all the women in the village. I knew my husband was spending his money on another woman, and buying her jewellery and clothes, but when I tried to tell him what the health lady had said, he got very angry and hit me,' remembered one of a group of widows in Uganda. Another said that when she produced a condom, she was suspected of having an affair herself. Her husband said that only prostitutes and soldiers used such things, and he would not use them as they reduced his pleasure. Often men, told they are dying of AIDS, do not want their wives to be told what is wrong with them, and refuse to curtail their sexual activities or undergo tests even if they are offered.

In 1994, southeast Zimbabwe, on the Mozambique border, the

hospitals are full of men dying from the complications of AIDS. 'We have such scarce resources, we are so overworked that we cannot follow-up the widows in the rural areas. When a man dies here this is no time to tell them the truth, and often we cannot do this until there has been a post-mortem,' explained a young Dutch doctor. He reported that bodies lay in the mortuary for days and weeks as young Zimbabwean doctors were often afraid to do post-mortems on corpses suspected of being infected. 'Even the doctors are ill-informed! Gloves, masks, and carefulness should protect them. And what can I do if there are no facts? I try and warn my patients but the men are so irresponsible. One of them said, after I had told him his test was positive, that he would sleep with as many women as he could if he had so little time left.'

It is wrong, however, to assume that it is only men who want sexual intercourse, or who are at risk of spreading AIDS. In Migori district, Nyanza, Kenya, widows have come begging for advice to an NGO working with women with HIV. 'I am dying with passion. I want sex but I am HIV positive and I do not want to kill. What can I do?' They are advised find an HIV-positive lover and use a condom; the NGO provides the condoms and food. The organisers are down-to-earth and practical. 'Widows need sex like any other women, and it is better for them to be inherited, and provided with food, than to be left out there to run around with man after man.'[19]

There are many rumours and false theories about how a man can protect himself, and some of these endanger the lives of very young girls. For example, one myth is that a man can be cured of the virus if he sleeps with a virgin; another is that safe sex with or without marriage can only occur with someone very young.

Enid, who lost her mother when a baby, was thirteen when her father died. She was sent to an aunt whose husband paid her school fees and looked after her. When her aunt died her uncle (by marriage) continued to support her. Enid neither knew nor asked what caused her aunt's death. Her uncle bought her clothes and jewellery and gave her money so that when she was fifteen she was induced to sleep with him, and he finally married her under traditional law. He became ill and she nursed him, but she did not know the true cause of his ulcers and cough. One day she discovered she had an infection. The uncle/ husband sent her to the hospital where they diagnosed HIV infection, and her pregnancy. At first her uncle seemed angry and accused her of sleeping with boys, but eventually he admitted that he had AIDS, and would soon die. His wife had also died from AIDS, but he had not told Enid because he feared she might leave him and there would be nobody to nurse him. He died shortly after; Enid nursed him to the end. Now she has an HIV-infected baby boy and she worries about what will happen to him if she should die. She is a member of the Philly Lutaaya widows' group and works to educate and inform young people in the villages about AIDS and how they can protect themselves.[20]

Due to the various false theories about AIDS, the female age of marriage in Uganda, which a few years ago was rising, is now decreasing. The consequence is an increase in the numbers of child widows (see Chapter 7). Young women, without education or training, become responsible for fatherless children, nursing ailing co-widows, and other relatives, as well as the offspring of co-wives who have died.

Infection in older, infertile widows may remain undetected since they may have less access to health services (see Chapter 8). This neglect may hasten in them the onset of full-blown AIDS.

Most widows are responsible for maintaining dependants, the young, old, disabled, and sick. Old widows may be left as the only surviving adult to care for sick children and grandchildren. In the Rakai district of Uganda in 1994, many households were composed of several widows and small children; their male relatives having died, these widows were left destitute and struggling to survive. Women-headed households, a growing phenomenon worldwide, make up over 30 per cent of all households in Africa.[21] In some countries, for example, Kenya, the percentage is higher (30 per cent).[22] In the years since the HIV virus was discovered the numbers of female-headed widowed households in Africa and southeast Asia have risen hugely as a result of male deaths caused by the pandemic, so that currently about half the women heads of household in Africa are widows.

Polygamy

Polygamy puts women at serious risk of contracting AIDS and, if they are themselves knowingly or unknowingly infected, of communicating it, through the husband to co-wives. Most marriages start with the man taking one wife, but during the marriage husbands take additional wives under the customary law, or have 'informal marriages' outside the law and its statements of moral codes. There is a blurring of definition between who exactly is wife and who mistress or casual sex partner. Whatever title is given to the relationship there will be several children left without support if the man dies. A polygamous man might die leaving as many as six or seven widows and around thirty offspring. Polygamy can, however, provide a mutual support system in widowhood, if there is harmony; but in the context of AIDS, co-widows can sometimes quarrel, blaming each other for the tragedy in their lives.

Particular groups of women, such as second and third wives, naturally find it difficult to introduce a discussion about condom use. If they are young and inexperienced, and their husband visits them only occasionally, they are in a weak bargaining position, only wanting to please him, and not wishing to provoke a quarrel or violence. Many widows are in this position having been remarried to a male relative who already has some wives; no matter how well she is counselled, a woman in this situation will rarely speak up for herself. Such remarried widows risk being thrown out if they refuse to have sex without a condom. In addition, myths and misinformation concerning AIDS exert a strong influence on women. In Uganda, some widows in polygamous unions believe that they are protected from becoming ill because the virus came from their husband and not from a stranger, and believe that their co-wives are equally safe. [23]

Prostitution

Women everywhere are at risk from men's visits to prostitutes, or other casual sexual encounters. This is particularly common when men leave rural areas to seek work in the city, and then return home to infect their wives. In Africa, and many other countries, men's reputations are often enhanced if they can boast of multiple sexual partners, but a woman with casual lovers is labelled promiscuous.

Widows may themselves be forced into prostitution because providing sexual services in return for money, or simply food, drink, clothes and shelter is the only outlet open to them to maintain themselves and their children. The shanty towns, 'bustis' and barrios of many Third World cities have their share of widows of all ages, forced to leave their rural areas in search of work. However, even in some villages there is also prostitution. [24] (See chapters 2 and 4.)

The Matharu Valley shanty town outside Nairobi is a long untidy cluster of shacks made from old packing boxes, corrugated iron, bedsteads, old cars, and rags. It is bulging with people, and 75 per cent of the population here are under fifteen. It is the natural destination in Kenya of widowed women fleeing the village when they have lost their access to land to seek work in the city. Wainigi is already in the last stages of full-blown AIDS. She is dying. Her thin arms and legs are blue and swollen with tumours. Wainigi came here with Nancy, her fifteen-year-old daughter, because her dead husband's family chased her away when she refused to cohabit with his brother. But she was too weak to work. A man said he would give Nancy domestic work but he set her up as a sex worker. Selling her body by day, Nancy is able to buy food and medicine and be with her mother at night. But the morning of her mother's death the social workers are unable to find Nancy. When, in the late afternoon, they eventually trace her to a brothel, Wainigi is dead.

AIDS widows are often victims of physical and mental violence. Their children are also vulnerable to abuse by others.

In Uganda, Norah's husband had died a year before from AIDS. Afterwards, her best friend's husband tried to have sex with her although he knew her husband had died from AIDS. Norah did not want to infect anyone, although she needed help. When she showed him the paper that indicated she was HIV positive, he beat her. Norah reported him to the Resistance Court (RC) chairman; but he too wanted an affair with her, asking, 'Don't you think you will have to pay me for helping you?'. The RC did, in fact, write the man a warning letter, but when Norah met him by accident in the street, he beat her again. She complained repeatedly to the RC. One day the man went to Norah's house. She refused to let him in, so he locked her and her child in. Norah was afraid that he would kill her.

Very often the surviving wife is blamed for the death of her husband from AIDS.

Sarah's husband Ndawala had died of AIDS, and she went to bury him in his village and to participate in mourning rites with her daughter of four and son of two, even though she had been separated from him for some eighteen months before his death. Her brothers-in-law saw her looking healthy and beautiful, and pointed her out to all the relatives, saying, 'She is the one who has infected him.' They threatened to beat her as a punishment and chased her out of the compound after seizing the children. A few weeks later, her older child, Nandawula, died of neglect and malnutrition. The boy, Musaka, is better cared for because he is the heir.

Sometimes the death of any AIDS widow is eagerly awaited.

Molly Kasule was thirty-two and her relatives knew that her husband had infected her before he died. 'Why are you not dying yet?' they asked her. 'Oh, soon you will be getting thin.' Molly had seven children aged between six and sixteen, and was asked, 'Why are the children not ill?' Now the little boy of six has tested HIV positive although he is still well.

It is not only the men who behave cruelly towards the AIDS widow.

Annie is thirty-three, a widow with five children. She is the tenth and last wife of her husband, and lived with him in the main house with the senior wife until she died. The co-wives dislike Annie and say that because she was so young when she 'caught' their man (she was eighteen and he was forty-seven) she had bewitched him and killed the senior wife by witchcraft. When the husband eventually died from AIDS, the co-wives tried to chase Annie and her children away; fortunately the husband had left a will.

The following case stories illustrate the economic, as well as social effects of becoming an AIDS widow.

Christine's husband worked as a truck driver and travelled between Uganda, Tanzania and Kenya. His wife cultivated a small plot of land growing groundnuts, sorghum and beans, which provided most of the food needs of the family. In his frequent absences, like other truck drivers he had casual affairs with prostitutes. Before he got ill he had borrowed money to buy a house, for he was earning good money. The couple also had a cow and some goats. Christine worked hard and was able to sell her surplus and feed all her three children who were all under nine years old. When her husband got ill, he had to stop work and Christine nursed him, found him special food and took him to the hospital in Kampala. The medicines were very expensive, so she sold the cow to pay for them. When he got worse she took him back to the hospital and stayed in the city, and therefore could not cultivate food. Eventually she brought him home to die. Before he died the moneylender was pestering her about the loan; although the house was unfinished he took possession of it. She took her eldest daughter out of school to collect firewood and water. After her husband died, her relatives made her spend all the money remaining on the funeral, as was customary. Christine herself became sick shortly afterwards and discovered she was infected. Finally, she sold the goats, and the relatives took back the land. They would not help her because they said she had 'killed' her husband, and they wanted nothing to do with her children. For a time some of the neighbours gave her food. When the children became ill because they were malnourished, Christine went to Kampala and tried to get work as a domestic servant.

Fortunately she went straight to TASO (The Aids Support Organisation of Uganda) and it found her work and gave her loans. But her children have lost all rights to their father's land.

Salome is a poor AIDS widow in a small village in the lake area of Malawi. She is only thirty-two but looks far older, with several small, ragged children. There are flaky white patches on their arms and legs. Almost all the youngest children have runny noses, and Salome says they get malaria, and cough and sneeze because they are so cold. They do not go to school, and when they are ill, which is often because of malnutrition, they have no warm covers, only bamboo mats which give no heat. There are some stuffed maize sacks for cushions on the floor. The children, if they are well, gather firewood to sell. An older, richer widow, who is a member of Malawi's parliament (her story is told in Chapter 3) visits Salome regularly with clothes and food. It is she who told me how the husband died, but his widow knows little about the cause, which was AIDS. She never visited him in hospital as she could not afford the transport, and had no one to leave her children with. She has no land, for her husband had worked the family's garden with his brothers, and now they do not want her near them. There was little to take, but the brothers seized the few blankets, some pots, and the furniture. Now there are only the bamboo mats and the stuffed maize bags. Like other widows in Malawian villages she has been passed over when women were being targeted to participate in credit and income-generating projects.

Orphans

A major social welfare aspect of AIDS is the question of orphans. (The term 'orphan' may include children who are fatherless, although the mother is alive). In some countries children whose fathers have died of AIDS have been forced by the authorities to leave school. [25] But in many cases, discrimination apart, a widow cannot afford to send her children to school.

The support of orphans is germane to the development of policies to improve the status of AIDS widows, because anxiety about their future is often their greatest concern. In Africa, and increasingly in Southeast Asia, AIDS is affecting the young, child-bearing population. Many AIDS widows may have been forced to break ties with the family, and they may have no close relative to whom they can entrust their young sons and daughters.

In some cases the debts run up by dying parents pass on to their young children, who become trapped in forms of debt bondage.

Exploitation of children in these circumstances is common. 'I had to support my mother with my body; that's all I could do,' said Nancy, the young girl from Nairobi (see page 84); she continued to work as a prostitute first to pay for her mother's hospital care, and then to pay her debts after she died. Some of these children are also HIV positive, and then pass on the infection.

In traditional societies, unlike in Western countries, the idea that children should be accommodated in institutions such as orphanages is totally unacceptable. So foreign is it to African culture that several governments have foreseen that other forms of support must be developed. [26] It is believed that institutionalised children would find it difficult to integrate in society once they grew up, and would be deprived of their cultural identity if they spent their childhood outside a family setting. In southeast Zimbabwe, in one orphanage outside Chipinge, the children look through bars at the life going on around them outside and live in cramped rooms, all ages crowded together. They go out to school, but once the lessons are over they are herded back to the barrack-like building, where kindly local people deposit gifts of food and vegetables for the cooks. Some of the inmates are the children of widows; with their fathers dead, they are classified as orphans because women are not expected to have sole responsibility for their children, and are rarely able to earn enough to support them.

Outside Harare, plans are already afoot to build a children's' village for orphaned young people, and to provide accommodation for them in small family groups with house mothers and fathers. In Uganda there are similar plans, spearheaded in 1993 by the First Lady, Mrs Janet Museveni, who established the UWESO training programmes in craft production for AIDS orphans. [27]

A major need of many AIDS widows in Africa is to be given opportunities to earn money so that school fees can be paid. Some rural AIDS widows say they want safe hostels for their adolescent daughters, from where they can attend secondary school - often at a distance from their homes - without fear of abuse or sexual harassment. Some widows are known to abandon their much-loved children in the hope that the authorities will rescue them and provide schooling which is way beyond their own power. [28]

Health and health care
Widows often die more quickly from AIDS than married women and men, because of their marginal status. Undernourishment, stress and lack of care all contribute to sero-positive widows succumbing early to the onslaughts of full-blown AIDS. (In Western countries AIDS need not

develop for twenty years following HIV infection provided the individual has a healthy life style.) Tender Loving Care (TLC) has been effective in bringing about sero-reversal in an orphanage in Kenya.[29] Widows generally are less able to afford nutritious food than other people; they may have less access to modern health care; and they may rely on inappropriate treatments from traditional healers when ill. Rural women, living at long distances from hospitals, may not be able to afford the costs of transport, or prescriptions, or substitute childcare when away from home.

> Elisabeth, an AIDS widow, stayed in her hut for three weeks; neighbours brought her water and firewood as her husband's family had abandoned her. Her legs were so full of ulcers she could only crawl. On her last day someone took her to hospital where she died in great pain. In the week before she died she had refused to be moved, saying that the money they had must be kept for the children's education.

Widows, whether or not they are HIV infected, need accessible and appropriate health care services. If their husbands have died from AIDS they and their children deserve sensitive counselling and practical assistance. The work of TASO of Uganda, described in more detail below and in Chapter 11, provides a model of what can be done.

Widows are often health carers as well as themselves needing access to appropriate health care. Older women, many of them widows, are often community health carers. They may be very much at risk from HIV infection, as it can be transmitted through blood passing into open wounds. Tradtional Birth Attendants (TBAs) have to be especially careful that small open abrasions they have suffered whilst working in agriculture are not in contact with blood from the patient. The same dangers apply to widows nursing sick relatives. Such traditional health care providers need some training on health risks, and protective clothing to avoid contamination.

What is being done?
Women, and in particular widows, have responded magnificently and creatively to the challenges described above. TASO, Philly Lutaaya and the Uganda War Widows Organisation in Uganda, the Widows and Orphans Society in Kenya, the Ministry of Widows in Ghana, the branches of FIDA have all developed innovative ways of supporting people with AIDS, and of co-operating with particular groups at risk based on the principles of openness, self-support and participation.

TASO (the Aids Support Organisation of Uganda) [30]

TASO was formed in 1987 by Noerine Kaleeba, a Ugandan widow whose husband died of AIDS in the UK, after contamination through infected blood in Uganda. Today TASO is a dynamic organisation offering care to more than 8,000 people with HIV/AIDS in six districts of Uganda. It offers counselling, education and social support to people with HIV/ AIDS and their families. TASO's philosophy is to promote 'positive living with HIV/AIDS'. It aims to restore a sense of self-worth and of social productivity. It encourages widows whose husband died of AIDS and who are themselves infected with the virus to come out about AIDS. 'PWA' stands for Persons with AIDS, and it is these women who are key activists, educators, and health promoters in their communities. Other counsellors are called ANONS (those who have not had the test), but all are aware of the social aspects of AIDS that are so distressing. Widows help other widows, listen to their stories, provide shelter for them when they are made homeless, help to raise loans for projects and for school fees, strengthen each other's resolve to live without men, educate their children about safe sex and women's rights.

TASO has done more than any other organisation in Africa to confront cruel prejudices and reduce stigmatisation. The office in a small street in Kampala bustles with life and laughter. Food is cooking, people come and go, and Noerine Kaleeba's office door is always open.

Irish Concern

A project in a village in southwest Uganda badly affected by AIDS provides a further good example of what can be done. Irish Concern supports a small group of twelve AIDS widows who, twice a week, after work, visit fourteen homes so that everyone in the village is contacted. When they find a sick widow, a dying child, an uncultivated garden, a need for water and firewood, they invite volunteer neighbours to help. Children have been recruited in the school holidays to dig and weed, or care for babies; neighbours are encouraged to provide cooked food, clothing and blankets. Once the self-help system was established in 1993, some of the founder widows began to pool their knowledge of herbal medicine in order to cultivate and market traditional herbal therapies. Each widow concentrates on growing one particular herb; Irish Concern funded the initial purchase of seeds. Since 1994 traditional healers and traditional birth attendants (TBAs) in the region have bought herbal medicines from Irish Concern, and accept their advice on how to treat a wide range of ailments. This project is now a thriving cottage industry. In spite of the tragic numbers of deaths that have depleted the population, the village, now mainly composed of widows and children, has become a resourceful and well-knit community; the gardens are cultivated and the widows are full of hope. 'Learning to live without men is what we must do,' said a wise older member, caring for several sick orphans and young widows.

Philly Lutaaya Initiative

The Philly Lutaaya project, supported by UNICEF, does similar work to TASO. It is named after a famous Ugandan musician, Philly Bongoley Lutaaya, who made public the fact of his HIV/AIDS infection before he died. The project practises TASO's creed about going public about AIDS, and helps widows to help themselves through income-generating activities, loan schemes, and counselling; when sero-positive widows succumb to the various opportunistic illnesses associated with HIV, Philly Lutaaya provides nursing care and food.

Ugandan Widows Efforts to Save Orphans (UWESO) has already been mentioned. The Ugandan War Widows Association supports war widows, many of whom are HIV positive or with AIDS. In Kenya the Widows and Orphans Society began in 1991 as a support system for AIDS widows, and in Ghana, Widows' Ministries - Northern Sector, a Church-based group, does similar work. The Uganda Association of Women's Lawyers (UAWL), and branches of FIDA (International Federation of Women Lawyers) all over Africa have also been effective champions of widows' rights in the context of AIDS.

There are doubtless many other successful AIDS widows' groups operating at the grassroots level elsewhere (Chapter 11 gives further examaples). All of them deserve funding by international agencies.

The challenges

The stigma attached to AIDS affects not only infected women, but also those thought to be at risk of infection or the source of it. Quantitative and qualitative information is needed.

Initially, the importance of the transmission of HIV to the foetus was not fully appreciated; nor in those early days was sufficient attention given to the crucial interrerlationship between women's status and HIV/AIDS. Neglect of this association has been a critical factor in the spread of the disease. Women, especially if they are poor, illiterate, and living in rural areas, are among the groups most difficut to reach in terms of sexual health information.

Women's lack of status within the family and the disgrace and humiliation of widowhood in many communities heighten their vulnerability to HIV infection and to other consequences of the pandemic. Both factors also affect their potential for advancement on the lines recommended in Forward Looking Strategies. AIDS widows, as the forgoing pages have described, are often exposed to discrimination, social rejection, and other violations of their basic human rights and dignity.

Prejudice and discrimination is not unique to women with HIV/AIDS, but is experienced by both sexes. However, while men's property and rights are generally protected by law, widows' lack of legal status often leads to their being denied legal protection. In societies in which widows were traditionally provided for by other family members, many AIDS widows, shunned by the community, are abandoned by the relatives because of the disgrace, and left without any support.

Older widows who would have normally been supported by their sons may find themselves burdened with the responsibility of caring for grandchildren and great-grandchildren, without any financial maintenance. Some of these carers may be frail or disabled; the children may themselves be ill (see Chapter 8).

As mentioned earlier, in some African countries AIDS has reduced the age of a girl's first marriage to puberty or near puberty with significant effects on their health, child-bearing, and opportunities for education, and increasing the likelihood that they will become young widows.

AIDS has had a serious impact on the fabric of social organisation, whether in the town or in rural areas. The withdrawal from the labour force of its most productive male members leaves widows with impossible responsibilities, as sole parent, health provider, breadwinner, farmer, and worker. Moreover, structural adjustment programmes (SAPs) have obliged many countries to reduce social services and support measures designed to meet the health-related costs of AIDS, thus increasing the burdens on widows. [31]

Conclusion

AIDS presents a global challenge of unprecedented proportions. It raises crucial health, humanitarian, economic, social, legal and feminist questions, and presents unique opportunities for effecting change, particularly for women.

It forces society to face issues that have so far been ignored, for example the poverty of unattached women, the relationship between poverty and prostitution, between widowhood and child deprivation. It also provides the impetus to examine sexuality and personal relationships, and the potential for women to take a more assertive role in this context. It highlights the need for men and women to be more responsible about sexual behaviour, and exposes the sexual double standards. AIDS can, in addition, be used as a challenge to protect the human rights of women and to combat discrimination against particularly vulnerable groups such as divorced women and widows.

If it could be said that anything beneficial had come of AIDS, it is this: many projects before have involved sex education, family planning and abortion, and tried to educate and help women, but have had little impact. Now, because of the harsh reality of AIDS, women are beginning to change. Through becoming economically independent, they can resist invitations from men and achieve some degree of personal autonomy.

Notes

1.   See D. Blake, *WHO International Consultation for Policy Makers on Women and AIDS in Preparation for the Beijing Conference*, Geneva, February 1995. The human immunodeficiency virus (HIV) is transmitted sexually mainly through sexual intercourse between men and women, and also through homosexual intercourse, contaminated blood and body fluids, and from infected mothers to infants perinatally. HIV is transmitted sexually in 80 per cent of cases. In Africa and Southeast Asia most cases arise from heterosexual intercourse.

2.   Statistics produced by the Indian Ministry of Health, 1994.

3.   'Global Battle to Conquer AIDS May Be Lost', *Independent*, 4 August 1994.

4.   WHO, 1994.

5.   See D. W. Cohen and E. S. Atieno Odhiambo, *Burying SM: The Politics of Knowledge and the Sociology of Power in Africa*, Heinemann, 1992, p. 113, for a discussion on AIDS and traditional customs.

6.   *Women and AIDS*, Rights and Humanity report to the WHO, 1992. A report on AIDS published by the Ugandan Medical Research Council in 1994 showed that in males aged 13 to 24, a crucial age group, the prevalence of HIV infection had fallen from 3.5 per cent in 1989 to less than 1 per cent in 1993.

7.   'Yes, AIDS Is Our Problem', *Independent*, 1 December 1994.

8.   This NGO is UWESO (Ugandan Widows' Efforts to Save Orphans), PO Box 8419, Kampala, Uganda.

9.   For example, in 1994 this author was told by a spokesman for the Ministry of Health in Bangladesh that there were only twenty-three cases of AIDS in the country.

10   'Global Battle to Conquer AIDS', *Independent*, 4 August 1994. Some 80 per cent of the prostitutes tested in Mombasa were found to be HIV positive or to have AIDS. Some of these were AIDS widows or orphans forced into prostitution through destitution, and so further endangering their own health and that of the wider population.

11.   Personal communication.

12.   Report from the AIDS Division of UNICEF, Lilongwe, Malawi, 1994.

13.   Personal communication.

14.   Personal communication from a spokeswoman for the Ministry of Health, Bangladesh.

15.   Bernadette Olowo-Freers and Thomas Barton, *In Pursuit of Fulfilment: Studies of Cultural Diversity and Sexual Behaviour in Uganda*, UNICEF Kampala, 1992, p. ix.

16.   WHO, *Women's Health: Across Age and Frontier*, WHO, 1992, Table 1 on p. 81.

17.   Olowo-Freers and Barton Thomas.

18.   Noerine Kaleeba, *We Miss You All*, TASO and Women and AIDS Support Network (WASN) Zimbabwe, 1991, p. 77.

19.   Personal communication, spokesperson of the Kenyan Widows and Orphans Society, Nairobi.

20.   The Philly Lutaaya Initiative of People with HIV/AIDS (PLI/PWA Project) is based in Kampala and supported by UNICEF. It helps people with AIDS who have volunteered to go public and share their personal experiences of living with HIV/AIDS with different target groups. It is named after a famous Ugandan musician, Philly Bongolay Lutaaya, who publicly acknowledged that he had AIDS some time before he died.

21.   United Nations, *The World's Women, 1970–1990: Trends and Statistics*, UN, New York, 1991.

22.   United Nations, *Demographic Yearbook 1987*, Statistical Office of the UN Secretariat.

23.   Conversation with Noerine Kaleeba, founder of the AIDS support organisation TASO.

24.   Personal communication from a group of widows in a Malawian village.

25.   Rights and Humanities, *Effects of AIDS on the Advancement of Women*, report to the UN Commission on the Status of Women, 1989.

26.   Zimbabwe is encouraging people to foster or adopt AIDS orphans. In Uganda, small, family-type children's cottages are planned.

27.   See note 8.

28.   Personal communication from a worker in the Widows Ministries in northern Ghana.

29.   See Margaret Owen, 'New Hope for Sero-positives in Italy', *Community Development Journal*, special issue on community responses to AIDS, Vol. 24, No. 23 (1989), pp. 210–217. Also Children of God Orphanage report from Nairobi, Kenya, where abandoned babies who initially tested sero-positive have reverted and where HIV-infected children have survived in good health because of the good environment (see Chapter 9, n. 8).

30.   Kaleeba.

31.   WHO Global Programme on AIDS, Report to the Director-General, 1992. See also *The Other Side of the Story: The Real Impact of World Bank and IMF Structural Adjustment Programmes*, Development-GAP, Washington, 1992; Oxfam, *Africa: Make or Break*, OXFAM, Oxford, 1993; and Susan George, *A Fate Worse than Debt*, Penguin, Harmondsworth, 1988.

CHAPTER 6

Remarriage

'Those who are excluded from family and society are the isolates. Those who have recently been deprived by death, illness, or migration of the company of someone they love are the desolates.' Thus wrote the British sociologist Peter Townsend of widows in a poor London borough in 1958.[1]

Widows very often feel isolated and desolated and if they must look forward to many years of life on their own, it is logical for some of them, as well as their family and friends, to think of remarriage as a solution to the problems of loneliness, poverty and low status. In the West, a widow's chances of remarriage may be low compared to that of a widower, but she cannot be forbidden to remarry, nor can she be made to remarry someone against her will. If she does remarry, she will not risk losing custody of her children although in most cases she will have to forgo rights to her former husband's pension. But living the remainder of her life as a widow, although she may experience loneliness, and often a great change in her life style and income, she will not have to suffer the dire social attitudes that are the lot of so many Third World widows. In some African and Asian countries, by contrast, customs such as widow inheritance, levirate, or other coercive conjugal arrangement for widows can be degrading to women. But they can also be beneficial arrangements, through which a widow is supported and integrated into her community: where obligations and duties are reciprocal, and everyone is looked after, including any offspring. Much depends on individual attitudes and personal relationships, so that it would be inappropriate to generalise. There are so many variations depending on ethnic group, education, locality, economic conditions, age and the particularities of specific kinship group. Some women feel secure in communities where old customs are still followed; others wish for change as reciprocity no longer operates and widows feel harassed and abused, as when they are forced into sexual unions that are not consensual.

Some of the more coercive practices relating to remarriage, which negate women's status, are gradually being brought to the attention of governments through the work of the CEDAW committee. States parties are asked to eliminate them in compliance with their obligations under the UN Women's Convention (See Chapter 1).[2] Where there exist limitations or restrictions or requirements relating to remarriage they are, for the most part, related to widows, and not to widowers.

There is a widely held assumption that the majority of Third World widows do remarry, and, if they do not, are supported by their families, and therefore present no great problems for policy makers. But there is considerable evidence that increasing numbers of such widows today do not remarry; nor, in many cases, do they wish to do so; when they do remarry, the evidence suggests that it is often due to pressure from their families and out of fear of destitution. Given the choice, widows who have had less than happy experiences of marriage and motherhood, often prefer to remain independent, working on their own account and retaining custody of their children. In some countries, widows are beginning to work together to explore means of managing their lives and those of their children independently of men. This trend is particularly noticeable among widows with HIV, many of whom work together in projects to prevent the spread of AIDS (see chapters 5 and 11).

In all countries, far fewer widows remarry than widowers: widows far outnumber widowers everywhere so there is often a shortage of suitable men. The existence of children makes many mothers wary of forming new permanent unions that might be detrimental to their welfare. Also, in certain circumstances, a mother with children may be a less attractive proposition to a prospective husband than an unmarried woman without dependants (although, in some cultures, a widow's children may represent the key to control over her husband's property and land, and therefore she may be pressed to remarry a male relative). Marriage to a 'stranger' may deprive her of her children who belong to her husband's kin. Sometimes these arrangements work well and the children are secure; but there are often cases in which the separation of mother and children in this way has tragic consequences, where children do not thrive or are not well cared for and sent to school, but exploited and abused. Economic and social changes have sometimes distorted patterns of family support that in previous times worked well for everyone.

Many widows in traditional societies, whatever their feelings, have no capacity to resist enforced remarriage. Without economic independence, or awareness of the modern laws or access to legal remedies, they are frequently oppressed by traditional practices that are degrading and harmful, and at times violent. Some customs in relation to nonconsensual remarriage represent infringements of fundamental human rights, and breaches of international treaties, such as the UN Women's Convention and the declarations of UN World Conferences such as the Vienna Human Rights Declaration of 1994, the Cairo Declaration on Population and Development, and the Global Platform of Action(GPFA) of the Beijing World Conference for Women, both of 1995. Widows have a right to be as free as everyone else to choose their partner.

Research

There has been very little study of the circumstances that facilitate or inhibit the remarriage of widows in developing countries (India is an exception.) [3] This is partly because if widows are studied at all, it is the currently widowed and not the ever-widowed whose lives are examined. Married women's marital history remains invisible to the researcher. Besides, remarriage of widows is a sensitive subject and it is frequently difficult to elicit information about its prevalence or its nature.

The international Demographic and Health surveys (DHS), for example, are restricted to women of childbearing age (that is, 15 to 49) and consequently do not capture the population of older women who are exposed to a high risk of widowhood and yet may still be remarried in some traditional societies. Furthermore, due to the prevalence of remarriage and widow inheritance among some ethnic groups, in them widowhood may be a transient phase in the lives of the vast majority of women under 60 years of age, but this stage in their life escapes capture by the cross-sectional data collected by most censuses and surveys. These classify individuals by marital status, that is, as single, married, divorced or widowed, and thus render invisible the numbers of women in the three latter categories who have gone through several marriages on widowhood. Because recent censuses and surveys have collected information on current marital status rather than women's marital history, the risk of widowhood tends to be underestimated because of the prevalence of remarriage. In addition, it is often difficult to define what constitutes remarriage: widows may find themselves in one of a variety of unions, which include concubinage, casual relationships, a leviratic arrangement, or a widow inheritance.

The collection of essays in Betty Potash's seminal book *Widows in African Society* describes many types of remarriage. [4] With the exception of this important book and a number of anthropological texts, the marital decisions of widows in most traditional communities have not been studied systematically.

With the exception of the excellent essays in Potash, the various types of sexual and procreative relationships that African widows enter into in some ethnic groups have often been misrepresented by Western anthropologists as forms of marriage when they are something else.

Potash suggests that the distortion may come from the unconscious ethnocentrism of these researchers, who themselves live in a conjugally structured society.[5] She argues that the celebrated levirate (described in Chapter 1 and below), in which a kinsman of the dead man becomes a consort of the widow and fathers her children who bear the name of the deceased husband, should not automatically be conceptualised as marriage. This type of relationship, from the point of view of the ethnic group itself, is always distinguishable from marriage. In many communities it is the deceased, not the levir, who is regarded as the husband. Among several ethnic groups in Africa death is not considered necessarily as putting an end to a marriage. The levirate can develop important differences in rights and obligations from those borne by the original couple. Moreover, to confuse levirate with marriage ignores the fact that in many cases widows involved in such relationships may live alone and have greater dependence and responsibility than wives enjoy.

The problem with much of the older anthropological work on Africa is that it is often not only ethnocentric but also anthropocentric - focusing on women exclusively in the context of their kinship group, and treating widows as passive subjects of customs and traditions. But today, as more women become involved in group projects and encourage each other towards greater economic independence, some of them are discovering that they do have freedom to live alone and manage their own affairs, to form relationships with men that may or may not be in marriage. However, there are still many communities, in Africa and in Asia, where no such liberty to take independent decisions exist, and where widows find themselves entrapped in further servile unions. It is these cases that deserve attention and actions to defend the women's privacy and dignity, as so often their problems are not recognised and their sufferings are hidden.

Patterns of widowhood and remarriage in developing countries

Widowers all over the world, in developed and developing countries alike, are often quick to remarry. After an earthquake affected areas of Maharashtra, northern India, in 1988, 80 per cent of the men who had lost wives in the disaster remarried within two months of their bereavement. In the West too, widowers often remarry within a year or two of the death of their wives, sometimes causing acute distress to their children.

There is a general almost universal notion that a man needs a woman for his bed, to maintain his household, to grow and prepare food, to fetch wood and water, to increase his status, and that man can not and should not live alone. (Ironically, women, so often portrayed as the vulnerable and dependent group, are expected to support themselves and their children in spite of the constraints on their obtaining paid work.)

Widowers often marry women very much younger than themselves, and may thus feel assured that they will have a woman to care for them in illness or old age. This tendency, common in both the developed and developing world, reduces still further the numbers of men available for remarriage to widows. [6]

Widows tend not to marry merely to satisfy sexual needs, but because they feel ill-equipped to live without a male protector and breadwinner. (Exceptions are rich widows, controlling resources, who are free to choose younger consorts as in, for example, the United States where it is not uncommon for wealthy widows, who are said to control a considerable portion of American wealth, to engage in serial marriages, outliving each successive husband and accumulating great fortunes.) If widows have sexual desires and would be happy to fulfil them within a secure relationship, the majority have difficulties in finding an appropriate mate for there will always be younger, more nubile women in competition for that rare creature, the considerate, devoted and available man.

In societies where remarriage of widows is required under traditional law, as in many cultures in eastern and southern Africa, widows often have little real choice as to their partner. Economically, socially and legally discriminated against, their only hope of reintegration into their community is as married women. Chapter 7 describes the situation of very young widows, who are extremely vulnerable to the coercion of not only their in-laws, but also their own fathers and brothers who cannot afford to support more dependants. Widowed daughters of husbandless mothers - divorced or widowed themselves experience similar pressures.

Whatever advances women have made in the legal and economic sphere, marriage generally is still in the gift of men rather than women. It is men, or male relatives, who make the proposals; in most cultures women are not expected to initiate discussions about permanent relationships. Western patriarchy has been 'softened' [7] by concepts of courtly and romantic love but still, even in developed countries, the male is freer to explore openly the question of remarriage than is a woman.

In Western societies widowhood is often associated with ageing, but this is not necessarily the case in developing countries. Demographic patterns vary. The stage at which women become widows depends partly on the marriage system. Where there is a wide age disparity between husbands and wives, many women will be widowed at a relatively young age. This is particularly true of second or later wives in polygynous systems. Data from the Luo ethnic group in Africa show how great this disparity can be [8].

Traditionally in African societies a widow, as an unmarried woman, is too valuable and scarce a commodity to remain unused; thus very soon after her husband's funeral, a widow is remarried or inherited by a male relative of the deceased. [9] In India, there are proscriptions concerning remarriage in higher castes. In the remarrying castes, a widow is usually not free to choose her partner. Going for '*nata*', that is, marrying outside the family, is often frowned upon, except among the scheduled or tribal castes. Remarriage is usually not given the same importance as a first marriage: it is often a perfunctory ceremony without celebration, feasting or gifts. In some castes a remarried widow never achieves the same status as a once-married woman.

'Death does not end a marriage' is a widely held belief in many African ethnic groups. Thus, a widow, if still fertile, is expected to continue to produce children for the deceased's lineage; in some tribal groups, there may be no negative sanctions if the widow takes a lover. The children may or may not be legitimate. An infinite number of arrangements are possible for the widow, not all of which can properly be called marriage. A post-menopausal widow may or may not be remarried. If she does not remarry because she is barren or too old, she may, in a few communities, acquire an enhanced status. Freed from traditional taboos limiting the activities of a married woman, she may gain an independence and power she never enjoyed before.

In West Africa, for example, among ethnic groups such as the Baule of the Ivory Coast, successful townswomen working as traders tend to be widows, with one or several marriages in their past. Unlike their married sisters, they are free to travel without attracting gossip and so are able to move between town and their natal village selling farm produce; they become focal points to rural relatives who decide to sojourn in the city. Such a widow might 'remarry' with a younger woman who will bear children for her in her husband's name. She may marry a very much younger man and support him so that he is able to find a second, younger wife to bear children as if they belonged to the widow.

Among the Bantu Nyika of Tanzania, the word for menopause is derived from the notion of a woman becoming a man, no longer sexually desirable - or sexually dangerous. She is not considered to have any sexual desires and so has freedom to choose her options: whether to remain in her husband's compound, or go to her natal home, or live independently or with or near her sons. A young, pre-menopausal widow is accorded sexual rights - she can ask a kinsman to 'scratch her back'. [10] In the Nilotic world, a woman is usually married to the men of the lineage in perpetuity, so that the union continues after her original partner is in the grave. The widows are called ' wives of the grave' (*chi lie*)[11]. In the Bantu world, by contrast, widows are not wives of the grave but the survivors of dead men, and the children they bear to their cohabitees belong to those genitors and not to the deceased. Where there is a levir, there may or may not be conflict between his marriage obligations and the levirate. The conflict may be resolved by the levir having no obligation to support the widows' children, who belong to the lineage.

Today, much has changed. Whilst some sections of communities, such as village elders and chiefs, strive to maintain customs and traditions concerning widow remarriage, widow inheritance, the levirate, and the rights of and obligations to children born to widows, the complex structural changes in traditional societies have caused conflicts with negative impacts on their weaker members. Kinship groups, fragmented through migration and unequal access to resources (education, health, land) experience conflicts sometimes manifested in greed and resentment. The welfare and protection of widows may not be the prime concern of poor relatives, but instead the acquisition of the deceased's property. Chapter 3 gives several examples of how customs concerning widow remarriage can be used to enrich a greedy relative at the widow's expense.

African widows certainly, in certain ethnic groups, have far more choices than widows in Hindu society, or in Muslim countries such as Bangladesh and Pakistan. Societies where the status of women is at its lowest, as, for example in Bangladesh and in some Indian castes, are those in which a widow or an unmarried woman has most to gain from being in a marriage. But in most of sub-Saharan Africa, women prove their economic work by working outside the home, in agriculture and trade, largely, and therefore they experience less financial need to accept a new sexual union. Many older widows in Africa - for example, the Swahili in Tanzania - frequently reject opportunities to be remarried, and may prefer to continue with a current lover who will visit but cannot dictate to them, or take over their affairs.

A Ghanean widow in her sixties explained her decision to retain her widowed state and avoid a new husband's domination: 'I have had so much of this bossing by men. I have been divorced once, and widowed twice. Why should I go into this again? I have my house; my garden; I grow my vegetables; I sell in the market. Everything I make is mine. Why should I have a man take it from me, spend my money on drink and other women, or tell me now what to do. I am the boss now'.

The levirate

The levirate, in which a widow is taken in marriage by her husband's brother or heir, has been a feature of many religions and cultures throughout history. It still occurs among orthodox Jewish sects. (The sin of Onan was not, as is often erroneously thought, the practice of masturbation, but that the dead husband's brother, when he 'went in unto his widow Tamar' 'spilled his seed upon the ground' and failed to raise up sons for the dead man.) The custom exists among several ethnic groups in Africa, and among some castes in India. It used to be practised in China.

Anthropologists describe the levirate practice as an expression of the concept of the social identification of kin with one another, and as a means of reproducing structural relations across the vicissitudes of the human life cycle. [12] It reaffirms the alliances between families that are created when individuals are bonded in marriage, and the belief that death does not end a marriage; widows are retained within the family as a part of its inheritance or as 'wives of the grave' who will continue to bear children in the name of the lineage and to the honour of the dead man.

The British anthropologist Radcliffe-Brown noted that 'all these customs of preferential marriage can be seen to be continuations or renewals of the existing structure of the unity of the sibling group since brother replaces brother'. [13] Leviratic arrangements have a large number of variables - for example, the identity of the levir, the consent requirements of the widow, the time and ceremony, the residential practices, the custody of children. The practice provides a solution to the problem of how to support a widow, harness her reproductive or productive resource, to ensure the lineage of the dead man continues, and maintain the relationship between kin groups. Anthropologists have noted a great diversity of conjugal arrangements designed for widows subsumed under the name 'levirate' or 'widow inheritance'. Sometimes the relationships parallel marriage, sometimes they do not. The widow may live with the levir, or he may have visiting rights; or, if she is an older woman, there may be no sexual relations at all, only symbolic ceremonies. The relationship may be permanent, temporary, or liable to be terminated by one or either of the parties. Some of these unions are described by various contributors in the Potash book.

Some caution should be exercised in reading some of the older, classical fieldwork reports of Western-educated anthropologists, mostly male, trained in what was clearly an anthrocentric framework, and writing some twenty years ago. In the last two decades there has been rapid and fundamental social and economic change in many Third World countries; brought about by urbanisation, education, and migration. Inter-ethnic marriages are becoming more common in many countries, accompanied

by increased assertiveness by women of their wish for independence.
During the hearing of a famous Kenyan case concerning the burial of
an educated Luo lawyer, the Kenyan counsel for the widow presented
his view of custom:

'The Luo cannot continue with customs that tend to isolate them from
the rest of the country. There are a lot of books written by
anthropologists; they refer to a society of the old order and do not
refer to contemporary society at all. Some of the things said in these
books - we are living in a modern Kenya - we find unacceptable and
not in keeping with us; the literature by anthropologists is no longer
applicable in contemporary Kenya.'

The book *Burying SM*, from which the above extract is taken, also
contains a Kenyan social worker's comments on the new implications
of and the exploitative aspects of traditional customs like the Luo
levirate:

Before AIDS was understood, and even now, when a man died from
unknown causes and his widow was quickly remarried by levirate, she
could spread the disease not only to her new husband and his other
sexual partner, but also to children she might bear. She could bear
children to carry her husband's name but she could also be abused as
a sort of servant.

Fear of spreading AIDS or of becoming HIV-infected has alerted
women to the risks of leviratic unions where one party may be a carrier.
   It is often very hard to clarify what precisely are the adhered-to
customs in any one ethnic group, for everyone, depending on what their
own status is and who they talking to, will give their own version.[14]
Traditions and customs are possibly too elusive, too ever-changing to
trap statistically within a report or a book. The 1986 SM Otieno case in
Kenya (in which the Kikuyu widow of an important and educated Luo
man tried to challenge his relatives' right to bury her husband under their
Luo traditions) illustrated dramatically the difficulty of pinpointing the
exact nature of a custom. In spite of the many experts who gave
evidence in court, it was clear there were as many versions of what was
a true Luo custom as there were pages of the transcript.[15]
   The accounts that follow of this custom may well be out of date, or
may never have been accurate. It is difficult to find out exactly how much
true choice a widow has today, for so much depends on such variables
as family dynamics, education, personal relationships, location and the

resourcefulness of the widow herself. Researchers need to study exactly what are widows' options, constraints and choices in these arrangements, for with so much economic and social change taking place, they may be expected to fulfil their obligations without receiving the reciprocal benefits they would have obtained under such arrangements traditionally (see below).

Among the Luo of Kenya, the levir is usually a married man living in his home; his primary obligations are towards his wife and legal sons who are part of his descent line. It is these sons who will inherit from him and carry on his name.[16] In a leviratic relationship the widow continues to live in the deceased's husband's home, and any children she bears through the levir will bear the dead man's name. Widows have no domestic responsibilities to the levir, nor does he have social obligations to the children.

On the other hand, among the Dukawa of Nigeria, the widow moves in with the levir, having her own hut in his compound for herself and her children. Her children belong to the first husband but her new husband has full responsibility for her and her children's care. For all practical purposes she is his wife, but her children are his brother's. Whether she is the senior or junior wife depends on her relationship with his existing wives and their ages. Since in this ethnic group the junior levirate prevails, she is most likely to be older than the levir and any other wives he may have.

Sometimes it happens that a junior wife is given to the heir or eldest son of the dead husband by another wife. She may be many years older than the son, and have to wait for him to reach puberty. This practice can sometimes prove embarrassing for such a son, if he has become educated and 'Westernised', is already married and does not wish to be in a conjugal relationship with someone whom he has regarded as one of his co-mothers.

This is what occurred to nineteen-year-old Sam, in Zimbabwe, who had gone to a school on the local Tea Estate and acquired five O-levels. He was newly married, in a registered civil law union, to a wife who also had a secondary school education. His father's youngest widow pursued him relentlessly, urged on by other members of the family, to take her in a levirate, but he admitted that he now found it impossible to consider having sexual relations with someone who had nursed him as a baby and whom he respected as one of his father's wives.

Sam's dilemma shows how education, mobility, and Westernisation can produce fundamental and lasting rifts between members of the same kinship group, and how men too can feel oppressed by customs they feel are now outmoded and inappropriate.

A different variation of the levirate is found in Swaziland where, according to law and custom, if an unmarried man dies, his family may pay the bride price, *lobola*, for the lover he leaves behind and find for her a relative to raise children for the deceased.[17] If the dead son is married, and leaves no issue or heir, his widow may be put under pressure to have one of his brothers or half-brother 'enter her hut' to raise seed for the lineage. The pressure will be greatest if she has no children at all; to refuse to take her husband's brother would be to indicate that she wishes to marry a stranger. But if she does take him, the children she bears will belong to the deceased unless the new man transfers cattle to her natal family, called 'dividing the womb', so that he can claim that the offspring belong to him.

Potash likens some of these African widows' lives to the Caribbean matrifocal family where women can take lovers and conceive children, but do not allow the male progenitor anything but a very limited role. Luo widows are not 'inherited'; they can choose who to take as a levir among the clan. They accept a levirate because they have no rights to return to their natal home and because they wish their children to remain in their dead father's community.

Widows who walk out of a leviratic union are often refused shelter by their fathers and blood brothers. In such circumstances they are often treated as loose women who have abandoned their own children. They risk censure because their walking out of their husband's family means that the brideprice of cattle - cattle which are needed to purchase wives for her unmarried brothers - may have to be returned to her husband's family, inevitably causing conflict and unpleasantness.

Today, there is considerable evidence - from newspaper reports, from the types of cases that widows take to women lawyers' co-operatives, from various reports by women's NGOS - that the custom of levirate is being abused.[18] The widow is forced to conform to a time-honoured tradition, but the levir may no longer reciprocate and support the widow. The Widows' Ministries, a widow-support group in Northern Ghana, reported in 1994 that:

In the Bolga District where the culture demands that the widow continues to produce children for the dead man, the new 'husband' having impregnated her leaves her to manage on her own until the child is weaned. Widows who are already victimised are made to bear increased burdens. The wives of the levir give the widow no peace. They insult her by calling her a witch, accusing her of casting an evil spell, They say she has killed her own husband and now wants to kill theirs. Most men return to their wives and their offspring after having landed the widow with even more children to support on her own. Some of these widows kill their babies, commit suicide or go mad.

Remarriage under law, custom and religion

In the West, and under modern statute law, there is no restriction on the remarriage of widows. Nor has the Christian Church, Catholic or Protestant, forbidden it. For Muslims, the Koran advocates the remarriage of widows as the Prophet himself married widows nine times, so in Islamic communities it is social discrimination and local customs rather than religious laws that make it difficult for widows to remarry. It is in Hindu law, and in the customs and traditions of local communities and particular ethnic groups in parts of southern, central and east Africa, that remarriage of widows becomes a matter of strict regulation either through proscription or prescription.

Muslim Law

Marriage in Islam is not a sacrament as in the Christian, Jewish and Hindu religions. It is a civil contract. Before the time of the Prophet it is said that the condition of widows was hard, but the Koran sanctions their remarriage, along with polygyny and concubinage.

'Marry such women as seems good to you, two, three or four'(4:4). These verses were revealed after the battle of Uhud (625AD), when large numbers of Muslim warriors were killed, leaving many widows. Encouraging men to marry widows relieved the community of responsibility for supporting them, and the Prophet himself led the way. His first wife was a widow fifteen years his senior and he lived alone with her until he was fifty. This and his other marriages were hardly liaisons fired by passion and physical desire, but, rather, as Islamic scholars are quick to point out, illustrative of attitudes to the poor and weak that are among the basic teachings of the Prophet as expressed in the Koran.

The Koran says, 'Such of you as die and leave behind them wives, they shall wait and keep themselves apart, four months and ten days. And when they reach the term prescribed for them, then there is no sin for you in aught - they may do with themselves in decency. Allah is informed of what you do' (2:234).

Nevertheless, much of Islamic law regulating personal and family life is inimical to women's emancipation and autonomy - for example, divorce by *talaq*, polygamy, purdah, restrictions on women's employment, criminalisation of abortion, the rights of men to custody of children, the halving of women's inheritance rights and the halving of their value, and the segregation of women in public institutions. Although there was a time many centuries ago when Muslim women enjoyed a condition in society superior to many women in civilisations elsewhere, today millions of women in Islamic communities are at the mercy of men, and this subservient position is reflected in the vulnerability of widows to coercive remarriage.[19] It is all very well to say that Islamic law encourages the remarriage of widows and does not prohibit it, but the questions to be asked are to what extent are widows able to make free choices about a second marriage, and what factors are influential in what happens to them on remarriage in terms of their legal and social rights.

Ideally under Muslim law, a woman should always be under the guardianship and protection of a man, whether father, brother or another male relative, and if she is widowed she needs to be remarried. If she is not she may suffer seclusion and indignity. This is the destiny of many Muslim widows in Bangladesh, Pakistan and India.

Although in many Islamic countries widows only rarely remarry, in Islamic groups in Africa widow remarriage is more common, and the *idda* or *eda* is strictly adhered to. This is the traditional waiting period before a widowed or a divorced woman can remarry. Theoretically it is required of both widows and divorcees to ensure that there is no pregnancy when the remarriage takes place. According to *sharia* law, during the period of her seclusion of four months and ten days, a widow's conduct is closely monitored to be sure she is not pregnant or engaged in a sexual relationship. (A divorced woman need only be secluded for three months, called 'three months of purity', representing the intervals between menstrual period.) The time requirements vary if the widow is past childbearing age or is pregnant at the time of her bereavement or divorce. Swahili widows in Tanzania used to spend their *edas* in their mothers' homes, where they would be looked after whilst they were cut off from normal social life.

In spite of what the Koran says and what is known of the Prophet's life, Muslim widows may still carry a social stigma, as they do in so many cultures. Similar pressures and constraints confront Muslim widows as are faced by Hindu widows in India and many African widows from Christian or animist cultures.

It is difficult for poor widows to make good second marriages. They are easily manipulated into remarriage against their will by both their in-laws and their natal family. Young childless widows are liable to find themselves being remarried to old men who are either widowers, or whose wives are too old for childbearing and who desire to have a nubile woman in their household as a status symbol and to bear them more sons.

In Bangladesh, many young rural widows are widowed for the second time when still in their teens, since their second husband is likely to be a far older man. I talked to some of them when visiting the fish pond project run by the charismatic Zavir of Prism (also described in Chapter 7).[20] They were vehemently opposed to being made to remarry; they wanted instead properly paid work in the village when the project ended. One young woman, the child widow also mentioned in Chapter 7, described how she came to be remarried:

> This old widower was so ugly. But he spotted me whilst I was out with the other widows and divorced women digging the fish pond. I was covered with mud and my clothes were dirty and torn. All the men think we are bad women. Because we work outside we have bad reputations; the village say we have relations with other men. That is why this old man came to stare at me for three days. I knew from the way he looked he was after me. But oh, so ugly, so small. Not like my young husband who died. I cried when my parents gave me to him because he didn't ask for any dowry; there were no presents, no feasting. I just had to look after him and his children and sleep in his bed. He was already ill when I was married to him. He could not come to fetch me. Even before he died his children, some of them older than me, were so cruel to me. But after his death they were worse, and threw me out. So here I am. If it were not for this project what would I do? I am now twice widowed and none will want me now.'

Another young woman working in the same project spoke of her remarriage to a sick man with many children whose two wives had become too old for him.

> 'He wanted me because they were too old to bear children and not good for sex. I was disgusted by him. I used to try and hide rather than sleep with him. But his other wives, far older than me, always found me and pushed me to him. I was not really like a wife.
>
> He gave me no presents when he married me. He just made the contract and took me. And they all used me as a sort of slave, even his children, because I had come with no dowry.'

Hard as it may be for widows who have no power to refuse a remarriage to a man they do not want as their partner, it is equally painful for women in Muslim marriages to have to accept their husband's marriage with a younger second, third or fourth wife, whether she is a widow or not.

Hindu law
There has never been a total ban on widow remarriage in India, as is

often assumed.

Anthropological studies have given ample evidence that in all non-Brahmin - that is, lower-caste-groups, widow remarriages are quite common. Some 60 to 70 per cent of non-Brahmin young widows in the twenty-to-thirty age group get remarried in central and northern India. In southern India widow remarriage is more prevalent except among the highest castes. Children born to remarried widows enjoy all legal rights to inheritance. It is said that very young virgin widows and child widows are allowed to remarry providing it is within their caste group.

The oppression of widows starts when they are forced into second marriages against their will, or when they go for nata, marrying outside the caste or clan, and are deprived of anything they had inherited from their dead husband, even when the assets were arrived at through joint effort.

Restrictions on the remarriage of widows among caste Hindus was imposed from 300 BC to 200 AD. Manu decreed that a widow should never remarry. Even a child widow (see Chapter 7) whose marriage was unconsummated was included in the prohibition. The restriction stems from the concept that marriage is a union of souls and not merely of bodies, and that widowhood is a punishment given by God. It was taught that the widow will join her husband in heaven after death, or in this world in her next birth.

To join her husband, she should commit *sati*, thus expressing to the living her devotion to him, and hastening her arrival in heaven for a 'thousand years of paradise'.

Remarriage of widows was therefore not an issue, as the custom of *sati* ensured that there were no widows living to marry again. Although the British enacted legislation making *sati* a criminal offence as early as 1829, members of the Indian elite were cautious in their advice to the British concerning legislating to permit the remarriage of widows and to prohibit infant marriages.

Widow remarriage was a sensitive issue, but it was logical that if she was no longer to immolate herself on her husband's funeral pyre, the widow should be given the freedom to remarry, especially if she was young. Alive, the conditions in which she was forced to live were considered by Indian reformers of the time quite inhuman. Not only was she considered inauspicious, and treated with scorn and contempt, but she was also subject to physical indignities and often sexually molested.

Once the legislation outlawing *sati* was passed, the numbers of Hindu widows increased, but although legislation to permit remarriage was contemplated as early as 1830, it was not effected until 1884 (in 1856 there was a half-hearted measure which had little effect), as the British continually sought the views of educated Indian scholars, lawyers and reformers, who advised caution. It was a sensitive issue. One advisor wrote: 'There is a native proverb to the effect that you wake a man if he is truly asleep but not if he is pretending; such is the present condition of Hindu society as regards widow remarriage. They are fully aware of the cruelty and hardship of enforced widowhood, and privately wish that the young might be remarried, and yet have no courage to openly declare their private wishes and risk criticism by the conservatives and the priests.' However, despite the nineteenth- century legislation, few widows in the higher castes do remarry. The inhibitions and prohibitions continue. Among the lower and scheduled castes, remarriage is approved of, although a widow may not necessarily be free to choose her partner.

Few Indian widows may actually want to remarry, fearing for the welfare of their children and especially their daughters, fearing too that the second husband will ill-treat them, and take any benefits such as pensions or insurance that they receive from their first husband. The exceptions are the child widows and the virgin or childless young widows. A second marriage tends to be a second-class affair, without the festivities, the presents, the celebration and the joy that traditionally accompany a first marriage. Sometimes entirely different rules are followed to perform them. Second-time brides have said that they never received the same respect that they had enjoyed in their first marriages, and were often looked down on as being second-class property. Often, a widow could not hope for a bright young husband, but might have to make do with someone old, or ill, or burdened with many children after the death of his wife. The situations commonly described did not make for happiness, and widows were aware of the problems. Certain local laws governing inheritance of the dead husband's property by a widow also discourage widow remarriage.

Remarriage of child widows
This subject is treated more thoroughly in Chapter 7, and therefore only a brief overview is given here.

In spite of modern legislation on the age of marriage, child marriage, even betrothals and marriages in utero still continue to be arranged in some communities of northern India. Child brides make child widows. Their fate is tragic, for them and for their parents and brothers. The anxiety of poor families to marry off their daughters is particularly intense when the child is the daughter of a widow and there is no money for dowry. Daughters of widows are vulnerable to early marriages, and become young widows themselves.

Even in the nineteenth century there was always a great deal of sympathy for those child widows whose husbands had died before consummation was possible. With the exception of priests and the fanatically diehard, increasing numbers of people thought that remarriage for these women was acceptable. For the parties involved, remarriage offers benefits. For the young widow it is her way to motherhood and status and the support of sons and daughters. And her in-laws are able to retain the property of their dead son or brother whilst waving their widowed daughter-in-law farewell. For her own parents and brothers it is a blessing, for it takes away from them the heavy responsibility of accommodating her for the rest of her life. In communities where there is a long tradition of supporting a widowed sister or daughter, this lifelong dependency can seem a threat to families living on the edge of poverty.

Widowed mothers

In India widowed mothers rarely remarry unless they are very young and there is only one small baby. Most widows questioned about their attitudes to remarriage say they do not want more children; they fear for the treatment of their first husband's children at the hands of a step-father, and in particular they worry for the welfare of their daughters. They also wish to retain a claim to their husband's land which they would have to relinquish on remarriage. Other reasons for not remarrying included fear of conflict with the stepchildren, and fears that the woman might not be able to bring her own children into the new household but would have to abandon them to her late husband's family. These fears were common to widows from both marrying and non remarrying castes.

Kamla is a remarried Bihar women in her mid-twenties. Her first husband died soon after her first child, a son, was born. She was badly treated by his brothers who wanted her dead husband's 1.5 acres of land. In desperation she sought refuge at her parents' home, and the brothers took possession of the fields. Her own brothers were nice to her for a bit but then their wives began to object and abuse Kamla. They said that as she was a widow she brought a bad name to the house and should be remarried. They organised an 'exchange' marriage in which her new husband's sister married her last unmarried brother, but the families lived two days' journey apart. The new marriage proved disastrous, for the second husband had been divorced three times, was impoverished, lazy, a drinker and a wife-beater. Once Kamla had given birth to a son for this man, he drove the first child away and began to be very violent. This child has now gone back to his maternal grandmother, and Kamla pines for him everyday. She still holds the title deeds of her first husband's land and hopes that one day, when her first child is adult, she can claim it back for him. She did not dare take action against her brothers-in-law.

If Kamla had had the help of a free lawyer, and the solidarity of a women's group, she might have stayed on the land and used it to support herself, thus avoiding the pain of being sold into a hapless new union with a man who clearly was going to be the very worst of husbands.

Factors influencing a decision to remarry

If widows are free to remarry, the contemplation of remarriage is often fraught with conflicts. Widows worry that remarriage may be upsetting for their children, that the new husband may mistreat the children of the former marriage; that remarriage is an insult to the memory of the deceased. The decision to remarry often results in bitter conflicts between the parents of the widow and those of the dead husband, and between potential step-children and step-siblings. Grieving widows may feel that it is impossible to love another man as the first husband was loved. They fear appearing disloyal. If the first marriage was not happy, there is all the more reason to fear a second marriage. Widows who have suffered unhappiness or abuse in marriage have little incentive to risk further unhappiness. Nor do they wish to endure a second widowhood.

Betty Potash lists factors other than the desire to re-establish marital or consort relationships which influence African widows' decisions concerning remarriage.[21] Among these are a desire for sex (the Luo), sex and companionship and the sanction against non-marital sexuality (the Dukawa), lack of economic self-sufficiency (Swahili), fraternal pressure (Hausa), loneliness and the possibility of inter-ethnic marriage, the burden of farming alone, and need for support for the education of children. However, her important book was prepared in 1986 before the full impact of the AIDS pandemic on relationships between men and women had been studied. Today, in African countries devastated by the spread of the disease, few women widowed through AIDS wish to marry again, especially if they are infected with HIV.

Studies show that, in Indian villages, the important factors determining remarriage among the remarrying castes, were the age of the widow and the number and ages of her children.[22] (Even in the remarrying castes, and in states where governments had given bonuses to widows should they remarry and incentives to the men marrying them, relatively few widows did in fact remarry unless they were widowed as child brides, or were still very young and either childless or with only one small child.) The studies show that remarriage was not a viable option for most widows, either because of external pressures or restrictions, or because of the negative images that women had of widow remarriage, through social conditioning or their experience of other widows' lives.

In Africa, as modern law marriage becomes more common - at present it operates mainly among the educated elite and not among the rural and urban poor - and men begin to make wills so that their widows can inherit, the customary reasons for remarriage will begin to fade away. But since socio-economic and legal changes are usually only partial, they sometimes have unexpected consequences.

For example, the pensions introduced for some formal-sector workers and government servants can be an attractive asset to greedy kin. Often in Africa and in India a pension is viewed by the husband's kin group as part of the inheritance that should belong to them: by marrying the beneficiary widow, they can appropriate this form of wealth. In the Ivory Coast, according to one study, a man married his uterine nephew's widow although normally remarriage to a close kinsman was forbidden. The justification was that the deceased had been a government employee and therefore his marriage was statutory and so carried a pension. In India, remarriage of 'riot' widows (those whose husbands were killed in the violence following Indira Gandhi's assassination) was encouraged by the state government anxious to find ways of avoiding paying pensions to destitute women. In Karnataka state, where pensions for 'destitute' widows are also available, the government made considerable savings by providing bonus payments, amounting to half the sum of the pension, to men prepared to remarry these vulnerable women.

Many widows in northern India interviewed by the author confessed they had suffered too much in their first marriage to wish to repeat the experience. They complained that the problems of widowhood cast a curtain over the problems of marriage.

' No, no! Never again. To have forced sex. To have to bear more children in poverty. To be beaten and treated like a dog. To have to watch another husband die and be widowed all over again. I would rather live on the streets by begging than be tied again to a man,'

This was the cry of one poor widow admitting that it was a relief, in the privacy of the workshop, to speak of this feeling which could never be expressed in public. Many Ugandan widows uttered similar concerns, remembering the violence, the drinking, the sexual infidelities and the horrors of watching their husbands die from the maladies associated with AIDS.

Wherever I went, during my short visits to six countries in Asia and Africa, to talk to widows, I always asked them for their views on remarriage. A word of caution to the reader here is necessary: first, I was not engaged in objective research, and therefore supply no quantitative data; second, I was unable to identify twice-married formerly widowed women who were willing to talk freely about the circumstances in which they decided to marry again; and, third, the widows I interviewed could never be classified as typical of the country, the ethnic group, or the region. The fact that they were speaking to me about intimate areas of their lives not normally discussed with strangers, or were exceptionally motivated and courageous to involve themselves in group projects where I could get access to them (BRAC in Bangladesh, SEWA or the Widows' Conference Participants in Bangalore, FIDA in Uganda, the Law Project Office in Zimbabwe) made them untypical. But the views they expressed are significant even if they do not represent the millions of poor widows whose voices I never heard. They prove that when women - or widows - work together to bring about change they become strong enough to take on the world: governments, village chiefs and elders, courts, judges, and the hardest opposition, the family.

In Britain, when I talk to widows about remarriage, I find most younger once-married women (divorced or widowed) hope they will find a second husband. In spite of the fact that so few suitable men are available and so few British widows remarry, many of those with twenty or more years of active life ahead of them, may fantasise about a new partner. Remarriage, although unlikely for widows over forty, is not seen as a misfortune.

I was unprepared, therefore, for the passion with which so many different groups of Third World widows rejected the idea of remarriage as a solution to their social and economic problems. (Rural Malawian widows were the exception: burdened with such large families - family planning information and services were banned for many years - my informants saw no way of surviving except through dependance on a man.)

Widows gave several reasons for their opposition to remarriage: First, because they had already experienced the harshness of married life, and had no wish to repeat it. Second, because they feared for the welfare of their children at the hands of the new husband, his existing wives, or his children. Third, in most cases of remarriage outside the family widows might lose any rights to the dead husband's property, and to the children. Fourth, widows could not expect to make a good match because of their inauspicious condition - the new husband might be a currently-married man wanting a second wife, a widower with many children, impoverished, old, or disabled mentally or physically. Fifth, several African women, widowed through AIDS, resisted the idea that they might infect or be infected, and rejected the institution of levirate and widow inheritance.

Conclusion

The Women's Convention and the Children's Convention, to which more than one hundred governments are parties, declare that women and children shall not be married without their full and free consent. Clearly, these articles pertain as much to remarriage as to a first marriage.

National laws in the majority of countries now have legislated a minimum age for marriage without consent, but girls continue to be married *with* parental consent when very young, risking early widowhood and further servile remarriage. Nevertheless, resourceful, organised, shrewd and courageous widows are beginning now to resist enforced remarriage, supported by imaginative initiatives developed with NGOs. But the widows who stand up for their rights are still the minority. Millions of poor, illiterate and powerless widows are unable to resist the imposition of unions - remarriage, widow inheritance, levirate, or some other sexual or residential arrangement - because they have no alternative means of economic support. In order to break this cycle of servile marriage and remarriage. Widows desperately need training, loans, credit, work and education for their children, especially their daughters.

Village councils and caste *panchayats* might work with widows' organisations and women's NGOs to provide community help to bereaved and unsupported women. Widows should have a representative on village councils and local and traditional courts so that the interests of widows can be represented. Widows should be able to appeal to local councils and traditional courts to protect them from arranged marriages they do not consent to. For example, a local council might intervene where the age gap between an old widower and a young widow is very great, or where other factors suggest that such a union would be exploitative and servile.

If widows were economically secure, controlling their own resources, they would be able to choose whether to remain as widows, or to remarry someone of their choice. Without opportunities to work and to earn, without security of house, land, or food, the poorest and most vulnerable of widows will continue to be at risk of a forced marriage, or subject to prohibitions on a marriage or relationship of her choice.

Notes

1. Peter Townsend, *The Family Life of Old People*, 1958, Routledge and Kegan Paul, London, p. 182.

2. UN Convention on the Elimination of All Forms of Discrimination against Women (also known as the Women's Convention), Article 16 on family law.

3. Jean Drèze, *Widows in Rural India*, Development Economic Research Programme Paper No. 26, London School of Economics, 1990, pp. 70-78.

4. Betty Potash, ed., *Widows in African Society*, Stanford Press, 1986.

5. Ibid, pp. 2, 15.

6. Jean-Claude Muller, 'Where to Live: Widows' Choices among the Rukuba of Nigeria', in Potash, ed., discusses the similarities between widowers and widows (p. 175).

7. Kate Millett, *Sexual Politics*, Hart-Davis, 1969, p. 36.

8. Potash, ed., p. 24.

9. Claude Levi-Strauss, <u>Tristes Tropiques</u>, Penguin, Harmondsworth, 1994.

10. Mariam K. Slater, Foreword, in Potash, ed.

11. Christine Obbo, 'Some East African Widows', in Potash, ed., pp. 94–108.

12. Jane Guyer, 'Beti Widow Inheritance and Marriage Law: A Social History', in Potash, ed., pp. 193.

13. A. R. Radcliffe-Brown, *African Systems of Kinship and Marriage*, Oxford University Press, 1950, pp. 1–85.

14. D. W. Cohen and E. S. Atieno Odhiambo, *Burying SM: The Politics of Knowledge and the Sociology of Power in Africa*, Heinemann, 1992.

15. April Gordon, 'Gender, Ethnicity and Class in Kenya: "Burying Otieno" Revisited', *Signs*, Summer 1995, pp. 883–911.

16. Betty Potash, 'Wives of the Grave: Widows in a Rural Luo Community', in Potash, ed., p. 45.

17. Thandabantu Nhlapo, *Marriage and Divorce in Swazi Law and Custom*, Websters, Swaziland, 1992.

18. See, for example, *Kampala Herald*, December 1993, and case dossiers at branches of FIDA in Kampala and Nairobi.

19. For a discussion of political change and Islamic personal status law see 'Revolution, the State, Islam and Women: Gender Politics in Iran and Afghanistan', Women Living Under Muslim Laws Dossier 7/8 (PB 23, 34790 Grabels, France).

20. Prism is a creative programme operating in the Maniganj region of Bangladesh. Unlike most development NGOs, Prism sets out to teach poor rural people about capitalism, avoiding handouts. The workers receive shares as part of their pay; people owning uncultivated land are encouraged to donate it to Prism in return for shares in the company; other individuals – such as the fishpond workers – receive shares in return for supplying their labour. Zavir comes from a wealthy landowning family; after fighting in the war of independence in 1972, he decided to use all his family land to help the poor rural people in his region.

21. Potash, ed., p. 24.

22. Marty Chen and Jean Drèze, *Widows and Well-being in Rural North India*, Development Economics Research Programme Paper No. 40, London School of Economics, 1992.

CHAPTER 7

Child Widows and the
Children of Widows

The following excerpt from *The Child Widows*, a biography written in 1966 by Monica Felton, gives a graphic impression of child widowhood in India in the early 1900s:

'Balam sobbed and sobbed and sobbed. She was a tiny child, smaller for her age even than Subbalakshmi, with a face that seemed to have been made for laughter. Now she buried her head in her mother's lap, her whole body shaking with grief.

'What is it?' her mother asked gently.

Balam looked up. 'It was the Head. She called Subbalakshmi by a bad name'.

'Surely not.' 'Yes, truly.' The Headmistress had been showing a foreign visitor around the school. 'This' she said, pointing out Subbalakshmi, 'is the little widow.'

'Mummy' Balam cried. 'Sister isn't a widow is she? It was wicked, wicked to say such a thing! How could anyone call Sister by such a bad word?'

It was a very bad word, a word which no lady would ever use..

Subalakshmi was beginning to discover, without ever being explicitly told, what it meant to be a widow. Although her own life was happy and sheltered she was becoming aware that there were many girls among her family's circle of friends and acquaintances whose husbands had died. She did not often meet them. They lived like ghosts haunting the kitchens and backyards of their parent's houses, pale, under-nourished, hard-worked.

She pictured again the baby-widow whom she had seen so long ago and whose cries still haunted her dreams. There were, she knew now, countless little girls all over India who were just as unfortunate as little Janak She seemed to see the bent heads and meagre, life-starved bodies of the young widows. [1]

The little widow of this biography came from a caring, educated and relatively progressive Brahmin family and went on, in spite of the then current attitudes in India to widowhood, to receive a university education so that she could teach and contribute to the intellectual and social life of her country. She was saved from some of the most degrading features of widowhood, such as tonsure. But she was never permitted to remarry, even though she had been widowed at the age of seven.

It is often assumed in the West that most widows are old women, and that their problems can be addressed in the context of ageing. But in some traditional cultures many girls are married when very young and become child or teenage widows. There is barely any data on how many girls are married and widowed when they are still minors, since such marriages tend not to be registered. [2] All modern age-of-marriage laws relate to couples marrying 'without parental consent', but children are married on the wishes of their parents, so there is no question of free informed consent to their unions. It is of little use for the legal minimum to apply only to couples marrying without consent; most of the extreme cases fall outside the boundaries of the law. If consent is to be officially assessed, the marriage has to be registered, which is rarely the case. One survey of 470 Gambian wives discovered that 36 per cent of them had not been asked for their consent, and did not even know that the marriage had taken place until after the wedding. [3]

In India, child marriage is now on the decline, in comparison to fifty years ago, but there are still many widows in their fifties and older who have lived in the 'inauspicious' state of widowhood since they were small children; child marriage and child widowhood still occur in the rural areas where legislation has little effect and access to education is poor. If child widows are from castes where they are free to remarry, even as adults they will have no freedom of choice of partner, and may find themselves married once more to older men, only to experience a subsequent widowhood. These young women will have had no education or training to provide them with the means to support themselves in a rapidly changing socio-economic climate.

So sparse is the literature on the prevalence of child widowhood that this chapter can only touch upon it by describing patterns of child and adolescent marriage and its consequences, and point to the need for research. [4] Studies of this neglected category of widows are needed in all those countries where early marriage is still the practice (see Figure 7.1). Countries need to pay special attention to the abuse of child widows that is derived from traditional practices.

The majority of countries have legislated to prohibit child marriage (in accordance with the international treaties reviewed below) and laid

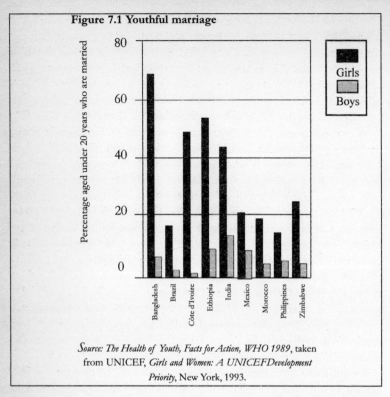

Figure 7.1 Youthful marriage

Source: *The Health of Youth, Facts for Action, WHO 1989*, taken from UNICEF, *Girls and Women: A UNICEF Development Priority*, New York, 1993.

down minimum ages for girls and boys to marry; but marriages under customary law are outside the remit of modern legislation, and in any case, changes in family law, where they have taken place, are badly enforced. Patrilineal inheritance (see Chapter 3) and patrilocal residence reinforce adherence to the view that a girlchild possesses little economic value to the family because she will go away on marriage. A whole host of factors influence overstretched and impoverished families to exercise son preference in relation to healthcare, nutrition, education and marriage plans.

Marrying a young bride can be an effective way of ensuring control over her productive and reproductive labour: she is seen as more malleable and her virginity is more readily guaranteed. She will also begin childbearing early – an important consideration in societies where large families, especially sons, are valued.

Women are often under the greatest pressure to produce sons and discriminate in their favour. They have often absorbed the notion that it is sons who are bound by duty to support them in old age, not daughters. Although in recent years many studies have demonstrated that sons do not necessarily take on such obligations, and that stronger emotional bonds often exist between a widow and her daughter and son-in-law than with her son and daughter-in-law, parents, and especially widowed mothers, are under strong pressure to send young daughters away into an early marriage. Because in many communities a bride must leave her parental home at the time of marriage to join her husband in his village, and may no longer be eligible to inherit from her father, a daughter is often seen as an economic burden: any value she represents, for example, her reproductive or productive capacity, will become the property of her in-laws' family; early marriage may relieve a poor family of an extra mouth to feed. The fact that girls are destined to marry 'away' also affects the value a family places on attitude educating her.

In some rural regions of South Asia, girl children may be betrothed before or at birth. In rural India, Bangladesh, and Afghanistan, girls may be sent to live with their husband's family many years before puberty, although the marriage will not be consummated until later. The average age of marriage in India is 14.3 years; in Democratic Yemen, most girls marry between the ages of twelve and fifteen, despite the 1978 Family Law which allows for a one- to three- year sentence for those involved in the marriage of girls under 16. On average, almost 50 per cent of African girls are married before they are 18. [5]

Poverty, ambition and avarice can affect the parent's choice of a husband for their daughter, especially when a transfer of resources is involved. The phrase 'with parental consent' often means 'regardless of the couple's wishes'. In the 1980s a Yemeni father living in Birmingham, UK, took his two young daughters of 12 and 14 to Yemen on the pretext of a holiday, and there sold them to two friends of his as brides. Beaten, raped, abused and imprisoned, the girls did not realise they had been 'married' when their father returned to Britain without them; it was eight years before one of the sisters was able to escape back to Birmingham, helped by Defence of Children International, although she was forced to leave the children she had borne in the Yemen. [6] Many children are 'sold' into marriages in this way, sometimes because the family is in debt, or because of the financial benefits accruing from the marriage contract. Their marriages are truly 'servile', and they may be exploited in many ways. Child widows may find themselves victims of abuse by other members of their deceased husband's family, including older widows and their children if the union is polygamous.

Concerns about virginity influence a family in arranging early marriage for female offspring. In Muslim orthodox groups, once a girl has reached puberty every care must be taken to ensure that she remains chaste. It is better to have her married than to put at risk her reputation and endanger the prospect of a good marriage. Among some ethnic groups in sub-Saharan Africa, a young girl may be married early in order for the family to acquire the bride price, which is needed to obtain a wife for older brothers.

In Bangladesh, Guinea, Mali, Niger and Yemen, more than half of the young women interviewed for a 1995 DHS (Demographic and Health) survey were married before they were sixteen. In seventeen other countries surveyed by the DHS programme, mainly in Africa, more than one quarter of all girls become pregnant before the age of eighteen.[7] Although these figures do not tell us how many of the young mothers are destined to become young widows, and there is no information on childless child wives, they give some indication of the numbers of young women who are at risk of early widowhood.

The outcome for young girls who become widows is very bleak, for they may have retained only very limited rights in the parental home and have little freedom to return there on their husbands' death. Today, in most cases, young and childless widows do remarry, but the chances of making a 'good' second marriage are poor (see Chapter 6). However, there are young widows in India who have never been given the chance of remarriage and must endure the disadvantages of widowhood all their lives.

International treaties
Although the definition of slavery in the 1926 Slavery Convention could usefully be applied to the condition of some women in marriages – 'the status or condition of a person over whom any or all of the powers attaching to the rights of ownership are exercised' – it is the 1926 UN Supplementary Convention on the Abolition of Slavery that deals explicitly with the slavery of women. The convention concentrates on the sale of women into marriage and the inheritance of widows. Article 2 stipulates: 'States Parties undertake to prescribe, where appropriate, suitable minimum ages of marriage, to encourage the use of facilities whereby the consent of both parties to a marriage may be freely expressed in the presence of a competent civil or religious authority, and to encourage the registration of marriages'. But despite the 114 ratifications of this Convention (as of December 1995) both early marriage and the 'servile marriage' that can result are not only still prevalent but in some countries are increasing.

The Forward Looking Strategies (FLS) document agreed in Nairobi in 1985 reflects common assumptions about age and widowhood and neglects the issue of child widows. Its only reference to 'widows' in the whole of the document is in Paragraph 286.

'The Plan of Action recognises a number of specific areas of concern for elderly women since their longer life expectancy frequently means an old age aggravated by economic need and isolation for both unmarried women and widows.'[8]

Paragraph 287 stresses the importance of extending and maintaining young women's access to health, education and employment, and refers to the obligation of governments to safeguard young women from sexual violence, abuse and sexual harassment. However, it makes no mention of child marriages, servile marriages, or marriages below the legal age, although the World Health Organisation has focused on the health risks of adolescent fertility for the child mother and her baby. Presumably the issue of child marriage was omitted because, during the lengthy and delicate discussions concerning the drafting of the document, several governments objected to any interference with traditional customs and culture.

According to the International Women's Rights Action Watch (IWRAW):

> there are a number of reasons to insist that girls are not married until they are of a sufficient age to make an informed choice.
>
> The first is that as a matter of basic human rights no person should undertake such a momentous act without full knowledge of its import, and no child can understand the full social and physical import of marriage. Another is that child-bearing at too early an age can severely damage a girl's reproductive and general health, causing such problems as obstructed labour, sometimes bleeding to death, and vesico-vaginal fistula, leading to social ostracism as well as health problems.

The IWRAW omits to mention in its report that many young women married as minors are in danger of becoming child widows, enduring all the disadvantages described in other chapters in this book. Nor has UNICEF as yet, in its campaigns to draw attention to the disadvantages of premature maternity and early marriage, focused on early widowhood as an outcome of unions where the age differential between the partners is great and the bride is a minor.

Article 16 of the UN Women's Convention (CEDAW) (128 ratifications) indirectly addresses child marriage, obliging states parties to enact domestic legislation to ensure that women have an equal right with men to decide on their choice of partner. It also requires governments to take measures to safeguard the reproductive health of women, and to promote their education and training. Early marriage deprives girls of education and acquiring skills that they will need later to support themselves when they are on their own. But in countries where plurality of laws exist, local legislatures have discretion in deciding whether or not to adopt reforms. Besides, as happens with other issues such as widows' inheritance rights, remarriage, access to land, and custody of children, local customs and solutions to disputes arrived at at the grassroots level tend to prevail over legislation emanating from the central power. Community attitudes may still favour the early marriage of girls and be opposed to them remaining in education after they have reached puberty, in spite of national laws, or in ignorance of them.

CEDAW's general provisions, in Article l, obligate governments to remove any discrimination in their legal age of marriage legislation, which in many jurisdictions sets a lower age for women than for men.

The sanctioning of child marriage is in breach of the general provisions of the UN Convention on the Rights of the Child (also known as the Childrens' Convention) which proclaim the child's right to to 'childhood', health and education (although child marriage is not specifically mentioned). However, there is no international consensus about when childhood ends. Enormous differences exist between societies and cultures as to the role of children within the family and the community, leading to inevitable differences in how the duration of childhood is viewed.[9] The onset of puberty may be the crucial indicator rather than a chronological age; or the ability to perform specific acts or the capacity for particular functions. In some communities, girls are married before the first menses. (But marriage can occur before this event, which may be late in some communities where girls have suffered from malnutrition and poor health). The Children's Convention recognises that there must be some congruity about the legal limits, and Article 1 declares that an individual is still a child when 'below the age of 18 years, unless under the law applicable to the child, majority is attained earlier'. A 1965 UN General Assembly Recommendation, a non-binding instrument, set 15 as the minimum age of marriage, and this was adopted during the 1990 UN Year of the Child. When the age of 18 was first proposed during the first reading of the convention, a minority of states argued against it as, under their national legislation, childhood ended at a lower age. This is because states with a high infant mortality rate and where life expectancy is low frequently allow children to participate at a lower age in the performance of duties that help the survival of all family members; this situation is particularly common in rural communities. In some states the laws regarding the upper limit of childhood reflect this social reality, and childhood ends at an earlier age than 18. Those states, relying on the General Assembly age of 15, drew attention to the fact that 14 was the age for the end of compulsory education in many countries as well as the minimum legal age for marriage (without parental consent).

Other states argued for adoption by the convention of the legal concept of 'emancipation', developed to accommodate situations in which young people have achieved *de facto* independence from parental control before the general age of majority, through, for example, marriage or military service. This concept is not part of English law, but it is found in the United States and in France.

Clearly, the international community is still some way from agreeing a universal definition of childhood, but there does appear to be a trend emerging in international law that the rights of the child should be as applicable to as many individuals as possible under the age of 18. This chronological age, for example, has been adopted by the African Charter on the Rights and Welfare of the Child.

The UN Children's Convention reinforces the human rights provisions of previous international treaties, and therefore states parties that do nothing to protect girls from early marriage and widowhood, or fail to act to protect children's rights to education and a 'childhood' are in breach of their international duties. By April 1995, the Convention on the Rights of the Child had been ratified by more than 180 out of 191 countries, each of which is obligated to take action – legal, educational, and administrative – to safeguard the childhood of all its young citizens. It has received a more rapid and extensive ratification than any other international treaty of its kind, reflecting the universal concern, in theory, about the importance of ensuring that childhood is protected, and that all children enjoy their human rights to shelter, food, health, education, and emotional security. The existence of this international instrument should provide strong leverage for national organisations concerned with children to lobby their governments to take action.

In addition, the declaration that emerged from the 1994 Cairo International Conference on Population and Development is relevant to efforts being made to safeguard young women and children from the perils of early marriage and early widowhood, as are the recommendations of the 1995 Copenhagen Social Summit.

National legislation

By 1995, more than 105 countries had enacted legislation on the legal age of marriage. But enforcement of national legislation is poor. Many births and marriages are not registered, marriages in any case are often conducted according to customary and religious laws, and the legal age for marriage without parental consent is often less for girls than for boys. Although legislation in many countries now outlaws marriage for girls below the age of sixteen or eighteen, local customs still dominate in many cultures. Most child mariages occur with the consent and active involvement of the parents and there is no legal regulation of such customs. The fear of AIDS has resulted in an increase in child marriage in some communities because of beliefs that the only safe unions are with virgins (see Chapter 5). Compulsory and free primary and secondary education for girls would help protect them from child marriage and child widowhood. [10]

Some jurisdictions have specifically outlawed child betrothal and child marriage. However, legislation on its own, without vigorous education campaigns and other initiatives to raise the status of women generally, is not enough to bring about change. Women as well as men may resist departures from customary norms (just as many mothers continue to insist on female circumcision of their daughters in spite of governments' efforts to eliminate the practice).

For example, the Afghan reformer Ananullah Khan introduced a family code in 1921 which stated that child marriage was against Islam and girls should be able to choose their own husbands. This code incensed the traditionalists and was never enforced; child marriage continued unabated. Among many Afghan groups women are regarded as men's property, the choice of husband is made by her family for reasons of lineage maintenance, gain and property. Hardly more than a child, all a girl can hope for is that, in return for brideprice, her family will marry her to a kind cousin whom she has known and grown up with. As in many traditional cultures, puberty defines adulthood for women, and so early marriage is common. On marriage an Afghan girl's natal family give up all rights to her, and (although contrary to Muslim law) she can inherit nothing when she is widowed.

Iran has turned back the clock. The sexual politics of the Revolution of 1979-81 resulted in legislation that was explicitly anti-female. Laws lowered the marriage age from eighteen to thirteen, as well as reinstating divorce by *talaq*, and enforcing fathers' custody rights, compulsory veiling, and restriction of women's employment. Legislation reiterated the Koranic rule that a woman's value and therefore her inheritance rights were half those of a man. Young Iranian women widowed by the Iran-Iraq war, are said to be relentlessly victimised. [11]

Education

Girls who are married in their childhood or adolescence are likely to be less educated than women who postpone marriage until they are older. Lack of education in childhood means that young widows are often unable to support themselves or any children they might have. This situation of dependency leaves them vulnerable to exploitation in new relationships – non-consensual remarriage, or other unions of a more casual nature -because they have no experience of how to live more independently. The cycle of disadvantage is often carried on through to their daughters, who in their turn will be married early and remain uneducated and dependent.

Many families, especially those headed by widows, would prefer their daughters to marry than be educated, for financial and other reasons. The knowledge that a girl has no father to defend her may make her more vulnerable to sexual harassment, assault or seduction. If she loses her virginity, or her chastity is in any way in doubt, her marriage prospects are severely damaged. In several African countries, widowed mothers talked about their terror of their daughters walking long distances to school, in open country where they could be waylaid. Nor are schools necessarily safe havens. Widows in Kenya spoke of seductions by male teachers, as well as by fellow pupils.

A Malawi widow spoke of these dangers:

'It is a long journey to the secondary school, sometimes it takes them more than three hours, and the young men offer them rides on bicycles. These boys are bad with them; they get them pregnant or into bad ways. So do the teachers. We do not like our daughters to go so far. You see, everyone knows they have no father to make a fuss, or protect them. Better they get married than have this bad thing happen.'.

Structural adjustment policies have escalated the costs of education so that even relatively comfortably off families find school fees expensive. In Malawi, parents must contribute 100 per cent of the costs of teachers' salaries and maintenance of school buildings and pay for books, stationery and uniforms. The opportunity costs of sending children to school are high: girls at home can look after younger siblings, collect water and firewood; boys can herd cattle, hoe and repair houses.

Widows' daughters are especially likely to be withdrawn from school. The direct costs of uniform, books and so on are beyond a widow's means. Male relatives may convince the widow that there is no reason for educating daughters who will be married, leave home, bring in brideprice; or they may promise education in return for custody and then renege on their undertaking and arrange a marriage instead.

Child widows, although of an age when their unmarried

contemporaries are still in education, are less likely to have access to further or continuing education, because of traditional constraints. Education policies need to target this group with appropriate programmes.

Widows who are working together in organisations and groups have begun to fight for the rights of their daughters to go to school. Alone, needing to earn a living, widows are often more conscious than other women of the importance of female education and training and of delaying marriage. Many illiterate women long for their daughters to have opportunities for advancement they have never enjoyed. They are profoundly aware of the injustices of traditional patriarchal attitudes since as sole breadwinner and head of the household they have had to struggle to maintain their families. They want assistance with school fees or free places for their children; hostel accommodation for older daughters at secondary school; crèches in schools where their daughters can bring younger siblings. 'How can we prevent our daughters from repeating our unhappy lives if the government does not help us to keep them in school? Look at me! I was married at fifteen, and a widow at sixteen. I don't want this wretched life for my two daughters,' said a widow involved in a BRAC (Bangladeshi Rural Development Committee) income-generating and education project. But efforts to improve the status of women generally, to encourage girls' education, and to eliminate child marriage under the religious law are frequently under attack by religious leaders (see Chapter 11).

Child marriage and widowhood in Hindu communities

Manu, the upper-caste law codifier, is seen by Indian feminists today as the man most responsible for the subordination of Hindu women; before his time, during the Aryan period, women had enjoyed relative equality compared to women in other societies at the time. After around 200 AD, women's position was eroded; they were married off at an early age, barred from religious ritual, and denied remarriage on widowhood. It was Manu who stated, 'From the cradle to the grave a woman is dependent on a male: in her childhood on her father, in youth on her husband, and in old age on her son.' The Mogul invasions of the sixteenth century added to existing regressive attitudes the practices of purdah and *sati*, although there is evidence of these rituals among high-caste families even before the Muslim invasions. In the nineteenth century, both British and Indian reformers worked together to abolish *sati* (1859), purdah, child marriage and the prohibition on widow remarriage (1856), but the laws had limited impact – as they do today – when all these customs continue among the less educated and lower castes.

The very low status of women, exacerbated by poverty, landlessness, debt and illiteracy in some states of India, especially Rajasthan, Maharastra, Uttar Pradesh and Bihar, and in certain other traditional communities elsewhere on the Indian sub-continent has impeded government efforts to eliminate child marriage, in spite of legislation on age of marriage and on dowry limitation. Son preference is so ingrained an attitude in many Asian families that the birth of a daughter is met with signs of grief, not joy. 'May you have a hundred sons' is a well-known blessing given to a Hindu bride at her wedding. It is sons who are needed to cultivate the land, make the blessings on the death of the father and support the widow in her old age. Sons have an economic value, and daughters are a burden and a cost. How to marry off a daughter is an overriding concern of poor families. When a woman is widowed with daughters it is an obsession, for how can a good marriage be arranged for a daughter when there is no money for a dowry?

The following stories emerged from the 1994 Bangalore Widows' Conference:

Pannabua, a Hindu widow, is now seventy years old. She was widowed when she was only seven, and, coming from a non-remarrying caste, her life has been always wretched. Naviben, from the same caste, is thirty, and was widowed when she was five. Pannabua and Naviben came together to the Widows' workshop in Bangalore in 1994. This was the first time they had ever left their villages, and they feared the gossip in their communities when they returned. Pannabua remembers: 'I was playing outside my house with my little sister and my cousin when my mother called me inside and said, 'Your husband's dead'. I asked, 'Who is a husband, mother?' I had never seen him. From that day my life changed. I was no longer allowed to play outside with the other children. I had to take off my jewellery. I continued to live with my mother, but she kept me indoors. I did all the work of the house, the cooking and cleaning and washing. From then on my life was a misery. I took refuge in God. When my mother died I went to live with my married sister and became their servant. Then Naviben heard about me and introduced me to this widows' group. If only I had had these friends to help me when I was younger.'

Pannabua had never lived with her husband, yet had still to conform to the traditional customs of Hindu widowhood, such as having her head shaved, giving up wearing the kumkum and jewellery, and living the life of an ascetic. It was never suggested that she be remarried.

Naviben, married at five, went to live with her 28-year-old husband when she was fourteen. She had never learned to read and write. When her husband was killed in an accident she was fifteen, pregnant with her first child, and too ignorant to resist her husband's brothers taking over his strip of land and claiming the accident compensation from his employer's company. Naviben with her daughter went to stay in her mother's house, from where she got involved with a self-help group of unattached women, including some who had been widowed from an early age. Of the twelve widows in the group, seven had been married as minors and only four had ever been to school.

Naviben spoke for them all when she said, 'If I had been educated, I would have known what to do about my husband's land, and his insurance. I could have a proper job and a pension when I am old, and I would have been able to educate my daughter so she will not have to live as I do.'

Bina, in rural Bihar, who also told her story to the Bangalore Widows' Conference, was married when she was six years old to a man of thirty-two without her widowed mother's permission or knowledge. It was all arranged by her older brother because the family was too poor to keep her or find a dowry. There was no celebration. Her husband's home already housed one child widow, her sister-in-law who was nine. Three years later Bina herself was widowed.

'I did not know then that I should observe ghugat, that is, I must not look anyone in the face. I used to keep looking at everybody. My brother took 300 rupees from my in-laws as if I had been sold, so I could never go home. I was tortured horribly in the three years of marriage, as well as after his death. My husband was a fierce, strong man and beat me with a thick stick, and would not let anyone interfere. I was made to collect dry leaves for the cooking fire; they never let me use any other sort of fuel. Sometimes they locked me out of the house for days and I slept under bushes. I know my husband hated me. If I crept into the house to sleep he would jump on top of me and beat me hard. They never let me wear good clothes or gave me any sari. After he died I had to wear a white sari without a blouse or petticoat and give up my coloured bangles. My mother died of shock when she learned that I was a widow like her, for I was still a little girl. My husband's brothers made me stay all alone in his hut; I had to cook all alone; I was not allowed to eat with the rest of them. Sometimes I did not eat for days. The brothers-in-law would beat me and pull my hair. Once, in the fields, they hit me so badly I nearly died. They would scream at me, "You are an unlucky one; you should not take a share." When I got really ill, the neighbours nursed me. The other child widow was just as cruel. But where could I go? I hated every leaf, every tree there. But this was my only home, and I felt I should never get away.

Bina's brother never visited her, and her natal family threatened that if she ever returned home they would maker her suffer also. Her sufferings finally ended when a married sister rescued her and brought her to the widows' ashram in Maddhubani. She became a member of the Self-Employed Women's Association (SEWA) working in its emporium and has learnt to read, write and sew. Recently she discovered that her in-laws had burnt down her house, but through SEWA she has become economically independent and strong. She says, 'We are making progress. We will show the kind of revolution that follows if widows are harassed.' (See also Chapter 11.)

Lakshmi is an old Hindu widow in Bangladesh, in the Maniganj district. She is very old and frail, and has to walk with a stick. She was married at ten and widowed at twelve, and prohibited from ever remarrying, for reforms in Hindu marriage law are not applicable to Hindus outside India. Lakshmi is one of the very few Hindus left in this community.

When her husband died, she continued to stay with his mother who had herself been widowed when she was fourteen years old. Later, her own widowed mother joined them so there were three widows living together, and Lakshmi worked as a servant to keep them. Because she was unmarriageable she was constantly harassed sexually. She used to work in the paddy for some of the richer families, and sell rice. Childless, for she was widowed so young, she now lives quite alone, dependent on begging or searching with her stick for spilt grains of rice on the village path.

Rampunit Deva's husband died before she had ever seen his face for she is from a purdah caste. She was only six years old. 'Then I had to go to live in his family.' One kindly brother-in-law and his wife treated her well throughout childhood, but once he had died everything changed, and the remaining brothers and their wives tortured her constantly in attempts to make her sign over her husband's portion of land. One night they called her to their room and poured boiling water and sliced chillies over her. Neighbours, hearing her cries, were just in time to prevent her attackers slitting her throat with a kitchen knife. With 75 per cent burns Rampunit Deva was in hospital for months.

Elementary education may not get all Indian widows jobs when their husbands die, but had it been compulsory and free, it might have protected some of those women from early marriages, or at least, enabled them, on widowhood, to manage more successfully their husband's affairs, and to get access to any services that were available, including training, income-generating and credit projects.

Child marriage and widowhood in Muslim communities

Under Muslim law, girls can be married very young. A Muslim marriage is a contract, so the parties (that is, the parents or guardians) can stipulate its terms and conditions. In practice, these conditions are very one-sided and rarely are brides aware of the details of the contract. A very young child wife will not necessarily know what stipulations are agreed concerning monogamy or polygamy; or *mahr*, dowry; or maintenance during the marriage, or divorce or death. (The *mahr*, a sum specified in the marriage contract in accordance with Islamic law, was traditionally to be paid to the bride at any time during the marriage or at its termination, through divorce or death. Muslim widows are supposed to have this money at their disposal to pay for their daughters' weddings.)

Child marriage is endorsed by many Muslim communities. (The Prophet married his wife Aisha when she was six and consummated the marriage when she was nine. The Koran states, 'marry such women as seem good to you, two, three or four'[4.4] and does not mention an age limit. But young widows, especially if they are from the poorest communities, are vulnerable pawns in the negotiations that take place to finalise a further marriage contract. In rural Bangladesh and Pakistan, and in Muslim communities in other parts of Asia and in Africa, girls continue to be married as children: elders believe that it is better for girls to be married young 'before they get into trouble'. There is always the fear that once a girl reaches puberty, she may be compromised, seduced, or raped, bringing dishonour (*zina*) on her family, and making it impossible to find a husband for her.

Where polygamy is allowed, a young girl can find herself the youngest co-widow and required to care for the older co-widows. Sometimes this can be a happy arrangement and the older co-widows may treat her as a daughter and be kind to her. But often the relationship is sour and there is much resentment and bitterness. Or she may be widowed before she has begun to live in her husband's family. Although widow remarriage is not prohibited in Islam, in some countries the child or teenage widow may find herself in an unfavourable position when her family seek to get her married for the second time.

Shamila lives in a village in Bangladesh. At eighteen-years-old, she is now a widow for the second time. She was married when she was eleven to her cousin of twenty, in order for the family land to be kept intact. She would have gone to live with him after her first menstruation, but he died suddenly in Dacca. Her parents were very poor, and had no money for a dowry, but they and her two brothers were determined to get her off their hands as soon as possible. The older a widow is, the more difficult it is to arrange a second marriage. They owed money to a man in the village who was always harassing them and threatening to take their land from them if they did not pay. He already had a wife who was sick, and children, some of whom were older than Shamila. A contract was struck to give Shamila to him in settlement of the debt. Shamila cried and begged her mother not to send her to the man, but her brothers beat her and showed her no mercy. She was fourteen when she was married to the farmer who was in his forties. There was no celebration, no gifts, to mark the marriage. Nor did the man come himself to fetch her from her father's house, but sent one of his sons instead.

Shamila was frightened. The marriage lasted only eighteen months because the man died. Shamila was the maid-of-all-work, looking after both the husband and wife, working in the fields as well as the house and forced to suffer the abuse of his children who resented her. After the death, her step-children accused her of bringing bad luck to the family, and chased her away saying she should have nothing from the inheritance although she was a co-widow.

Her brothers did not welcome her return, as it meant they would have to support her and provide her with land. Fortunately for Shamila, her village was the site for an innovative experiment in rural development run by PRISM (see Chapter 11) and she was soon involved with a group of women digging out fish ponds.[12] These women, who included other widows, were looked down on by the rest of the community because they worked 'outside' and did not keep purdah; but the solidarity of these 'sisters' has helped Shamila to come to terms with her situation. She still hopes to marry one day 'somebody of my own age', and to have children.

The women, widowed, divorced, abandoned, all very young, laugh rowdily together as they work digging up the earth and hoisting it up the bank in baskets. They know the men in the village disapprove of them. A village elder spoke: 'It is against all tradition. Women must stay in the house. If women will work outside they will be interacting with other men and leaving us.' Shamila answered, 'Next time, when we are landowners, we will be rich enough to choose our own husbands and we will tell them what to do!'

Bangladeshi widows rarely marry again once they have had children, or reach their late twenties. Nor, when questioned, do many wish to be remarried, as they have often suffered ill-treatment in their previous unions. However, when it comes to deciding how to support their children, widows – often against their deepest instincts – may be persuaded to give up their own young daughters to marriages they fear will be harsh. Dowry is not a feature of the Islamic marriage contract, but it has crept into the culture from India, and from before partition, so that daughters of poor widows, without a dowry, have to take whatever man is prepared to marry them. He may be a divorcee (with a history of violence), a widower with many children, an already married man who wants a younger bed companion, or someone who is old or sick.

'Why wouldn't a man want to marry again when his wife starts to look unkempt, is asthmatic and thin? My father has married a girl of fifteen, younger than me, because my mother cannot please him sexually any more,' explained a young male sociology student in the University of Dacca, without a shred of disapproval. 'These young girls are fortunate that in our culture a man can take more than one wife, for it is only older wealthier men who can afford to marry a girl who brings no dowry with her.' As in many other traditional communities, excessive expenditure on marriage ceremonies can undermine the status of women, weaken the financial status of the family, increase poverty, and often brings about a wide disparity of age between the spouses because only an older man can afford a wife.

Unfortunately, many of these child brides are treated like unpaid servants or as mistresses, never succeeding in earning the respect of older wives or of their husbands' children. And when they are widowed, they are often deprived of all rights to their share of the inheritance; nor are they welcome back in their own natal family.

Customary law
Governments in countries where customary and religious laws operate alongside or in conflict with modern legislation have not been able to do much to enforce laws on the age of marriage. Traditions are very deep-seated, illiterate people may have no knowledge of or understanding of the new legislation.

Enforcing legislation on the minimum age of marriage is only possible in countries where all births, marriages and deaths are registered. In developing countries, especially in rural areas, these rites of passage take place unrecorded by the statutory authorities, so that a girl's exact age may not be known. However, legislation, while badly implemented, is important because it demonstrates the commitment of governments to improve the status of women and conform to their obligations under international treaties. It cannot change behaviour in the short term, yet its existence is an important tool for education programmes on the rights of family members.

Betrothal vows made on behalf of children not yet born still occur in various traditional societies, where it is important, for example, to conserve land rights within a family, to cement a union between kin groups, or barter one child in exchange for receiving another from that same family as a marriage partner for a son or daughter. In some poor communities an unborn child may be promised in marriage as a settlement of a debt. A poor landless Asian family unable to find dowry for a daughter may find this to be a solution to an unwanted pregnancy, should a girl be born. One of the young Bangladeshi women working on the Prism fish-pond project told her story:

'I went to my husband's house when I was twelve years old, for I had been promised to him in my mother's womb. I used to hide under my mother-in-law's bed I was so frightened of him. He was twenty-five. When I was thirteen his mother took me to him, and locked me in. She said she would beat me if I did not stay with him. He raped me, and I gave birth to our first still-born child when I was fourteen. I am now seventeen, and a widow with two children.'

Polygamy, decreasing among more educated and urbanised people, is still common in rural communities in Africa; in some regions it is seen as one solution to the severe drought and crop failures of recent years. It makes sense for men to have several wives who can farm widely and in scattered plots. Girls who are still children may find themselves not only child brides, but sharing widowhood with a number of co-widows.

Widows' children
There is already much anecdotal evidence all over the developing world that the children of widows, especially daughters, suffer special disadvantages, reflecting the low status and marginalisation of their mothers. Millions of children of widows live in wretchedness and poverty, often withdrawn from education and exploited in child labour, or forced

into early and unfortunate types of marriages. Generations of children growing up without proper shelter, food, health care, family, education, and training can threaten the economic and social fabric of society. Widowhood, looked at from this angle, is no longer a feminist issue, but a serious development problem.

A useful area of research might be the consequences of widowhood for children, since children are the most important natural resource of a nation, and represent its potential development. Targeting the children of widows would create more public awareness about the injustices associated with widowhood in general and why it is an important issue.

The following statements describe some of the situations that widowhood enforces on children.

'I have no father and I have to keep my mother and work the land so that we can eat,' explained an eleven-year old boy from Emol, Guatemala, whose father had been killed during the 'violencia'.[13] 'My children cannot go to school for since my husband died there is no money for school fees,' said a widowed mother in Malawi. 'Her fourteen-year old-daughter is working as a sex worker since she came to Nairobi with her AIDS-infected dying mother,' reported a nurse volunteer working in the squatter slum in the Materu valley. 'My little girl of three years old died from malnutrition and abuse when my husband's relatives threw me out of the house and took my children from me because they wanted the land,' recounted a young widowed mother at the offices of FIDA in Kampala, Uganda. 'My mother got me married very young to an old and ugly man, because as a widow she could not afford a dowry to get me a good husband or keep me in education, or food on her own,' sobbed an eighteen-year old widow in Bangladesh.

A Masai widow in Kenya explained some of the pressures she felt:

'A widow with children has a lot of problems, But you can do a 'harambee' – a joint get together fund-raising to get help with school fees, food and clothes. The trouble is you are not always blessed with good children. But other bad children who have fathers don't get criticised in the same way. You are so disadvantaged as a widow. Your own children defile you. I am the man and the woman, the father and the mother. Then people point and say "look at these bad children. It is because only a woman is in charge of them" '.

Children bear the brunt of society's neglect of the widow. Children taken into custody by relatives under the guise of local custom are frequently in danger of exploitation, ill-treatment and neglect. 'The way to the property is through the children,' commented a woman leader of a group of widows in Zimbabwe. Many of the street children who beg, deal and take drugs, and become involved in crime and prostitution while trying to survive in the cities and towns of the Third World often have only a mother alive; the father is dead, disappeared or has abandoned them.

Child labour

There are no reliable estimates of the extent of child labour, and figures vary from 150 million to 300 million. Child labour is difficult to define, for different cultures define work and childhood in separate ways; nor are there any precise figures for the numbers of widows' children or orphans involved in illegal work.

It is probably a universal experience, in all rural areas of developing countries, that as soon as children reach the age of eight or nine they begin to help in a wide variety of work – for example, taking cattle out to graze, weeding, fetching firewood and water, caring for younger siblings, doing craft work. Such activity does not attract attention because it is unpaid family work. It is assumed that, as long as a child is occupied in a family group, the work is tailored to its physical capacity. But when children are sent out to work for an outside employer there is a different and often dangerous type of relationship which can give rise to exploitation. The formal sector, governed by employment protection laws, does not employ children, but the informal sector labour market is uncontrolled; here poor children can be found working long hours, in insanitary conditions, for a derisory wage.

Widows hope they can bring up their children as their husbands would have wished, without too many changes, without deprivations, but as extreme poverty threatens, children become a vital economic resource. Some widows' children only work with, or under the supervision of, their families: in agriculture, domestic jobs, the family business or cottage industries. This last category may involve semi-industrial work: making carpets, leathergoods, and also street trading (selling newspapers, cleaning shoes, selling sweets or family-grown foods). But there are children who work without any family supervision in so-called apprenticeships – often for as long as ten to twelve hours a day – in industrial work (illegal in most countries but very largely unmonitored by the countries concerned), or are hired out or sold for agricultural or domestic work.

In countries where it is normal for households to have a servant, many of them are children. Families where both parents work often keep

another child from a poor family to look after their own children in their
absence. In Africa and the Indian sub-continent a servant can be as
young as ten. Often a widow's child in a rural area may go and work for
better-off members of the extended family, but in many cases children
are grossly overworked and ill cared for in stranger households.

> In March 1994, Salma was only ten when her widowed mother in the
> village agreed to hand her over to an inspector of police who needed
> a servant in Dacca. Alone, she had to care for five children under
> seven; cook, wash dishes and clothes, and clean the house. She worked
> eleven hours a day (sometimes more), seven days a week and was
> continually screamed at, hit, and abused.
>
> One day a neighbour heard her screams. She had been locked up
> in the kitchen with one bowl of rice, whilst the family returned to the
> village for a three-day stay.
>
> This writer visited her in a women lawyers co-operative refuge the
> week after her rescue. Her body was covered in bruises and cigarette
> burns; bald patches on her scalp showed where her hair had been
> pulled out. She spoke of her gruelling hours of work, how she was
> given the scraps to eat from the family's meals, how even the children
> aped their parents' behaviour and shouted at her. 'My life quite
> changed after my father died. My mother had to do what the
> inspector said'. Efforts to prosecute the inspector were stalled:
> Salma's mother was his tenant and she was induced to sign a
> statement that her daughter was happy in his house, and had been
> well-treated, that her injuries were self-inflicted.

Some of the worst cases of exploitative child labour are to be found in
the carpet factories of the Middle East. A 1994 BBC television
documentary, shot in Morocco, revealed how despite a damning report
to the International Labour Organisation (ILO) from the Anti-Slavery
Society in 1975 and legislation forbidding employment of under-
fourteens, children as young as five years old are still made to work at
the looms for as long as eleven hours a day in unpleasant and unhealthy
conditions. Finally there are the children who have been abandoned by
their families, thrown out of the home, or have run away and are
prepared to do any work to keep alive. Among all these groups, the
children of widows are to be found, although, to date, there has been
no research specifically addressing these child workers. [14]

Many children of widows may be forced to live on the street. In
Bangladesh, widows' children who have accompanied their mothers to
the city for work might earn a few *taka* as tempo boys (finding

passengers for the rickshaws and taxis) or work in the garment factories; girls may be coerced into prostitution, sometimes under the guise of domestic service, or through the tourist industry. In Bombay, according to Dr Ghiladi, who works to rehabilitate child prostitutes, many of the little girls sold to brothels by their relations are the children of widows. Some men are prepared to pay more money to have intercourse with a young child, and many of these girls become infected with sexually transmitted diseases and AIDS, resulting in their early death.

There are calls occasionally for the abolition of child labour, or for the boycotting of manufactured goods produced by such toil, but the reality is that children's work, whether unpaid in the home or poorly paid outside, is crucial to the survival of millions of poor families. Children's worth to the family increases as a result of widowhood, because their mothers look upon them as support in the absence of other normal support systems. Dona Ana, a widow in a Guatemalan village, described their value: 'The other women can lift a heavy load, but I need my children's help for I can hardly walk. They take my husband's place.' In Guatemala, widows' sons as young as seven might be sent to find work on the coast in the company of another adult. From the age of thirteen they travel together to work as shoe shine boys and ice-cream vendors in the towns, or harvesting coffee and cotton in the *fincas*. In India children are often forced into debt bondage, working as agricultural labourers or knotting carpets from the age of ten to pay back a dead father's debts incurred whilst he was ill. In the Indian subcontinent, land-poor and landless widows are often deeply in debt which encourages debt bondage, for this type of bondage is almost without exception related to land tenure relationships. [15]

Much of the illegal work children do in small workshops (carpet weaving, embroidery, tailoring), or in the streets (collecting paper and rubbish, peddling drugs, and begging), or working in the putting-out system, severely affects their health, but widows are rarely able to afford health care when their children fall ill or have worksite accidents. Among purdah families in India, Pakistan and Bangladesh, little children sit up all night with their widowed mother homeworkers, engaged in piecework, rolling *bidis* (cheap cigarettes made from leaves rolled round shredded tobacco), embroidery, and toymaking.

The link between widowhood and child labour merits research. The absence of an adult male in a household and the limited prospects for remunerative female employment often compel a widowed mother to allow, encourage or even force her children to undertake wage labour in spite of miserable conditions of pay. [16] Children as young as four years old can collect wood, sell prepared food, go out and beg with a baby sibling tucked under one arm. Maids may be as young as eight years old in households in Latin America, although older girls are preferred. Widows who find employment as live-in maids are sometimes allowed to bring a daughter with them as an extra hand. Domestic service is not regulated, the hours are long, the work is hard, and the pay may be only in food, not money. Mistreatment, sexual abuse and physical punishment are common. The men of the house may see widow and daughter as property and treat them as sexual slaves, throwing them out when they become pregnant.

Conclusion

The appalling conditions in which many widowed mothers find themselves means that their children are denied a proper chance in life. Even if the needs of widows themselves continue to be neglected and ignored as a national priority, the plight of their children – who are, after all, every country's most valuable national resource – should galvanise governments into action; the UN Children's Convention, ratified by so many countries with such swifteness and enthusiam, offers considerable leverage for those campaigning on behalf of such disadvantaged children everywhere.

Notes

1.   Monica Felton, *A Child Widow's Story*, Gollancz, London, 1966.
2.   UNICEF could not provide any figures. However, its 1995 report *The Progress of Nations* draws attention to the prevalence of child marriage in some Asian countries, and the lack of quantitative data.
3.   UNICEF, *The Situation of Women and Children in Gambia*, UNICEF, Gambia, 1993.
4.   The Human Rights Watch report *Child Widowhood in Southern Nigeria*, Washington, DC, 1995, one of the rare reports on the subject, came to the attention of the author whilst revising the manuscript.
5.   Organisation of African Unity/UNICEF, *Africa's Children, Africa's Future*. Report of the International Conference on Assistance to Africa's Children, Dakar, Senegal, November 1992.
6.   Ayesha Raif's 'Sold', a dramatised documentary about the two Yemeni daughters was broadcast on BBC Radio 4 on 19 June 1995.
7.   UNICEF, *The Progress of Nations*, 1995, p. 2.
8.   United Nations, *The Nairobi Forward-looking Strategies for the Advancement of Women*, UN, New York, 1985.
9,   Geraldine Van Bueren, *The International Law on the Rights of the Child*, Martinus Nijhoff, 1995, pp. 36–9.
10.   For the benefits of female education and its constraints, see World

Bank, *Letting Girls Learn: Promising Approaches in Primary and Secondary Education*, World Bank Discussion Paper 133, 1991. The issue of child marriage is not discussed, however, under traditional constraints except in Box 3.3, p. 29.

11.   See 'Revolution, the State, Islam and Women: Gender Politics in Iran and Afghanistan', Women Living Under Muslim Laws Dossier 7/8 (BP 23, 34790 Grabels, France), pp. 34–5.

12.   See Chapter 6, note 20.

13.   Judith Zur, *Widows in Highland Guatemala*, University of London, 1993.

14,   J. Challis and D. Elliman, *Child Workers Today*, Quartermaine House, 1979.

15.   Judith Ennew, *Debt Bondage*, Anti-slavery Society, London, 1981. Debt bondage also occurs in Latin America, the Middle East and Africa.

16.   Jean Drèze, *Widows in Rural India*, Development Economics Research Programme Paper No. 26, London School of Economics, 1990.

CHAPTER 8

Older Widows

The world's populations are ageing rapidly. Populations have a greater life expectancy than ever before because of improved medical care and public health programmes. Although at present developing countries still have a higher proportion of children to old people (unlike the West where the balance is reversed) the absolute numbers of old people in developing nations are large and ever-increasing. By the year 2020, nine of the twelve largest elderly populations will be in developing countries. From 1985 to 2020 the rate of increase in the numbers of elderly people in countries such as Mexico, Indonesia, Brazil and China will be up to fifteen times higher than that of countries such as Britain.[1] National resources in developing countries are least likely to be adequate to deal with the rapid increase in the very elderly, mostly widows, who need maintenance and medical care. More than half the elderly of the world live in these countries, and by the year 2025 that proportion will have risen to three quarters. The fastest-growing segment of the elderly population is that of those aged eighty years and over.

An important effect of the different life expectancies of men and women is that the greater proportion of the elderly are women, and widowed. This is an increasing reality affecting women across the globe. Since women generally get married at an earlier age than men, and men die younger, many women can expect to live a long period of their lives as widows. A Family Life Cycle Table for Kerala and India for 1981 showed that whereas in Kerala and India as a whole the expected duration of widowerhood for a man was 3.5 and 6.2 years respectively, a wife's expected duration of widowhood was 14.7 and 11.5 years. In many developing countries, a vast majority, perhaps 70 per cent, of all elderly women over sixty are already widows. But the incidence of widowerhood among old men is much less.

Women are never prepared for the disadvantages and precariousness of widowhood, despite the very high chance that many will find themselves in that state at some period in their lives.. Elderly widows may have been widowed several times. They may have been remarried to the first husband's kin on several occasions, always outliving the

Table 8.1 Demographic change and older-women: Life Expectancy and Gender Gap - Selected Countries

	Life expectancy* Men	Life expectancy* Women	Gender Gap** (no of years that women outlive men)
Sweden	73	79	4
Australia	71	78	7
Soviet Union	64	74	10
China	62	66	4
Japan	73	79	4
Philippines	59	62	3
Indonesia	49	51	3
India	46	45	-1
Egypt	54	56	2
Mauritania	41	44	3
Guinea Bissau	39	43	4
Ethiopia	38	41	3

Note that in India, unlike any other country listed, average female life expectancy at birth is less than that of older males.

*   Life expectancy at birth: the average number of years a person may expect to live.

**   Gender gap: the difference in years between female and male life expectancy.

Source: *UN Demographic Yearbook*: 1980 or latest year available from: *The New State of the World Atlas*, Kidron and Segal 1987 New York. Reprinted from Kasturi Sen, 'Women in Later Life: Health, Security and Poverty', *International Health Exchange*, May 1994.

husband. Each time such a bereavement occurs, depending on the culture, religion, her age and that of any children she has, she finds that she is severely disadvantaged if a new husband cannot be found to support her.

But once a woman gets to the menopause she is unlikely to find another husband. An elderly widower, on the other hand, even when he is a very old man, will be quickly helped to find another wife. Old men are four times as likely as old women to be living with a younger partner. This vast difference between the marriage opportunities of old men and old women exists too in both developing and developed countries. A financially secure and socially successful man in the UK in his seventies or eighties may easily manage to find an attractive and supportive younger woman to share his last years, even when it is clear that such a union must involve, in the not too distant future, terminal nursing care, whereas widows past the age of forty-five are most unlikely to find a suitable partner. It is almost universally thought that a man requires a woman in his household: society concludes that a man cannot manage on his own without a woman to look after him, clean, cook, look after his garden and warm his bed. More compassion and thought is given to the domestic needs and comforts of widowers than is given to the practical and emotional or social needs of widows in their old age. Thus, even approaching the end of life, sexual inequalities remain. There is barely any research on this aspect of ageing, but it could be that as old traditions are eroded, old women, the survivors, suffer worse treatment by family and society than old men.

In Britain, according to the 1991 census, 43% per cent of women over the age of 65 were widows. In Third World countries the proportions of women who are widows after this age are far higher: 75 per cent in the Republic of Korea, 70 per cent in India, 41 per cent in Mexico, and 35 per cent in Cuba.[2] While widows of all ages may suffer marginalisation and discrimination, old and very old widows confront special disadvantages once they are no longer able to work and thus become totally dependent on others. Only some of the causes of elderly widows' vulnerability can be attributed to their years. Their marginalisation is largely as a result of the low status of women in general, and their lack of legal rights. A large proportion of elderly household heads in developing countries are women, but unlike their counterparts in developed regions, their households contain often two or more members who may be non-earners. It is not unusual to find elderly widows, unable to earn, caring for grandchildren and dependent old people, so that a disproportionate number of women-headed households are living in poverty.

Possibly, it might be argued, the cruel gender-induced deprivations women have had to endure have made them even stronger than men in their third and fourth age. Besides, men are more likely to die earlier from accidents, in war, and from disease. Just as the human female is stronger than the male as an infant, so she is in old age. The gender differences in life expectancy are particularly noticeable in the over-75s and over-80s. (Bangladesh and Chad are exceptions). Female numerical superiority tends to be greater in urban areas than in rural ones. For every 100 elderly men in Africa, Latin America and the Caribbean, there are 116 elderly women (in developed regions the ratio is 100 to 152).[3] These figures are taken from 1988 statistics; the proportion of women over sixty is probably much higher today because of improvements in life expectancy and lower child-bearing rates. In the early 1980s only six countries in the world recorded a life expectancy for women lower than that for men: Bangladesh, Bhutan, Nepal and Pakistan, the West Bank and Papua New Guinea. The 1995 World Population Data Sheet shows only minimal progress; Pakistani and the West Bank now have the same life expectancy at birth as men – that is far lower than everywhere else in the world. The great majority of women surviving into old age will be widows.

Today Third World communities have desperate problems to face as contraceptive use takes hold. 'As survival-seeking Asians, growth-orientated African tribesmen and *macho* males of Latin America', as Paul Harrison, development journalist, describes them, are converted to the small family, who then will there be to look after the elderly, and especially the vast numbers of elderly women?'[4] What if a widow has only one or two sons, or none, or only a daughter? How will she survive old age? Her increased longevity may bring her not necessarily happiness, but, on the contrary, an augmentation in suffering and long-drawn-deprivation and isolation. Her sons, poor themselves, may have their own families to support, or may have migrated, searching for work, many years ago. Her married daughters may live far away. She is no longer able to work. She enjoys no pension, either through her own labour, or through her dead husband. She has inherited nothing. In China, already the success of the one-child-family policy is placing severe strains on the one child required to support parents and grandparents, and often great-grandmothers.

One of the most pressing considerations for populations of countries where there is not, and is not likely to be in the near future, a system of state universal old age pensions is insurance against old age (see Chapter 2 for a more detailed discussion of pensions). Social security gets only 5 per cent or less of GNP in developing countries as against fifteen per cent in Europe. Most rural and urban poor families rely on their children for financial help in old age. Only a very few elderly people have pensions from their work in the formal sector.

In developing countries, with some exceptions, a woman becomes less useful as she ages since she can no longer bear children. In rural areas she may have been abandoned by her husband or offspring and required to provide care for her grandchildren and elderly parents.[5] Older widows will mostly have missed the benefits of social change over the last two or three decades in terms of education, employment, health and culturally prescribed roles experienced by younger women, and they are consequently more marginalised. In polygamous societies, however, benefits may arise for some elderly widows because a younger co-widow may care for the older woman on the husband's death.

A Masai widow spoke warmly of her husband's younger wife: 'We are together in this world. Her troubles are my troubles, her children are my children. She helps me by collecting firewood when I am too weak, and she tends the animals when I cannot get up. I would die without her for my sons do not bother with me, they go off to the city and are no good to me anymore.'

In monogamous societies, when children have migrated far away leaving the widowed mother alone she may have nobody to care for her, cultivate her garden, buy her medicines, or take her to hospital. Old widows in a group discussion with this writer in Zimbabwe spoke of how neighbours and friends were more likely to give practical help to them than were faraway sons and married-away daughters.

The elderly, so many of them women, are especially vulnerable to the adverse impacts of ecological, political, economic and social changes. Yet older women, of whom so many are widows, play a key role in both economic development and in social and family stability. Their productive resources and care-giving roles, so long as they are still able to function physically, together make a crucial contribution to the economy, although their work is mostly invisible and unreported in labour statistics or in figures for the gross national product.

Older women, mostly widowed, with their greater longevity face the prospect not only of nurturing even older dependants - the 'old old' - but that of raising the dependants of their middle-aged and younger descendants who have deserted them, migrated or died. For example, in certain districts of Uganda it is the old grandmothers who care for the orphans whose parents have died of AIDS. In the Rakai district, entire villages are inhabited only by old women and their young grandchildren; because the middle generation has been wiped out by the pandemic.

In general, older populations in the less developed regions of the world are predominantly rural and projected to remain so beyond the year 2000. An exception is Latin America, which is highly urbanised, with all but 15% of its population of the Southern Cone living in towns; here, the problems facing isolated elderly widows in an urban setting need addressing. It is thought that rural-to-urban migration has a particularly deleterious effect on old women living in the towns since an urban economy absorbs those who might otherwise be at home caring for elderly relatives.[6] Nor is urban housing usually designed to suit an extended family. In several Latin American countries, urban widows suffer severe isolation.

The continued neglect of the concerns of elderly, mostly widowed women, is perhaps difficult to understand when there has been such a worldwide increase in the female population over fifty, and when the social and economic implications of this 'greying' or ageing of populations relate particularly to women. The United Nations estimates that this group doubled between 1955 and 1990 - from 250 million to 500 million. Projections of 1990 show that in 35 years the figure will have more than doubled again to reach 1.1 billion. This is equivalent to the total population of all the more developed regions in 1975, or twice the population of Africa in 1985. [7]

In China, already, the success of the one-child family policy is placing severe strains on the one child required to support parents and grandparents, and there, as in the majority of countries, it is women who survive into very old age, rather than men.

Images of old widows

In fairy tales, legends, myths and nursery tales the old widow portrayed as a hag, harridan, witch, or sorceress is a familiar character. Marina Warner has shown how fairy tales reflect the insecurity experienced by older women. [8] For example, in 'Rapunzel' the old woman's desire to snatch the baby girl reflects her material need for younger helping hands at home and the fear of redundancy sensed by a widow whose son's marriage has deprived her of control in her own household. Many stories from around the world depict widowed mothers harassing their daughters-in-law whilst showing a possessive adoration of their sons. Widows are often the butt of crude 'mother-in-law' jokes. The vilification of old widows belongs to a long tradition and arises not just from intergenerational strife but from rivalry and guilt about the weak and dependent. Often an old woman appears in stories as possessed of magical evil powers. She is rarely described in positive terms as someone worthy of respect for her experience and her wisdom, or as a human being who has a right, in old age, to be cared for and supported in recognition of her past contributions to her family and community. Such stereotypes of old women are almost universal, and are to be found in the literature of all societies, from time immemorial. This fictional depiction affects both collective and individual attitudes. Small children are taught to fear the sight of old women, and from that fear may come first taunts, then threats, and finally violence. The old widow living alone, even in developed countries, is easy prey for physical assault, robbery, and even rape. In parts of the Third World, old widows accused of being witches are expelled from villages, or assaulted, murdered, or driven to suicide. In Ghana, according to one official source, no one knows how or where some of the old widows die, for no one asks when they have disappeared. [9] The archetypal witch is female, old and ugly. [10] Women who outlive their husbands or worse, who survive their children, are the most likely to be suspected of witchcraft. In societies where death in childbirth is common, a woman surviving into old age is seen as an anomaly, as unnatural. In India, in the last decade, publicity about the involvement of widowed mothers-in-law in dowry deaths has contributed to this negative image.

Old widowers are rarely described in such terms.

The value of elderly women
It is wrong to categorise all elderly women as a 'vulnerable' group and to see the issues concerning their lives exclusively in the context of welfare policies and programmes. Some, although unfortunately a minority, of elderly women live healthy, active and positive lives. It is important to distinguish between older women who are fit and active and those who are infirm and require care, remembering that chronological age is an imperfect indicator of capacity and potential. In the poorest states of India, for example, the ageing process for many women is accelerated because they have had such harsh lives, overworked, having had too many pregnancies, without adequate nourishment or health care; their lifeexpectancy is short, and at forty or fifty they may look like old women. Yet in other areas of the world there are millions of women in their sixties and seventies who are still active, strong and working or capable and wanting to work.

In Africa, Latin America and the Caribbean, many women of this age are crucial to the rural economy, running farms and working in agriculture, supplying all the food needs of their families as well as producing crops for marketing. Theirs is a significant contribution to development and to the survival of communities but it depends on their access to resources, such as land, and the protection of their rights to remain in their homes and keep their possessions. (See Chapter 3.)

Older women, all over the world, contribute much - although their contribution is unrecognised - in several areas of the economy: in sustainable development, health, family planning, midwifery, child care, agriculture, food security, cottage industries, education, and community leadership.[11] They are needed to fill the gaps left by cutbacks in social services resulting from structural adjustment policies. In the Dominican Republic, for example, research has shown how valuable are the contributions to the economy made by older women: special programmes use retired teachers for pre-school education and administer a revolving loan fund targeted at older women enabling them to start small businesses and cottage industries. Older women are used as health promoters and mentors to teenage pregnant girls.[12] The talents, skills and experience of these women need recognition. Active old people live healthier and happier lives than those whose contributions to the economic good are unwanted or ignored.

Education

Studies conducted among elderly women in all regions of the world show high levels of illiteracy compared with that of the female population as a whole, since the older generation of women is least likely to have received any schooling. This deprivation compounds their powerlessness, making it difficult for them to learn about and obtain access to any services which may be available for old people. (Chapter 2 provides examples of how illiteracy and ignorance of civil rights are major blocks to many elderly Indian widows obtaining special pensions.) Illiteracy intensifies the generation gap, increases the isolation of old women and makes them dependent on others to acquaint them with their social and legal rights. Help of this nature is not always altruistic; intermediaries may demand payment for their services, or be less than honest in their handling of an elderly widow's affairs. On countless occasions widows relying, in order to acquire their lawful dues, on the good faith of others (local officials as well as relatives) have found themselves victims of embezzlement and fraud. Moreover, lack of education often makes it difficult for them to understand and pursue legal remedies.

Old widows who have received some education do not necessarily fare better. For example, those in the West who born in the 1920s usually received education that was geared to them being wives and mother, and not independent beings needing to earn their own living. In the UK, as in Third World communities, old widows are the women most likely to find that they have been defrauded by people they trusted to deal with matters - such as property, service management and financial affairs. (Even this author, in spite of her legal training, found herself the victim of an embezzlement of her dead husband's estate in another European country.)

Female-headed households

In the Caribbean, there is a predominance of female-headed households composed of three or four generations of women and their offspring; old women tend to be more valued and cared for in old age because they are integrated in a matrilineal kinship group, and have over their life-span been involved in child-care and economic support in the warmth of women-centred households. This is also the case in some African countries. In Botswana, for example, the presence of elderly widows in a household is associated with increased children's school enrolment, as the widows are available to cover the children's chores during their absence.[13] This role of child-minder and household helper is also evidenced in surveys of elderly women undertaken in China, Korea, Malaysia and Sri Lanka. These extended female households provide support for very old and infirm women that is missing in patriarchal societies.[14] A much higher proportion of female than of male household heads are widowed.

Studies in Indian villages show that elderly widowed women in India are more often living alone than living with sons or daughters.[15] Findings like this expose as myth the assumption that the old in developing countries are generally supported by their sons. The sons themselves may be too poor to carry the burden of another dependant in addition to their own children, or have migrated or emigrated far away. Often daughters-in-laws resent the incumbrance of an old mother-in-law with out-of-date ideas, who puts impossible strains on the family budget and on intra-household relationships.

Old women living on their own are considered more needy than those living in households where there are adult males, although much more research is needed on the subject of intra-household distribution of resources (see Chapters 1 and 2) and there are obviously wide regional variations.

Health

Female longevity masks the fact that women do not necessarily experience longer periods of good health. Women who have survived gender-biased neglect during infancy and childhood and the risks associated with miscarriage, clandestine abortion, pregnancy and childbirth in their fertile years are prone to a wide range of disabling conditions and chronic health problems, even though they are likely to outlive men once the dangerous pre-menopause years are over. The problems they are prone to include conditions such as arthritis, diabetes, high blood pressure, anaemia and osteoporosis as well as other age-related changes in functional capacity such as visual and sensory impairment.

In this context, also, a much neglected area is women's mental health. Higher rates of anxiety and depression are found among women (of all ages); some illnesses are brought on by the effects of poverty and isolation, which in old age may reach their peak. The double shifted-work by women inside and outside the home also takes its toll. Recent research undertaken by the International Research Centre on Women (IRCW) shows that as a consequence of their earlier life, women in their older years have increased feelings of powerlessness, dependency, insecurity and lack of autonomy which can cause deterioration in mental health.

Whilst both men and women are vulnerable to certain contingencies of life such as illhealth, disability, unemployment and, of course, old age, it is the combined effects of being a woman and experiencing one or more of these risks that puts a woman in a far more disadvantaged position. The poor health of old widows is, in many cases, the culmination of years of neglect and discrimination. Born, raised, married and becoming mothers in an age when son preference was seen as a natural phenomenon, when family planning services and general health care were virtually nonexistent or inaccessible, and when girls were married young and given no education or training to fit them for economic independence, old widows illustrate vividly the consequences of a lifetime of subordination under male dominance. When the infirmities of old age prevent them from engaging in any economic activity, they become destitute.

Women's increased longevity is not always seen as a bonus, either by them, their relatives, or society, for in the main longer life expectancies have not been accompanied by the establishment of statutory support such as pensions or retirement homes (as in the West) for women whose families are unable to maintain and care for them. The concept of institutionalising old people is alien to traditional societies, and furthermore health and social services in developing countries tend to be delivered to younger women through maternal and child health care, rather than to those women who are past childbearing. The majority of governments in the less developed countries do not yet, when life expectancy is still quite low, see the necessity of extending the public health infrastructure, but there will be serious problems in the future if health care is not extended to elderly women.

Economic deprivation among older widows is likely to be reflected in higher morbidity and mortality compared with married women in the same age range. This pattern emerges from recent studies among women of different marital status in Bangladesh [16] and in some Indian villages. However, the mortality rates for older widows can be quite different depending upon their living arrangements, for example whether they head a household, live alone or live as dependants with adult sons or daughters. Old widows living alone emerge as the group with highest mortality. Chen and Drèze found, in their Indian study, that mortality was lowest where the widow headed her household in which an adult son was present.[17]

Elderly women fortunate enough to have continued in happy marriages into their old age but who then lose a husband when they are infirm are also most vulnerable, since it is often when the male head of the household is no longer in charge that old widows are treated harshly and their lives are shortened through psychological and physical deterioration. Women who lose their partners in old age and have no close family to comfort them may experience an intense disorientation, sense of loss and isolation, which can lead to permanent mental disfunctioning. (It is often in these circumstances that old women may be regarded as outcasts, teased and jeered at by children, and branded as witches. These widows, not surprisingly, have the highest mortality rates.

In societies where there is a high outward migration of selected groups and old widows remain behind just at the very time when they are in need of support from the younger generation, mortality rates can also be high. Studies in India have shown that where widows live as dependants in households which are not their children's, their mortality rate is higher than that of married women of the same age living with their own children. This suggests that intra-household neglect is an important source of enhanced mortality for dependent widows.[18]

The invisibility of old widows

In some societies, old widows simply seem to disappear from view, no longer taking any active role in the home or in society. They become 'invisible'. Some aged Indian widows who are members of relatively affluent, high-caste families, or Muslim widows in purdah societies may suffer more deprivation through their incarceration within a family than others from poorer and lower castes who are permitted to move outside the home. Very little is generally known outside about how resources are distributed within a household and how equitable is the elderly widow's share of food and other comforts, including emotional support. Older widows are the most silent sufferers of abuse in all its forms. They are often unable to participate in new movements to help women fight discrimination. Sometimes - as studies in India and Bangladesh have shown - widowed mothers-in-law do have economic and cultural/social power as the head of the family, and sometimes make use of it in excessive domination, to the point of cruelty, of young and exploitable daughters-in-law. As mentioned above, the harsh mother-in-law devoted to her son and an accessory in dowry-associated harassment is a familiar figure of the Indian sub-continent. The Director of the Ministry of Women's Affairs in Bangladesh told me she felt most sympathy for the young wives terrorised by their husbands' powerful widowed mothers. However, this scenario is far less common than that of the widow who is powerless. Research conducted in India reveals how elderly widows are often victims of severe neglect and abuse. Although we know a little about elderly widows who live alone or are heads of household, we know much less about how old widows fare when they live within the households of relatives.

> Sohagi Hembran comes from a West Bengal village. Her own sons seized family land from her when she was past seventy, so that thereafter she had to live as a casual labourer. She often faced extreme penury and starvation. Shashi Barik in another village was also over seventy when her daughter's husband forced her to sign away most of her land into his name. Once he had possession, he and his wife refused to care for her any more. 'For want of food she became weaker every day'.[19]

A front-page article in a Uganda newspaper in 1993 entitled 'In-laws Evict Widow, 72' tells the story of how two co-widows evicted from their homes, robbed and beaten by the brothers-in-law, attempted to get protection from the traditional courts (the RCs or Resistance Courts).[20] The older widow appealed eventually to the District Administrator to help her regain her property and to recover the three children of her co-wife who had been forcibly married to and made pregnant by a clan member. Maduda Albina said, 'I am being humiliated because I did not produce a child in that home, but all the same those children born to my co-wife are equally mine since it was our collective work that raised the animals for the bride-price.'

In the rural areas of Bangladesh, old impoverished widows are a common sight as they walk from village to village begging, 'Sha'Allah Sh'Allah'; they can be heard wherever people congregate for festivals, for weddings, for funerals, for it is the custom to give to beggars at these times, and old women predominate in this crowd. In Bangladesh and India, aged widows are easily recognised for they wear no coloured bangles or nose rings, petticoats or blouses. In the city slums of Dacca, in Delhi, Bombay and Calcutta, these elderly women lie down in the streets and die. Many of them have migrated from the rural areas in the hope that they would find charity if not alms. When they are questioned, their stories are always of lost children, forgetful sons and cruel relatives.

> Along a path in a village in rural Bangladesh, a wild, white-haired ragged figure is stumbling along with a stick. Occasionally she sits on the ground, using her stick to collect together bits of wood and rubbish, leaves and twigs she can use for firewood. She hunts with her long nails for rice that might have fallen by the wayside as it was being carried home. She is a Hindu widow in a Muslim village, and she is entirely alone. She was widowed when she was seven years old and for

years lived with her widowed mother and widowed mother-in-law.
Since they died she has seen no other relatives. She doesn't know how
old she is. People laugh at her and call her names. Sometimes they give
her some rice. She is too old to work. When she was younger she
sorted paddy. She is now a beggar. She has known only abuse,
suffering, poverty. Her toothless gums yawn open as she tries to smile
at us. 'I must have done something bad in my last life, very bad, to
live like this now.' She says she is glad to be old and near death.
Another laugh, a sort of cackle as she whispers, so the other villagers,
crowding round will not hear, 'At least now the men no longer attack
me. I am so ugly I interest none any more'. Her neighbours jostle and
giggle at her. They stare with curiosity because we are talking to her,
but they show no kindness or pity.

What can be done?

It is important to distinguish between the work capacities of elderly
women over the age of sixty, and of those aged over seventy-five. The
former should be enabled to work in some capacity for as long as they
are able: the satisfaction of work with the knowledge that one is still a
useful member of society is one of the best ways of keeping young and
preventing depression, illness and death. Women over seventy-five, on
the other hand, will probably need some care, although even very old
people have attributes and abilities that should be appreciated and used.
For example, such women may be a source of information about the
history of the family, the village, the region and the country. Their
wisdom and knowledge of the past are to be valued and recorded;
children can learn much from them; and, even in very old age, these
women could be invited by teachers to talk in school about how things
were in the past.

Elderly women may continue to work as long as they are able. Women,
unlike most men, are adapted to diverse tasks in the home and outside.
In rural communities especially, older women may always find some
useful work. Studies in India, however, showed that even in the informal
sector women were laid off work at a younger age than men. But so long
as old widows can work, they are seen to have some economic value. In
return for child-minding, cleaning the house, cooking and other domestic
tasks, they will be fed and accommodated; transmitting to the young in
stories, songs, and habits, the ancient traditions of their communities may
ensure they are respected. A generation ago it was often the
grandmothers in villages who instructed the granddaughters in all they
should know about their bodies and how to conduct themselves in their
relationships with their peers and elders, and imparted to them the codes

and values that would keep them safe; with migration and urbanisation these good practices are dying out. The problems start when the widows become older still, and unable to work for their food and lodging.

Food-for-work and public works programmes need to take into account the skills, capability and special needs of widows between the ages of sixty and seventy-five. Primary health care programmes could do more to recognise and encourage the skills of elderly women in cultivating and applying herbal medecine (see Chapter 5 for an acccount of a herbal medecine project in Uganda) and as traditional midwives or family planning promoters (many of these are old women paid not in cash but in kind). They could be targeted for training in hygiene, and to train younger women, so upgrading their status.

Although very old widows in developing countries receive pensions, and where they do the sums involved are often derisory and are frequently misappropriated by bureaucrats or relatives, in many countries of the Third World there is little likelihood that in the foreseeable future governments would be able to provide pensions for their elderly people - men or women. (Pensions and other forms of support are discussed in Chapter 3.)

In Varanasi and in other towns of India, ashrams may provide refuges for elderly widows. There they live out their days, depending on alms from the temple worshippers and from begging. In return they sing songs for the visitors to the shrines. The Varanasi (or Kashivasi) widows are the special ones who live the religious life with a view to obtaining *punya* (forgiveness of sins), and reaching *mukti* (state of grace) at death. Often these white-clad elderly women have lived in the ashram for many years, even from childhood, having been brought there by their relatives, frequently under compulsion, because their inauspiciousness made them a burden. They may come from all over India, representing different linguistic groups, but Bengali widows form the majority. Ashrams provide some solution to the problems of supporting elderly women. In 1988 67 per cent of the women in them were aged between sixty-one and seventy-five; 99 per cent had been married as children; 60 per cent were childless and most were illiterate. The ashrams provide safety, security, and the company of other women.[21] There the widow can pursue the religious life, avoid contact with men, and exemplify the life of ascetic austerity which is expected of her. 'We live in Kashi to wipe out our sins so that after death we may join our husbands. We bathe in the Ganges; we fast; we grieve and we pray,' explained, through an interpreter, an old widow in Varinasi. In the ashrams widows can pray for their husbands, prepare for the day when they will join them in death, perform religious ceremonies, avoid painful contact with relatives, and demonstrate their fidelity. Private charitable trusts run some of the community homes for the destitute; groups of widows live together in community houses. Other destitute Hindu widows find shelter in Christian missions such as those run by Mother Teresa and her staff. And in some African countries, Christian missionaries and churches have established refuges for widows, but these have sometimes been misunderstood by local communities: widows have been abused and mocked as mistresses of the priests.[22] However, these solutions to widowhood in old age may not serve the needs of elderly widows of the future who may have had more education, be less religious, and may require other forms of support.

Clearly, other community options should be explored to look after old widows who have no other relative to turn to. Some of the new NGOs formed to provide support for widows in Kenya and Uganda provide good models which could be adapted in other countries, for example, schemes that encourage younger widows to share their homes with older ones and the development of local reciprocal care arrangements (see examples in chapters 5 and 11).

In developing countries, placing elderly parents in residential homes or institutions is not generally considered acceptable. Old and widowed women living in government-managed homes for the destitute in India were socially disowned.[23] Stories of the abuse of elderly residents of institutions in the West are widespread. Old age pensions and old age homes and orphanages are concepts alien to most traditional societies. Most people pride themselves that their cultural practice is to respect elderly people and not subject them to the horrors common in developed societies. Yet the reality often is that the elderly are mainly female and widows; they are not respected; and they may end their lives begging on the streets or through the villages, with nowhere to shelter and no food to eat. An elderly Zimbabwean widow recalled how her daughter-in-law greeted her when she went to her son's house to ask for food. 'Get away, you old woman. You are always coming here to take our food. Go away. We don't want you here.[24]

Conclusion

The 'greying' of populations, the feminisation of poverty, and all aspects of elderly widowhood should be of concern to every government on both humanitarian and developmental grounds. Long-term policies need to be developed that will provide for and protect widows in their old age, either through pension schemes or through self-help efforts supported by NGOs.

Governments and NGOs need to explore how to use the resources of older, but still active, women in productive and creative ways.

Education and self-help programmes such as have been introduced in the developed countries might be adapted for introduction in Third World communities. Older women's organisations in the West might network with groups in the least developed countries, exchanging skills in various fields, such as managing environmental degradation, family planning, health, caring, and education. Voluntary Service Overseas (VSO) already has a programme recycling the skills of retired people in Britain for the benefit of communities in the developing countries, but much more effective work could be done through targeting older Third World widows for training as communicators, educators, reporters and informers about the issues concerning the elderly in their local communities. A 'widow-to-widow' programme might help older women in both the North and the South.[25]

Governments and NGOs must address, as a separate issue, the needs of frail, disabled, destitute and isolated old widows, and support NGOs involved in providing them with support. They must also support research efforts to analyse the causes of destitution among elderly widows and introduce policies and laws that will ensure that widows enjoy legal protection of their human rights under the UN Women's Convention. Female poverty at the end of life is a consequence of all the inequalities a woman has endured from birth. If women are to be exhorted to bear fewer children, then governments must, in return, protect their old age.

Neither the Mexican (1975) nor the Copenhagen (1980) UN World Conferences on Women addressed older women's problems within the perspective of the life cycle, or acknowledged ageing as a process in every woman's life. In 1985 the Forward Looking Strategies (FLS) adopted at the Third World Conference on Women held in Nairobi devoted an entire section, paragraph 286, to elderly women, but focused on them only as a 'vulnerable' group, failing to separate them into age cohorts, tainting ageing with negative connotations, as if there was a 'cut-off' point in women's lives after which they were no longer useful members of society.

In 1991 the UN Social Development Commission approved the set of Principles for Older Persons which have since become a Declaration of Rights of Older Persons. The declaration aims to encourage goverments to incorporate the principles into their national programmes, and focuses on rights under four main categories: independence, participation, care, self-fulfilment and dignity. In 1995 the Social Summit at Copenhagen committed governments to take action to reduce poverty.

In September 1995 at the Fourth World Conference on Women held in Beijing, governments renewed the commitments made at previous world conferences and agreed to implement the Global Platform for

Action (GPFA). Paragraph 116 points to the particular vulnerability of elderly women to acts of violence; Paragraph 101 to their health needs; Paragraph 47 to the poverty of those who fall outside support systems and female-headed households; but there is still insufficient attention given to widowhood. NGOS should, however, use those sections which refer to elderly women as tools for putting pressure on governments to address the various issues raised in this chapter.

On the positive side, however, the Vienna International Plan of Action on Ageing, the UN Principles for Older Persons recently adopted,[26] and the designation of the year 1999 as the International Year of the Elderly show a more heightened awareness of the resources that older people possess. The establishment of a new NGO, Empowering Widows in Development (EWD), as a result of a workshop held at the NGO Forum at the time of the Fourth World Conference on Women, should at last ensure that the voices of widows are heard at all levels.

Notes

1. Kasturia Sen, *Women in Later Life: Health, Security and Poverty*, International Health Exchange, 1994.

2. United Nations, *The World's Women, 1970–1990: Trends and Statistics*, UN, New York, 1991.

3. Ibid.

4. Paul Harrison, *Inside the Third World*, Penguin, Harmondsworth, 1979.

5. Information from Lela Gulati, 'Widowhood and Ageing', paper presented to the Rural Widows of India Conference, Bangalore, 1994. The author works in the Centre for Development Studies, Thiruvanthapuram, Kerala. She notes that '70% of the aged women will be widows for whom the support of the family cannot be taken for granted'.

6. N. Youseff and Hetler, 1984.

7. Natis Sadik, ed., *The State of the World's Population 1990*, UN Population Fund (UNFPA), New York, 1990.

8. Marina Warner, *From the Beast to the Blonde: On Fairy Tales and Their Tellers*, Chatto and Windus, London, 1994.

9. Information from the Widows Ministries, Northern Ghana, 1994.

10. See Sir James Frazer, *The Golden Bough*, 3rd edn, Macmillan, London, 1955.

11. Julia Alvarez, Keynote Address, *Mid-life and Older Women in Latin America and the Caribbean*, Pan American Health Organisation and American Association of Retired Persons, Washington, DC, 1989.

12. Alvarez.

13. M. Chamie, *National, Institutional and Household Factors Affecting Young Girls' School Attendance in Developing Societies*, USAID, 1983.

14. Joycelin Massiah (University of the West Indies), report prepared for

the UN Meeting on Vulnerable Women, Vienna 1991.

15. Lela Gulati, 'Ageing of Widows in Kerala', paper presented to the Rural Widows of India Conference, Bangalore, 1994.

16. Omar Rahman, Andrew Foster and Jane Menken, 'Older Widow Mortality in Rural Bangladesh', *Social Science and Medicine*, 34(1), 1992.

17. Marty Chen and Jean Drèze, *Widows and Well-being in Rural North India*, Development Economics Research Programme Paper No. 40, London School of Economics, London, 1992, p. 9.

18. Ibid.

19. Bela Bhatia, 'Widows, Family Support and Land Rights: Three Case Studies', paper presented to the Rural Widows of India Conference, Bangalore, 1994.

20. *New Vision* (Kampala), 21 December 1993.

21. Baidyanath Saraswati, 'The Kashivasi Widows', in *Widowhood in India*, Sri Dharmasthala Educational Trust, Karnataka, 1988, p. 103.

22. Michael Kirwen, *African Widows*, Orbis, Maryknoll, NY, 1979.

23. Saraswati.

24. Personal communication from a widow in Chipinge, southeastern Zimbabwe, 1993.

25. 'Age Potential', European Year Conference, 1993.

26. See in particular Annex 4.

CHAPTER 9

Refugee Widows

The sudden uprooting and exodus of thousands of people in diverse regions of the world has become an all too familiar feature of our times. The majority of refugees - the United Nations High Commission for Refugees (UNHCR) estimates as many as 80 per cent - are women and children. [1] In 1994 the UNHCR reported that there were approximately 20 million displaced or refugee women. During 1995 the numbers increased as the war continued in the former Yugoslavia and the crisis escalated in Rwanda and Burundi, displacing more people both within their own countries and outside them. The UNHCR count may well have been an underestimate since the definition of 'refugee' is complex and it is impossible to monitor and classify every exodus of people, or to enumerate and analyse the motivations of all the individuals involved. As yet there is no disaggregated data on widows in the refugee population.

Only in recent years has much been written about the special plight of women refugees or specific action taken to document the issues facing them. [2] Many of these women are widows, having lost husbands (as well as fathers, sons and other relatives). Family groups consisting only of widows, old people and small children are a common sight in refugee camps. There might be three generations of widows in a traumatised family group; or widows who have no one but the children they have managed to save, theirs and those of others - relatives, friends or strangers; or widows left completely on their own. Seeking refuge are also those who do not know if they are widows or not, having been seperated from their husbands in situations of extreme violence and danger. They may never be sure if their husbands have been killed, 'disappeared', imprisoned, under torture, or have deserted them. The ambiguity of their status exacerbates all their other difficulties; in consequence they have to confront complex problems and difficulties as they struggle to come to terms with their loss - not only of husband but of home and country - and attempt to build a new life.

The causes of refugee women's flight from their homes are always beyond their control. They suffer special disabilities and traumas on their nightmarish journeys to safety: in camps; in the countries of reception; and when they return from exile. The woman refugee, without an adult male to protect her at any of these stages, faces particular difficulties. Some of these are the common lot of all unattached women; other problems stem specifically from the special status of widows in custom and tradition, and the conflicts inherent in situations where established community patterns have disintegrated because the new environment can no longer accommodate them. Women are rarely participants in the decision-making processes that are responsible for insurrection, war, the abuse of human rights and the degradation of the environment, yet they and their children bear the harsh consequences of political instability in terms of homelessness, poverty, and insecurity.

Left to bring up the children on their own, refugee women face huge social, economic and psychological difficulties. Some react with incredible resilience, taking on responsibilities they would never have dreamed of in their previous life, courageously challenging old taboos and customs in oder to ensure the survival of their dependants. Through sheer necessity they confront unimaginable vicissitudes and become strong, independent and creative, and leaders of other women. Others, alienated and marginalised, having suffered some of the especially terrible experiences that men have devised to subdue women - for example, of rape and torture or watching loved ones being tortured - never recover from their ordeals and may remain in a traumatised state indefinitely. Ultimately, of course, how refugee women respond to the horrors of dislocation depends on a variety of factors, of which personality, character and resourcefulness play a crucial part. It is important to identify the special problems these women face so that policies can be developed to provide the right support. Many will need help and protection for the rest of their lives. This chapter calls for planners and aid agencies to focus on refugee women so that the issues can be better identified and their problems alleviated.

Traditional support systems break down almost totally in situations of war and natural disaster where large numbers of people flee their homes. Widows in their traditional settings and communities, lived within an established pattern of gender-divided labour. As refugees, they are often suddenly forced to undertake tasks usually performed by men. Women who have come from societies where purdah or seclusion is the rule find themselves in alien surroundings having to deal with strangers, male officials, police, wardens and doctors. Traumatised, physically exhausted, emotionally drained, frightened, in grief and mourning, they may be solely responsible for the first time for what remains of the family group. They need sensitive support, and women with an understanding of their own culture to counsel them. Even when they have been the victims of violence, traditional attitudes may prevent them from receiving any sympathy if what has happened to them is seen as a sin.

Men often feel their identity and status is threatened when women's roles change and they show that they can shoulder responsibilities that were previously in the male domain. Refugee women from traditional cultures who bravely organise themselves into co-operatives, deal with male officialdom, or take on casual work outside to earn money to buy essential goods, for their dependants may be treated with contempt by the men of their communities and branded as 'loose'.

In the 1980s Afghanistan refugee women in camps in Pakistan found themselves facing particular difficulties since their culture decreed that they should never be seen by men outside the close family group. The widows and other single women had no one to collect food for them in the camps, and no means of obtaining supplies. The Pakistan government set up a widows' camp in Nasir Bagh where over three hundred widows lived with their children. Within the camp the widows could move about freely, and attend an all-female staffed dispensary and school. There the widows waited for their sons to grow up and take over the role of household head. They knew that only then would the community acknowledge them as a real family, and be prepared to assign them a house on their return to their village of origin.

The Nasir Bagh refugee camp in Pakistan became home to many disabled and elderly people. In 1984 there were 227 families of widows and orphans there (mostly fatherless). In spite of the custom that widows remarry a husband's relative, refugee widows at Nasir Bagh have not remarried. They have learned over the years to retain more influence over their children's activities and over their own lives, and are unwilling to surrender this new-found autonomy within the family. They became used to being interviewed by male foreign visitors and journalists, and to receiving the gifts offered by them. Many widows did not want to remarry because of the suffering they had endured or because they were still in mourning. While many of the older widows knew that they would never return to their homeland but would die in the camp, younger ones were preparing for their return as heads of households.

One group of widows had this to say to a foreign reporter, 'After all, as the heads of our families we have many responsibilities. When we return home to Afghanistan, people will discover that there are many more adults than men. The task will be tough; we must start preparing right now for the day we rebuild our country.'[3]

Kerala is a refugee village in the Bajaur district of Pakistan but unique because it is home to Afghan women and children who in 1979 fled from their destroyed village of the same name across the border in Afghanistan. Its origins are tragic, for 1,700 men and boys were slain in the Afghan village; the survivors who escaped, mostly women, numbered some five thousand. Pakistani farmers were shocked to wake up one morning and see a vast and haggard crowd of mothers and orphans, exhausted with four days of walking, begging them for help. The Pakistan government decided to build them a special village. But unlike the famous Nasir Bagh camp, which has received all sorts of visitors over the years, few ever come to Kerala as it lies within one of the most closed areas of tribal Pakistan. It is a unique settlement, the houses built high above the road so that no passers-by can look in and break the traditional rules of seclusion. The women always seem sad, grieving, dressed in black even years later. Very few men survived, so customary remarriage to a male relative is rare. One important feature of this community is that in spite of the paucity of males, the village council still has an exclusively male membership, the difference is that it takes its orders from a hidden caucus of women.[4]

In some cases, refugee widows may find themselves not only cut off from their own families, tribes and people, but forced to live in close proximity to their enemies. This happened in 1995 in Rwanda and in Zaire where fleeing Hutus and Tutsis have ended up in the same refugee camps. This has been particularly traumatic for widows who recognise the men who butchered their husbands. Many live in fear of being recognised and also abused and killed to stop them informing those who might avenge their husbands. Widows without a male to protect them are especially fearful and vulnerable and may have to watch their children being killed in retribution for crimes that their own dead husbands are alleged to have committed. The events of 1992-95 in the former Yugoslavia made thousands of women into refugee widows, and at risk in flight and in temporary settlements to the vengeance of the superior ethnic group.

Discrimination, sexism and ageism

During the flight from their homes, women alone are continually in danger. There have been many complaints from women concerning how they are treated at border posts by guards and police who can exploit them, find faults in their papers, threaten to return them to the other side of the frontier, demanding money and jewellery as the price of transit. In the resettlement camps, widows are likely to be at the end of the distribution queue, and neglected in terms of training for income generation, language skills and loan schemes. Extension programmes often bypass them, and they are usually the last to be resettled. Refugee camps everywhere tend to become residual dumps for elderly unwanted widows and for children. But in general, out of fear, widows do not complain. In the host country widowed refugees may meet with racism, sexism and ageism as well as the multiple problems of disorientation, homesickness and poverty. Immigration policies in the West may also discriminate against widows applying to join children who are already settled, especially if there are other adult relatives in the country of origin or elsewhere who could provide alternative shelter.[5]

Documentation

In traditional societies, papers such as title deeds to land, marriage certificates, identity cards, ration cards, health certificates, and bank books are held by the man. Even where women are *de jure* or *de facto* heads of household it is often sons and other male relatives who, possibly being more literate, will look after such things. Identity cards and passes that confirm refugee status and the numbers and names of family members are essential in order to qualify people for allocation of accommodation, food, clothing, health, education and training services. Official papers are vitally important when resettlement or repatriation is planned, or agencies are trying to trace missing relatives and reunite the family.

Without proper documentation, widows may have the greatest difficulty in proving their case for refugee status. Morover, to obtain refugee status in their own right under the UN Convention Relating to the Status of Refugees demands a sophistication that many women in flight do not possess. Papers may have disappeared with the dead or disappeared husband. They may have gone missing on the flight, or been stolen. Sometimes widows are tricked by men touting in the camp into parting with money to obtain false documents which are subsequently discovered to be false.

A widow returning home to a devastated country to reclaim her husband's land may not be able to prove her land rights. This has happened on a large scale in Mozambique. Women have seen their husbands killed and have fled the country, but on return their claims are disputed and they can present no official evidence of their ownership. In 1994 the World Bank supported NGOs working with Mozambican returning refugee widows wanting to reclaim their husband's clan land abandoned in the 1970s at the height of the civil war.[6]

The stories of the Vietnam boat people in South China sea provide further illustrations of the risks women take, when they try to cross hostile territory. In one reported case a whole group at sea was attacked by pirates and threatened with death or return to where they had escaped from unless they surrendered the women. The men agreed to surrender the women for sex rather than be captured and slaughtered. Somalian widows reported terrible experiences as they travelled to the camps in Kenya. Mozambican widows have told similar tales. In 1995, Muslim, Croat and Serbian women - among whom thousands were widowed, raped, and beaten in flight - testified to the horrors they endured as woman were caught up in civil war.

Nor are women safe once they have reached the refugee camp. The design of these camps is often so poor that they present obvious dangers for women. The communal latrines and washrooms may be some distance from the dormitories, and the walkways may be so badly lit that women are liable to attacks. Some camps are surrounded by barbed wire, virtual prisons. They can seem inhuman places where inhuman acts take place. In camps, as in Rwanda, refugees have to share the same quarters as members of a hostile faction responsible for the torture or executions from which they are fleeing, the traditional mechanisms for protecting vulnerable women disappear.

Health

For all refugees, health is a major problem. Rates of disease, malnutrition and mortality are always very high in refugee communities. Often it is the women who suffer most, and particularly widows, who have no man to help look after them. Many widows give up their own share of food for their children and suffer the consequences. Mental health is also a major issue: many widowed refugees fall victim to extreme depression.

If health care is extended to refugees, the priority is often the children or pregnant women. There are often few female health practitioners, and often medical staff are from a different ethnic group and do not speak the same language. Pregnant widows are at particular risk of suffering the consequences of pregnancy and childbirth in poor conditions, unattended by traditional midwives and often in unhygienic surroundings. Some refugee women are so malnourished that they cannot lactate adequately, or their bodies nourish the baby at their own expense. Lack of vitamins and minerals in the diet lead to diseases such as scurvy, pellagra and anaemia.

Women who are widows are more likely to be deprived of essential reproductive health care than those married women who have access to contraception or antenatal care. However, widows may well be victims of rape and also need care. Many widows may be suffering from post-traumatic stress disorder following the terrible experiences they have been through.

Violence
Women without a male protector are everywhere vulnerable to harassment, abuse, and violence. Widowed refugee women as well as the daughters of these widows are especially in danger - even in the country of refuge. Refugee women have recounted unbearably cruel stories to aid workers.

Ayusha, a Somali, fled with her children to the Mal'afa camp in Kenya; she suspected that her husband had been killed but had no certain proof. In the camp a very much younger man befriended her and helped her, found food and obtained papers for her. They began a relationship, but it was frowned on by the community for he was no older than her eldest son. To make the relationship official she asked to be allowed to marry him, but her older sons complained to the elders that their father was still alive somewhere in Somalia. They tried to kill their 'stepfather', but he escaped, so they knifed their own mother to death, leaving behind some very young orphaned children.

In northern Kenya, the women go outside the camp perimeter to gather firewood. With so many people pouring across the border, the women have to walk long distances to find wood.

Mina, a Somali widow, was raped by a gang of bandits when she was on her way home to the children. Fawzia, a Somali social worker employed by the UNHCR in Nairobi, got involved with Mina when she was already eight months pregnant. Mina had tried to kill herself on several occasions. The rape in itself was a brutal violation, and she had been badly beaten and lacerated internally. To have conceived as a result of this shameful attack meant that the consequences of her degradation would remain with her forever. As far as the community in the camp was concerned, she was 'polluted'; she was ostracised, and people pointed their fingers at her and gossiped. This made it all the more difficult for Mina to obtain papers, rations, and services for her children. She could not face anyone, even the officials. She hated the baby she was expecting. Under Kenyan law she was not eligible for an abortion, for rape is not a ground. (Some social workers have managed to get other raped and pregnant women into the various illegal abortion clinics in and around Nairobi. As the time of Mina's confinement drew near, Fawzia feared she would lose her mind. Fawzia managed to arrange for Mina to be transferred to

a camp on the coast where no one would know her. Mina had her
baby, and with a lot of counselling has succeeded in adjusting to it.
Now Fawzia and the UNHCR are trying to get her and the children
resettled in Canada under the 'Women at Risk' programme.[7]

Tradition, change and conflict

Traditional communities tend to grow more reactionary when
threatened by a new environment. Flight and insecurity increase the
feeling that old customs are being attacked and that women and young
people are endangering themselves. The elders, usually men or older
women, try to keep control of such developments. They view the greater
freedom that some refugee women exercise as an affront to their cultural
identity, and so they become not only critical of changes in behaviour,
but strict in condemnation of any flouting of the old patterns. Even
when a woman is the victim and not the free agent, she must bear the
collective indictment of her clan. Sadly, the raped women and the
abandoned, divorced, or widowed women who have accepted new male
companions to assist them can expect no understanding from the older,
more conservative generation.

> In 1990 the borders between Somalia and Kenya were closed so that
> refugees could only travel at night. Julia, aged thirty-three, was
> crossing with her husband when they were both attacked with knives
> by a group of men waiting by the frontier. Her husband was killed
> in front of her, but not before he had been made to watch his wife
> being gang-raped. Afterwards they threw her in a pool of her
> husband's blood and raped her again. They scarred her face and left
> her for dead. Other refugees following them managed to get help and
> she was taken to hospital, where she was found not only to be
> pregnant but also to be HIV positive. Once recovered she was taken
> to the camp, but the appalling nature of what had happened to her
> did not prevent her from being regarded as a fallen women. She
> committed suicide after leaving her baby in a pit latrine.[8]

The shame of rape, the horror of giving birth to a child of a husband's
murderer, the agony of widowhood in such circumstances, and the
knowledge that she is HIV-infected as is the child, lead many women
to end their lives. Others simply disappear, or are killed by their relatives
for the crime of dishonouring the family.

> Shuma, a Somalian refugee widow, was raped by two men who made
> her husband watch before they killed him. She knew she had

conceived, but in the camp she let no one know and never went for any medical checks. When her time came she walked to the airstrip and delivered herself all alone and left the baby at the edge of the field. Her brother, already suspicious, realised she had given birth and searched the fields until he found the little boy, dehydrated, suffering from exposure and covered in insects and insect bites. Somehow, the dedication of the medical team saved the baby's life. But the young man never admitted to the nurses that the baby's mother was his sister. When the UNHCR official questioned him, he answered, 'I do not know who the lady is.' Later, Shuma was found and brought to the hospital where she was united with her son and helped to establish breast-feeding. But in spite of all her sufferings the community did not accept her. Instead everyone came to stare at her, and she was pointed out as 'the woman who was raped and left her baby in a field'. Shuma felt totally degraded, as if she was an animal in a cage. She became very sick, and suffered a complete breakdown. She also tested HIVpositive. She begged to be allowed to leave the hospital and give up the child. Eventually she was allowed to go back to her hut. This baby was taken to an orphanage outside Nairobi and is HIV-positive.

Kurdish widows raped and made pregnant by Iraqi soldiers encountered hostility from their own community when they tried to return to their ancestral lands accompanied by the children born of the violations. Such gross sexual torture of war widows is an old device deliberately encouraged by leaders who wish to reward their victorious soldiers; the humiliation experienced by the defeated group through the seizing of its women has been exploited in war since time immemorial; only in the 1990s has the gravity of the crime been acknowledged in international law. International abhorrence over the revelations of the Serbian 'rape camps' in the former Yugoslavia in 1992 helped to ensure that by 1993 the rape of women by enemy forces in war was designated as a 'war crime'. The perpetrators or inciters of such crimes may be charged before the International War Crimes Court sitting at The Hague.

Repatriation

To return to one's homeland after hostilities have ceased, and sometimes after years of exile, is never easy. The often long journey, often by foot, which might last many days, may be exhausting as well as dangerous for the unaccompanied woman. Knowing that there is no man at the other end to help build or repair the house and cultivate the land deters some widows from even attempting the journey.[9] To revisit the scene of so much barbarity and violence, to see the place where once a homestead stood ravaged by war, the fields untilled, reverted to scrub and bush, occupied by hostile straangers, may be deeply disturbing. Widows with young children may have not merely to confront resistance to their land claims but find ways of acquiring agricultural tools, seeds, fertiliser, and extension services. They may need male labour to do specific farm tasks. Widows may face community censure if they attempt to undertake activities normally reserved for men. But a returning widow who must depend on a 'stranger' male to give her assistance may find that she is expected to provide sexual services for his work if she cannot pay him with cash (see Chapter 4).

In 1994, thousands of refugeee widows returned to Mozambique from Malawi and Zimbabwe. They met with considerable hostility from those who had stayed behind when they tried to reclaim the land belonging to their former husbands, since they had lost all documentation or proof of identity. During the long years of the war and their absence, other families had cultivated the family land. Other widows found their land had been ruined or laid with mines. In 1994 the World Bank funded a project to clarify the customary law on land ownership in the rural areas, with returning refugee widows as key participants.[10]

Even if widows are reunited with family and children, the occasion is not always a happy one. In 1995 some widows returned to Mozambique after twenty years to meet their now grown-up children, who were still scarred from their experiences of fighting as guerrillas. Some as children had been forced by the rebel army to kill their fathers, and were then kidnapped and forced to fight as child soldiers. Learning what has really happened in the intervening years can rob the returning widow of any joy she might feel on seeing her children again.

Conclusion

Since the early nineties, the UNHCR has expanded and intensified its special programmes aimed at refugee women, and has increased the numbers of its women staff, appointing where possible and appropriate women from the same ethnic background as the refugees. There is much greater awareness now of the peculiar problems relating to gender that need addressing. In 1989 a new position was created within the UNHCR: a senior coordinator for refugee women, along with a steering committee on refugee women. In 1990 the UNHCR was given a mandate to try and prevent people from becoming refugees - political or economic - by providing incentives for them to return to their villages of origin. One of the programmes developed focused on assisting widows to claim title to their land, and teaching them to 'know their rights'.

National and international NGOs have initiated creative and innovative projects which provide useful ideas for programme planners involved with similar situations worldwide. For example, in Bangladesh the Gonshashtya Kendra, highly regarded for its innovative grassroots-based development initiatives, provides culturally acceptable and accessible health services for Rohinga Muslim refugees in Dumdumia refugee camp.[11] Oxfam female engineers and health educators in the camp have led the way in highlighting and responding to women's concerns. Health educators, responding to the women refugee's own agenda, arranged gatherings and group meetings and set up women's centres, called 'health education centres' to make them less controversial. These were constructed by the women themselves with materials devised by Oxfam. New ideas for garbage disposal, construction of bathing places for women, watching water sources, guarding and protecting latrines and other communal places came from discussions at the women's centres. Evaluation of this project showed that women felt better about their situation through these informal contacts. However, widows are not specifically targeted and it is thought that some, particularly older widows, are excluded either because they feel unable to join in collective activities, believing the generation gap is too wide, or because community bias against them is too strong.

Although the special needs of refugee women are now well documented, those of widows deserve more attention. Greater recognition is required of the obstacles they face under traditional, customary and religious laws when policies, programmes and projects are being developed to make them more independent, whether in the resettlement camps, on repatriation, or in the new country of reception. For example, there should be an increase in the numbers of female staff of relevant international humanitarian organisations along escape routes, in reception centres, camps, settlements and in other areas where refugee widows find themselves. The physical security of these refugees must be safeguarded. All refugee widows should be given special priority when identification and registration documents are issued, whether their status has been determined individually or as members of a group. Training of staff working with refugees should sensitise them to the complex aspects of widowhood. Immigration policies in all developed countries that can provide a safe haven should be reviewed to ensure that they are humanitarian and do not discriminate against the widow who wants to join members of her family.

It is not enough to rely on the UNHCR for the formulation and implementation of policies to improve the welfare and future of refugee widows and their dependants. Many refugees fall under other mandates such as those of the Red Cross, the United Nations Development Programme (UNDP), the United Nations Relief Agency for Palestine Refugees in the Near East (UNRWA), the United Nations Childrens' Fund (UNICEF), The World Health Organisation (WHO), the World Food Programme (WFP) and other UN agencies. These agencies need to co-ordinate their programmes and share experiences with each other on the needs of refugee widows under their protection. Ministries in asylum or host countries, countries of transit or of repatriation - foreign, interior, education, health - need to work together to provide them with appropriate services. But for policies to be developed that are truly effective, much more action research is needed, with the full involvement of the refugee widows themselves.

Notes

1. Report of the United Nations High Commissioner for Refugees, 1993.
2. See, in particular, Susan Forbes Martin, *Refugee Women*, Zed Books, London, 1992; Chaloka Beyani, *Refugee Women in International Law*, University of Oxford; and UNHCR policy document on women refugees, 1993.
3. Kyra Nasir Bagh Nunez, *Refugees*, UNHCR, November 1984.
4. Annick Billard, *Refugees*, UNHCR, June 1985.
5. For example, UK immigration rules impose severe restrictions on widowed mothers joining sons and daughters in the UK. Stringent criteria govern eligibility, and it is difficult to convince immigration tribunals of compassionate grounds for entry. Further information is available from the Joint Council for the Welfare of Immigrants and the UK Immigrants Advisory Service, London. The author has worked for many years on immigration applications to the UK.
6. Personal communication from Daniel Owen, World Bank, Maputo.
7. The Women at Risk programme also operates in Australia.
8. The child, which survived, was brought to the Children of God Nyumbani children's home in Karen, Nairobi, and with loving care thrived and eventually tested HIV negative.
9. Informal conversation with widowed Mozambican refugees on the Zimbabwe border, 1993.
10. Owen, personal communication.
11. See *Links*, journal of the WID Division of the Commonwealth Secretariat, June 1994.

CHAPTER 10

Human Rights, Equality, and Legal Protection

'The human rights of women and of the girl child are an inalienable, integral and indivisible part of universal human rights.' So states the 1994 Vienna Declaration and Programme of Action on Human Rights. With this statement, the forty-year omission of women from documents by the human rights fraternity was overcome at last - at least on paper. All aspects of women's human rights and their violations should now be capable of being dealt with in the mainstream of machineries of the UN's human rights system. The commitments to women made at the 1993 Vienna World Conference on Human Rights are reaffirmed clearly and strongly in the Declaration and the Global Platform for Action(GPFA), the documents that came out of the Fourth World Conference on Women held in Beijing in 1995.

The Declaration and the Global Platform for Action (GPFA), the documents of consensus of the Beijing conference, are structured very much in terms of the rights of women; these rights are described as being an 'inalienable, integral and indivisible part of all human rights'(Paragraph 14). Chapter 1 of the GPFA makes clear that the approach to women's advancement into the new millennium will be through human rights. Furthermore, acknowledging the rights of women to enjoy their full human rights, the UN Human Rights Committee has appointed a special rapporteur to receive individual complaints by or on behalf of women subjected to forms of violence. The GPFA fails to mention widows specifically as a category of women who are vulnerable to grave assaults on their human rights, including physical and emotional violence. But the appointment of the special rapporteur and the recognition of the human rights of women in general in the Beijing GPFA can provide scope for the protection and enhancement of the status of widows.

More than 3 billion women are subject, systematically and casually, to a wide range of violations of their human rights simply because they are female.[1] Although states have obligations under the various UN charters and human rights instruments to promote women's human rights actively, they have not provided adequate protection. The power of men over women, whether in the public or in the domestic sphere, has remained, in many regions of the world, absolute. This is because international and national legislation and policy remain in the power of men, and women are still not sufficiently integrated into the decision-making processes at all levels.

Many of the laws, modern as well as religious and customary, administrative policies, actions and attitudes associated with widowhood and widows represent grave breaches of the various international and regional human rights charters and declarations, namely, the 1979 UN Women's Convention on the Elimination of All Forms of Discrimination against Women, the 1990 UN Children's Convention,[2] the Social, Political and Economic Charters,[3] the 1993 International Declaration on the Elimination of Violence against Women and the 1995 GPFA. Governments who have ratified such international treaties or agreed declarations are under an obligation to eliminate practices that are harmful to women and to extend to them protection both in the private and the public spheres, using every means in their power: law reform, education, administrative changes, monitoring and research. But few governments have done so. The equality guarantees in the national constitutions of many countries are rarely used in the courts to prevent discrimination against women. In Zambia, the constitution excludes from its equality guarantees matters comig under customary or family law: just those areas in which widows are most oppressed.

National laws and policies concerning personal status and the family, inheritance, land ownership, credit, education and health services continue to discriminate against women, but their impact on widows in particular, and the wider effects of the marginalisation of widows on society as a whole, have not been sufficiently addressed by governments or the international development agencies.

The purpose of this chapter is to give examples of infringements of rights in the context of widowhood, and to describe some of the initiatives which might be or have already been taken to empower widows to enjoy their fundamental rights.

It is to be hoped that the committee for monitoring the UN Convention on the Elimination of All Forms of Discrimination agaist Women (CEDAW) will in the near future focus attention on the status of widows within the context of the convention and consider inviting states parties to report on what they are doing to identify discrimination and eliminate it.

In the 1990s at last some efforts are being made to redefine the notion of 'human rights' to include 'women's rights'. The 1948 Universal Charter of Human Rights used the male personal pronoun 'he' and never 'she', as if women were neither human nor capable of possessing 'rights' on their own account; that error set the pattern of thinking for the next forty-five years. The very words 'human rights' would seem to any rational reader to encompass universality, with no discrimination implied. But in the last few years it has required intensive effort on the part of feminist legal activists and scholars to convince a male-dominated UN human rights body that women are part of humankind. It is shocking to realize that only in 1993, at the World Conference on Human Rights, was the rape of women in war recognised as a grave breach of human rights and as a war crime. Was this because the atrocities happened in the former Yugoslavia, in Europe, and to white not black women? The special horrors innocent women, many of whom are widows, suffer because of wars and insurrection are never the events which inspire the UN to send in a peace force. Other gross violations of privacy, person and property occurring in periods of peace still remain unacknowledged as human rights infringements.

To future historians it may seem extraordinary on philosophical, ethical, linguistic and intellectual grounds that there had to be such arguments. The resistance to the demand for recognition of women's claim to be regarded as part of humankind came from many different quarters. 'Cultural relativism', the opinion that there could be no such thing as 'universality' in human rights given the diversity of cultures, was used in the attempt to stop any international monitoring of what happens to women under interpretations of customary law which is so often debasing of women's status.

For quite other political and economic reasons, women's right to family planning has been elevated to a human right at successive world population conferences, culminating in the Cairo Conference of 1994. Yet widows are often excluded from the benefits of health and family planning services simply because they are no longer 'married women'; their health is thus unjustifiably endangered. In the rush to try and reduce the Third World's population growth, the development agencies and the international community have targeted only one aspect of women's lives, continuing to ignore them as potential participants in development. Yet it is the legal responsibility of the World Bank, the main agencies, governments and NGOS to respect the prohibition of discrimination found in international and regional human rights conventions. By continuing to ignore this legal obligation to reform discriminatory laws and policies, whether found in statute, custom or informal regulation, they are complicit in the perpetuation of the marginalisation of women.

Women, and widows in particular as a category of women partiularly oppressed by the dictates of male-interpreted 'custom and tradition', will have much to gain if officials, administrators, lawyers and judges take on board the human rights dimension of sex discrimination, so that all actions taken are monitored within this framework. The long-overdue US ratification of the Convention on the Elimination of All Forms of Discrimination against Women was announced as one of the priorities of the human rights programme of President Clinton when he came to power in the USA.

Although Canada, France and the United States have finally accepted in the court that fear of gender violence is a valid ground for requesting political asylum, up till now there has been little use of the rich resources of international and national human rights laws, national constitutions and legislation to protect widows specifically from exploitation, abuse and discrimination. But such use is starting. Gradually, women's lawyers' associations are becoming more courageous in testing the weight of modern law against the arguments of discriminatory 'living custom'. There is now a growing feminist jurisprudence firing women's organisations and paralegals in developing countries to take to court actions which are against the stated modern law and have as their justification an interpretation of custom that is always anthropocentric, chauvinistic and patriarchal.

But it is not enough to view widows as exclusively victims of oppression; they are human beings with much to contribute, whose work needs acknowledgement, and whose legal and economic autonomy must be guaranteed. Recognising that women are one half of humanity could release women's potential contribution to their national economies to the good of everyone.

Third World women's rights have often been ignored by Western agencies because of the sensitivity of intrusion into custom and tradition; their own governments are also often fearful of interfering in the intimate areas of personal status and family arrangements. Yet the human rights framework has special relevance for women in general and for widows in particular. Widows in particular are often unaware of their rights under the modern law, and are often powerless to challenge local or judicial decisions because of their low status, and lack of education or legal representation.

Using the law to improve widows' rights and status
The constitutions of most countries now contain 'equality' provisions, though these have generally little effect on the unequal conditions of

the majority of their female citizens. In virtually all the written constitutions of Commonwealth countries and in many other jurisdictions also, the following human rights and fundamental freedoms are observed: the right to life, liberty, security of the person, equality before the law and the protection of the law; freedom of conscience, expression, assembly and association; the right to privacy in personal and, family life and, in nearly all cases, the right to property. Most constitutions forbid the enactment of sex-discriminatory legislation. All rights and freedoms are guaranteed regardless of race, place of origin, colour, creed or sex. Some constitutions contain specific provisions relating to women. For example, that of Bangladesh declares a policy of integrating women at all spheres of national life.

Widows could use these constitutional guarantees to challenge a whole range of legal and executive decisions made against their interest. In 1994, a widow in Ghana cited the equality provisions of her country's constitution in her legal action against a forced leviratic marriage, and won. There is enormous scope in this area of the law to protect widows against blatant infringement of their personal and property rights.

However, some constitutions specifically exclude from the general anti-discrimination provision all matters to do with marriage, divorce, and inheritance. Where they do, this exclusion is itself a breach of the CEDAW and should be removed. In the meantime, it should be possible for widows to challenge discriminatory actions by depending on the articles of CEDAW.

The UN Convention on the Elimination of All Forms of Discrimination against Women, now ratified by 135 countries, is the definitive international legal instrument requiring respect for and observance of human rights for women. Yet it has paid little attention to the position of widows. Now that the United States has finally become a states party, it should be easier to ensure that the convention's principles are adhered to in all USAID bilateral and multilateral aid programmes and that the US can take the 'global stage to help other governments understand the necessity and the methods of paying attention to the human rights of women.'[4] It provided a framework for advocacy and action leading up to the Fourth World Conference on Women in Beijing.

The importance of the convention lies in its ability to impose legal obligations on ratifying governments to act to get rid of discrimination, and to empower them to use positive discrimination in favour of women (for not more than a temporary period) where expedient. So, for example, it will not be illegal discrimination if governments abolish school fees for girls if this is a way of accelerating women's road to equality.

CEDAW has not delivered to women all it promised, however; governments have been slow to act, and have often continued to 'reserve' on implementing those sections of the treaty that are most pertinent to women's lives, but the potential is there and should be used. Nor have human rights and women's lawyers' groups been active enough in using CEDAW in test cases so as to establish case precedents establishing the rights of women. Sometimes lawyers themselves are unclear as to the status of the treaty in their own country constitutions, even when it has been ratified. [5]

As far as widows are concerned, one of the most pertinent sections of CEDAW is Article 16 on family law:

'State Parties shall take all appropriate measures to eliminate discrimination against women in all matters relating to marriage and family relations and in particular shall ensure, on a basis of equality of men and women:
a) the same right to enter marriage
b) the same right to choose a spouse and to enter into marriage with their full and free consent
d) the same rights and responsibilities as parents, irrespective of their marital status
h) the same rights for both spouses in respect of the ownership, acquisition, enjoyment and disposition of property.
i) The betrothal and marriage of a child shall have no legal effect, and all necessary action shall be taken, including legislation, to specify a minimum age of marriage and to make registration of a marriage in an official registry compulsory.

In Africa and in many countries of Asia, where widows are neither free to remarry nor to resist a new conjugal arrangement, whether marriage or a levirate, CEDAW could offer them protection from these forms of personal violence. Being forced to bear children in the name of the dead husband through impregnation by his brother, against the woman's will, is a practice that governments have a duty to eliminate through all possible means. As chapter 6 describes, widows often lose all rights to their husband's property if they remarry, and to their children. To make progress on forced marriages, therefore, governments need to do more in the way of positive discrimination in women's education and employment so that they do not become dependent on the husband's male relatives on his death. When a court of law adjudicates on the issue of free consent to remarriage, it must take into account the circumstances of the widow and the degree to which she was under duress. A sensitive and imaginative court, as clearly the Supreme Court of Ghana proved to be in the levirate case, could greatly advance the position of women and show how CEDAW can be used to interpret existing domestic law.

All the articles of CEDAW are relevant to discrimination against widows, including the general Articles 1 and 2. A violation of the convention arises when a state party tolerates laws and practices that, on their face or in their application, discriminate. Therefore a government's tolerance, shown by its refusal to intervene, of traditional customs that devalue and degrade widows is an infringement of its international treaty obligations. Although there is no international sanction, no women's human rights courts at which a government can be arraigned, there looms the possible embarrassment of being publicly shown up in the international arena as having failed to fulfil a legal duty.

Worth particular mention because of its relevance to many of the case stories cited in this book is Article 14 on rural women. This obliges governments to ensure that women enjoy equal rights to such things as credit, loans and extension services, and equal treatment in land agrarian reform. Where widows have been denied access to the husband's land, or discriminated against in land development, allocation, and registration, or refused credit, they should be assisted to take action against the officials on the ground that their actions breach the convention. In some countries, the traditional courts, most headed by male elders, have exclusive jurisdiction over land disputes, which means that widows have little chance of winning their claims. Judicial reviews of such decisions could help educate those who administer traditional courts that the CEDAW articles must take precedence over customary law if the latter is discriminatory of women. Article 15 demands that governments ensure that women have equality before the law and shall be treated equally in all stages of tribunals and courts. Restrictions on a widow's right to inherit property are among the most widespread discriminatory aspects of customary legal systems. In addition, women are also often poorly served by the police, who often do not respond to women's complaints.

One important reform that governments might adopt is to ensure that women, possibly widows, are represented on every village council in Africa, every *panchayat* in India, every *shalaya* in Bangladesh, and in traditional courts, and that they participate in decisions regarding land distribution to widows on the deaths of their husbands. A move in this direction would be in keeping with the overall intention of CEDAW to integrate women into the political process at local and national levels.

Widows' rights have few advocates in national legislatures, or at local government level. This is true in the surprising numbers of Third World countries that have been or are headed by widows; Kalida Zia in Bangladesh where the rival opposition leader was also a widow, Mrs Bandaranaika in Sri Lanka, Indira Gandhi in India, Corazon Aquino in the Phillipines were widows, but this did not help to inform public policy, in much the same way as Margaret Thatcher's reign as the first woman Prime Minister of Britain did nothing to improve the status of ordinary British women.

Article 12 of CEDAW requires states parties to work to ensure 'health care services, including those relating to family planning' are available to women. This article could be used to facilitate access to health care for widows. Surveys have shown, for example, that Indian widows face a death rate nearly twice that of married women. Reliance on this article could improve the provision of care and counselling for widows whose husbands have died of AIDS, and who need special support if they are HIV-infected or have AIDS themselves. Also the article should be invoked to improve the attitudes of family planning associations and other primary health care providers to widows who may need contraception or abortion services, or treatment for sexually transmitted diseases, cancer, or the gynaecological and other ailments that affect women of later years.

Considering the higher mortality of widows, compared with married women of the same age, in many developing countries, the vulnerability of widows to rape, unwanted pregnancy and unsafe clandestine abortion, the providers of health services need to assess the needs of widows and shape programmes for them, making it easy, not embarrassing, for them to come forward or be visited. Neglecting consideration of the reproductive health needs of unmarried women, such as widows, is discriminatory.

Education and employment are covered by articles 10 and 11, and the removal of traditional practices that are harmful and degrading to women is covered by Article 6. One of the biggest constraints on widows' dignity and autonomy are the discrimination against them in the economic field and their exploitation as informal-sector workers, in such notoriously unregulated and oppressive activities as agricultural labourer, domestic servant, homeworker and, sweatshop casual worker. CEDAW restates the 1948 Universal Declaration of Human Rights that 'the right to work is an inalienable right of all human beings'. CEDAW could be used to improve widows' remuneration, provide them with minimum wages, equal pay, sick pay, bargaining power, and improve their employment opportunities by putting pressure on governments to support NGOs' training programmes and loan schemes. Through their obligations under CEDAW, governments could be influenced to begin to look at the present employment discrimination against widows, and the effect this has on the quality of their lives and that of their children.

Widows' employment prospects and their unwished dependency on male relatives emerge from their lack of education, and the discrimination they suffered when they were growing up. Because women's literacy levels are lower than those of men, they are not only often hindered in work opportunities when they become widowed, but are unable to deal with or administer their family affairs, which may allow ruthless people to take control. Differential literacy rates are an indicator of breach of Article 10: 'States Parties must take all appropriate measures to ensure women equal rights with men in the field of education and the reduction of female dropout rates.'. One appropriate measure governments might take is to support research into the dropout rates of the daughters of widows, which are known to be considerable; other measures could include the introduction of subsidies for girls' education, scholarships and hostel accommodation for widows' daughters, plus assistance with uniforms and books. Aside from financial reasons, widows often explain that daughters stay home from school to care for younger siblings whilst the mother goes to work; or that they fear for their daughters' chastity on the long walks to the nearest school. Providing free crèche facilities in schools for small children, and girls' hostels near secondary schools would help to implement Article 10. Raising the level of education of widows' daughters would help to reduce the incidence of adolescent pregnancies, early marriages and early widowhood.

Periodically, every two years, states parties to the convention report to the CEDAW committee on implementation. For the last few years NGOs have been invited to add their comments to the official government CEDAW report, or send in their own comments. The CEDAW committee has also taken the initiative of sending out questionnaires to governments on particular topics of current interest. In 1993 it received answers from governments on domestic violence.

The government of Ghana was the only country voluntarily to offer the practice of traditional funeral and widows' mourning rites as an example of 'degrading or violent treatment'. In order to try and address this problem it amended the Criminal Code by inserting a new section:

(1) Whoever compels a bereaved spouse or a relative of such spouse to undergo any custom or practice that is cruel in nature shall be guilty of a misdemeanours

(2) For the purposes of subsection (1)...a custom or practice shall

be deemed to be cruel in nature if it constitutes an assault within the meaning of 2 sections... of this Act.

Whoever compels a bereaved spouse or a relative of such spouse to undergo any custom or practice that is immoral or grossly indecent in nature shall be guilty of a misdemeanour.

Although widows' organisations say that this law has had very little impact on the degrading customs practised in relation to widows in Ghana (see Chapter 1) - whether because women do not know their rights under the law, have no access to legal representation since FIDA cannot penetrate all the rural areas, or if they are aware of but too fearful of their male in-laws to dare to seek legal remedies - the action of the legislature in Ghana is to be praised. It is a start. The amendment amounts to recognition that there is a problem and that it can be used to educate communities and give clout to women's organisations working to improve the lives of widows.

National legislation: inheritance

Several countries in Africa and certain Indian states have enacted legislation to give equal rights to women in inheritance, declaring that daughters should inherit equally with sons and making it illegal to disinherit the widow. Muslim law for centuries has given some inheritance rights to women (see above). Yet neither the more recent modern equality legislation nor the old Muslim laws have generally had much effect on widows' rights.

The Kenyan parliament recently debated a bill to give daughters rights to their fathers' estates. But the reaction of the mostly male legislators and (male) public opinion was negative. Protesting letters to the press argued that such a move would deter women from marriage, motherhood and obedience to men.

The Indian state of Maharashtra has recently passed similar legislation as part of its programme to improve the status of women. The legislation includes proposals for the joint ownership of property by husband and wife, and for daughter inheritance. Nevertheless, widows will require much paralegal education and support if the new laws are to be relevant to them. In Zambia, under the 1989 Intestate Succession Act, if there is no will a widow is entitled to 20 per cent of a husband's property, while 50 per cent goes to the children, 20 per cent to the deceased man's parents, and the remaining 10 per cent to other persons whom the deceased maintained immediately before his death. But there have been widespread objections by husbands' relatives to this poorly enforced new law. They argue that the widow gets too much as she is likely to control the 50 per cent due to her children.

Grabbing widows' property has continued in spite of the legal reforms, and is a phenomenon of poverty and social change practised increasingly all over sub-Saharan Africa. In many countries associations have been formed to protect women and help them to use the law, but with a few exceptions governments give little support to these initiatives. NGOs working to empower widows and help them to get their legal rights are often themselves subject to threats. In several countries, will-making courses have been introduced into the programmes of various NGOS and women's legal groups, such as FIDA, but still many people are resistant to writing wills, and even when a husband has left a will the relatives may ignore it. In Zimbabwe, a legal aid service based in Harare now has a standard letter it sends off to the husband's relatives, since the majority of the cases it is asked to deal with are property claims by widows. (They see only the tip of the iceberg, those widows aware of their existence and able to travel to find them in town.)

Here is the format letter for the pension (there are others for furniture, house, child custody, accident compensation, and widow inheritance):

We assist the above named who has approached us for assistance. We have been advised that you were a brother to the late......... We have been further advised that you are demanding that you and some other relatives should receive a share of the money that the widow received from her late husband's employers.

Be advised that what you are proposing is unlawful as the deceased left an immediate family, namely.........

Also further note that these children are all minors and that the money the widow got is insufficient to cater for the family needs.

We hope you shall stop harassing our client as your actions are potentially criminal. If you persist in your actions we shall be left with no option but to pursue legal remedies. We hope this will not be necessary. We look forward to your co-operation. Thank you.

The Harare Legal Project does not always manage to win, or take every case of this nature to court. The relatives are often able to pay a lot of money to a private lawyer, and threaten the widow if she dares continue with the case. Emily Lboyo, a lawyer at the project, felt that lawyers consciously abetting a breach of the rights of a widow under the law should be disciplined by the Law Society. She knows that there are thousands of widows made destitute in this way who have no access to a lawyer.

Women in Law and Development Africa (WiLDAF) produced a booklet, *Inheritance Law. What It Means for Families in Zimbabwe* for use by women's groups and other NGOs[6.] Written in very simple language - a feat since the various laws of inheritance pertaining in Zimbabwe are far from simple as there are several types of marriages - it sets out the situation under both modern and customary law, identifies the problems with this plurality, and explains all the various procedures necessary to make distribution of the property easier and quicker. It presents some proposals for change and invites readers, on behalf of the government, to say what they would like to happen.

National legislation: Protection of person and property
Penal codes, the ordinary laws of theft and robbery should protect the widow from assaults against her person and her property but they frequently do not. The WiLDAF booklet states clearly that in relation to Zimbabwe 'the law says that it is a crime for anyone to interfere with the dead person's property or take it away, before the court has decided how the property is to be distributed. The widow or widower and the dependent children of the dead person have a right to stay in their home, without interference from anyone.' The problem is that, first, widows are often ignorant of the law; second, they are too frightened to use any knowledge they have to challenge their relatives, third, justice at the local level in village councils or traditional courts tends not to favour a widow. Similar situations occur in many other countries.

The most hopeful developments have emerged where widows have come together in solidarity and been informed of their legal rights by a trained paralegal - the Bangladesh Rural Advancement Committee (BRAC) project described on page 192 is a good example of this approach. It is often better for rural widows living in small communities to reach a just settlement without the need to go to court, which is expensive, slow and can lead to permanent bitterness between the parties.

In Uganda, a group of widows went to the assistance of one of their members who had been robbed of all her household property and was being assaulted by one of her husband's brothers. They all went together to his house. 'We came with sticks and garden tools to defend our sister. There were ten of us all marching and singing to his house. He was so frightened he jumped out of the back window of her hut he had taken possession of, and ran away. He never came back. We were too many for him.'

In a north Indian village, one widow decided to go to the village

council and claim her rights to her husband's land. No woman had
ever done such a thing. 'She has started something and we will follow
her' said the other women as they spoke admiringly of her courage
and success.

Making the Concerns Public

Women and widows' organisations can play a crucial part in making
public cases of blatant discrimination and suffering involving widows.
Both NGOs and governments can successfully use the media to whip
up public opinion in widows' favour. For example, Ugandan widows are
now militant, resourceful, courageous and strong. They have had years
of war and danger in which millions of women lost their husbands,
followed by the terrible scourge of AIDS and the harsh economic
climate resulting from structural adjustment programmes. These widows
have organised themselves into groups which have close links with the
Ministry of Women's Affairs and are instrumental in lobbying for new
laws and in monitoring their enforcement. In the ministry an equally
zealous and hardworking legal research team has been doing its own
study of how matters of inheritance are dealt with in the Administrator-
General's office. This has been publicised in the press.

The Kampala office of the women lawyers' organisation FIDA,
groups like TASO and Philly Lutaaya, and the Uganda War Widows
Association are all working together to bring the issue of legal protection
of widows to public awareness. In March 1994 a huge demonstration was
organised, with hundreds of widows marching, and carrying placards,
with speeches from women activists and lawyers before a platform of
parliamentarians and ministers. They were asking for tighter laws, for
enforcement of the penal law against the 'widow robbers', and for more
support and protection from the police and district and village officials,
elders and chiefs.

Customary law

Women are more likely to have their lives governed by customary or
religious law than by the modern law in many developing country
jurisdictions. There is often a conflict between these different systems,
especially in relation to what sort of marriage has been contracted. The
confusion surrounding the rights of widows in many countries often
stems from the difficulty of clarifying the type of marriage. Child
marriage and polygamy are not allowed under modern laws, but they
still take place in many traditional communities. Dowries in India and
Bangladesh, brideprice in Africa, may be constituent elements of
traditional marriages without which the marriage is incomplete.

Sometimes widows learn that either the dowry or the brideprice was not fully paid, and so their legal status is questioned and their rights are contested. Uncertainty about status and legal rights is bad for all women, as daughters, wives and widows. It is important that there is certainty in all matters of the personal status of women.

The Women's Convention, CEDAW, has attempted to provide some norms for governments to follow. Although it is not possible to generalize on the status of widows under customary law since there are so many differences in the cultures of different ethnic groups, it is clear that some features in customary and religious laws in some countries are regarded, at least by feminists and human rights activists in those countries, as being degrading and harmful to widows. Such practices as forced remarriage, ritual cleansing by sexual intercourse, shaving and scarification, seclusion, prohibition on social participation, proscribed ways of dressing, eating, and residing, derogate from the dignity and status to which all women are entitled.

However, the most difficult problems concerning customary law are that it is unwritten, and that it varies in detail from place to place and from ethnic group to ethnic group. Customary courts are not courts of record, there is no jurisprudence or case law, and decisions are usually made ad hoc in order to arrive at a settlement or conciliation. Nevertheless, governments should regard the Women's Convention as the dominant legal influence and amend their legislation to conform to its articles. Where widows' rights are the subject of adjudication in religious or customary courts, governments should legislate that in the case of conflict between customary law and the modern law, the modern law should prevail.

Conclusion

One overriding defect in the Women's Convention is that breaches of its articles by states parties carry no sanctions; there is no international tribunal at which governments' guilt of infringements can be accused and penalised. Governments do not, however, welcome the embarassment of being publicly shown up as anti-women, and therefore the monitoring of governments' implementation records by the CEDAW committee plays an important part. Widows' organisations worldwide can network to make sure that the CEDAW committee is kept informed of instances where governments, NGOs and other agencies have omitted to take account of widows' rights and needs, failing to comply with the Women's Convention or other human rights treaties. There is scope here for action in such areas as land rights, inheritance law, credit, education of daughters, employment, and health and social services. NGOs and women's and rural development groups should also conduct such monitoring.

Some of the reasons for inequality are well known and apply to all women; other causes are pertinent especially to widows because of their peculiar social status. There are the general causes such as illiteracy and geographical and social isolation which make it hard for women to learn about their legal rights. There is the problem of the conflict between different systems of law and custom; where there is confusion it is harder for widows to make their claim. Another obstacle is that some constitutions do not make sex a prohibited ground of discrimination, and governments may have 'reserved' on those articles of CEDAW that cover most aspects of widows' lives: marriage; custody; inheritance; land. Another big obstacle that widows face in attempting to challenge decisions at the village level, or in bringing a dispute to a lawyer or court, is their fear of social ostracism. Members of SEWA (the Self-Employed Women's Association) attempting to bring widow agricultural labourers in Gujerat, India, into a minimum wage framework were threatened by the tobacco plantation owners: 'We will kill you'. Similarly, the Bangladesh Rural Advancement Committee (BRAC) staff organising Bangladeshi widows to defend their inheritance and residence rights were menaced by the fundamentalist Mullahs and conservative male village elders. A branch of FIDA in Uganda could only hope to arrive at a 'settlement' for a certain widow who had been robbed of her property and her children, rather than retribution and punishment, because the widow herself feared for her future if her tormentors were arrested.

Widows' rights awareness programmes need to be targeted not simply at widows, but also at those in the community who are responsible for administrative and legal decisions. Police, for example, should be disciplined if they fail to take action, under the penal law, when relatives evict, rob or assault a widow. Village chiefs and elders, magistrates and judges, officials in the state bureaucracy, land registry staff all need to be not only educated about widows' rights, but made aware that they will face penal sanctions if they fail to uphold the law.

And widows must be helped to help themselves, by organising together, networking nationally, regionally and internationally, and by taking collective action, citing CEDAW wherever appropriate. Women's' organisations and women's lawyers groups and university law faculties can help to build up a body of jurisprudence and case law, showing how instruments such as CEDAW, the UN Convention on the Rights of the Child and the regional human rights charters have been used to promote women's rights. The Ghana Supreme Court's decision that a nonconsensual levirate was discriminatory could be used as a precedent in other actions in Commonwealth countries. The Supreme Court of Canada's decision that degrading customs imposed on women can be defined as 'persecution' for the purpose of seeking political asylum could be of weight when widows begin to challenge harmful funeral and mourning rites. The World Bank's programmes, where they ignore widows' access to land and an ecologically balanced environment, or need for employment, can be challenged in collective actions on the grounds that it ignores international legal norms. Widows can be empowered to effect change using legal resources. Test cases resulting from their efforts can make sensational news, and the media can be an effective educator.

NGOS can pressure their own governments and outside agencies to support their work for widows and their children by using those declarations in international and national laws which endorse this effort. If governments fail to assist widows with education subsidies for their daughters - education being crucial to women's improved status - they can report this omission to the CEDAW committee, or directly to the UN Commission on the Status of Women.

Notes

1. Georgina Ashworth, *A Diplomacy of the Oppressed*, Zed Books, London, 1995, p. 5.

2. Convention on the Rights of the Child. UN Doc. A/Res/44/25 (1990).

3. International Covenant on Economic, Social and Cultural Rights, 1966, and International Covenant on Civil and Political Rights, 1966. Both entered into force in 1976.

4. International Women's Rights Action Watch (IWRAW), *Women's Watch*, Vol. 8, No. 2, September 1994.

5. Commonwealth Secretariat, *Manual on Implementation of CEDAW*, Commonwealth Secretariat, London, 1986.

6. Women in Law and Development in Africa (WiLDAF), *Inheritance Law: What It Means for Families in Zimbabwe*, WiLDAF (PO Box 4622 Harare, Zimbabwe), n.d.

CHAPTER 11

Conclusion:
Widows Organising for Change

Previous chapters have described the various ways in which widows throughout much of the world are discriminated against, and are unable to enjoy their fundamental human rights. The anecdotal evidence available demonstrates that where widows can control some resources - house, land, pension, inheritance - or are able to work productively with fair remuneration they are more likely to be regarded with respect than if they are seen only as potential burdens on other kin members.

In order to improve their capacity to obtain the legal, economic and social rights due to them or, where those do not exist, to campaign and lobby for reforms in law and more equity in the interpretation of local custom, widows need to work together by forming their own associations, either under the umbrella of other women-based NGOs or as new grassroots associations. Collective action for her rights is usually more effective in the long run than individual widows fighting alone. Such activities can generate useful media attention, and media reporting can often help to make the concerns of widows into public issues that the whole community becomes aware of.

'Widows must be spirited agents of change' Jean Drèze writes at the end of his study of widows in some northern Indian villages.[1] Widows should be seen not exclusively as powerless victims of male patriarchy and greed who need public support, but as often resourceful and independent heads of households, contributing to the economy and the community. With greater freedom than many married women who are limited by the conventions of the conjugal state, they can be powerful catalysts for social change.

Christine Obbo, in a similar vein, an anthropologist who has conducted field work among ethnic groups in Kenya and Uganda, concludes that in the final analysis whatever the systems of family, marriage and inheritance may be, the important variable is how widows adapt to their husbandless state.[2] This holds true for widows everywhere, whether in the First World or the Third. 'Widows must be wide-eyed, resourceful and tough,' she was told repeatedly during her fieldwork.

Likewise, in the course of conducting interviews for this book, I was continually reminded of how important it was for widows to confront the reality that people they might consider to be sources of support - relatives, officials, strangers - were likely to take advantage of them, and they needed to manage their own affairs without the mediation of others. It was noticeable how much better widows fared when they joined forces to fight injustice and to work together. Many widows, abandoned by the husband's family and unable to return to their natal kin, found that when in need help came from other widows.

Women working together can provide mutual help, especially in times of crisis, as when the husband falls ill or dies, and in the critical period after bereavement. Such support can cover not only the essential physical and emotional requirements - shelter, food, and clothing, consolation and comfort, providing loans, access to income-generating projects, assistance with school fees - but also protecting the widow from extortion and violence, and helping her to obtain legal advice and representation to safeguard her person and property.

The brillliant, funny and honest Zimbabwean feature film 'Nuria,' essential viewing for all widows and their organisations in Africa and indeed in all developing countries, illustrates the value of collective action in telling the story of an urban widow at the mercy of her feckless and scrounging brother-in-law who seizes her house, furniture, children, car, and savings, and then tries to possess her as an additional wife.[3] It is the other women in her sewing group, some of them also widows, who accompany her to a lawyer; the film ends with Nuria's triumph in the court, winning back all the property she lost, while the relative is led away to prison.

Things can change
Shramjivi Samaj

Shramjivi Samaj is a local trade union of the poor in northern Gujerat, India, whose members are mostly women. In 1988, it brought together five hundred poor widows from different villages in the region who gathered in the main square of the largest town to share common problems, and convey a list of their immediate demands to local officials. The culture of the local communities marginalised widows, regarding them as burdens, and discriminated against them in many ways, but their daring amazed the village elders, for their militancy and the precise articulation of their grievances defied tradition. Indeed, the widows amazed themselves by their actions, going public in a patriarchal society where their widowhood was seen as inauspicious, and they were expected to bear their dishonour in silence.

The widows, who were of all ages, ranging from the very old to some who were still children, expressed their anger at the corruption in the local bureaucracy which blocked their access to the small pensions they were entitled to. They demanded legal protection, the right to stay on in their houses; to enjoy the benefits of the modern Hindu Succession Law of 1956; to retain their dead husband's portion of land so that they could feed themselves and their families. They also asked for proper remuneration for the long hours they worked as informal-sector workers in, for example, the tobacco and vegetable fields, as head-loaders, bidi-rollers, paper collectors, and as piece-workers. They wanted schooling for their children and the right to participate in local decision making by having a member on the *panchayat* (local council).

The event was a brilliant success, for the widows had rehearsed intensively for the occasion, holding meetings at the wells, in the fields and, wherever they could, in each other's homes. The local radio and press co-operated and gave them the publicity they needed. Issues that had barely been brought to light before were discussed in public for the first time, and the widows felt encouraged and confident to continue their fight for justice. One consequence was that many more widows began to apply for the state pensions, and the administration, attacked by the media and other political parties for its corruption and indifference, was forced to yield to at least some of the claims made.

Dwip Unnayam Sangstha

Hatia island, Bangladesh, is where the cyclone and tidal wave struck in 1991, killing 3,500 islanders and destroying 90 per cent of the homes. Widows and divorced women, who face a miserable life at the best of times because the status of women in Bangladesh is one of the lowest in the world, suffer the most. Purdah is strict, and widows are often subject to violence if they leave the *bari* or household area. Widows suffer shame if they are forced, as sole breadwinners, to go outside to work. But since 1985 women there have begun to fight back. A remarkable grassroots organisation, Dwip Unnayam Sangstha (DUS)(Island Development Society), financed mainly by Oxfam, has been working to form groups among the landless divorced and widowed women. In 1992 there were over two hundred women's groups, which started off as saving clubs but soon grew into self-help and development groups helping to finance small business ventures such as paddy husking, hiring fishing boats, aquaculture and advising on legal rights.

The DUS work in gender development has been startlingly successful. Groups networking together managed to force a pay rise of 12 taka a day for domestic work and one group paved a muddy track between the bazaar and the well. The DUS has also attacked more fundamental injustices such as male violence. Sabia Katun spoke to the development writer Paul Harrison in 1991.

> 'One of our members was a widow. The neighbours' children were stealing her fruit. When she complained the neighbour beat her with a stick and left a bruise on her arm. Our group sent her to the District Chairman, who did nothing. Then we all went to see him and threatened to go to the police if he took no action. After a lot of pressure, he finally sent a council member to judge the matter, and the neighbour had to pay a fine of 500 taka to the widow.'[4]

The DUS and other Bangladeshi organisations are helping women to take control over their destinies; attacking the discrimination against widows in inheritance and land allocation, and opposing violence, divorce by *talaq*, the dowry system, and son preference.

Organisations for widows in Uganda
Uganda has produced some of the most innovative and effective self-help associations. The long civil war, that only ended in 1986, and the spread of AIDS have made millions of Ugandan women, of all classes, into widows, and forced them to explore ways to support themselves and become independent of men.

Bringing widows together to protest and demonstrate in front of officialdom - judges, village chiefs, administrators, police, members of parliament - has proved an effective way of lobbying for change. The experience of speaking publicly and of articulating needs gives confidence to widows to continue to fight for their rights, and it can show politicians that widows are voters whose loyalties are worth retaining. Such events also provide good copy for the media, thus extending the circle of awareness. In 1994 the Ugandan Ministry of Women's Affairs arranged precisely the same type of event as that organised by the Indian NGO Shramjivi Samaj in Gujerat (see above), so that one afternoon the main streets of Kampala were full of marching widows holding banners and shouting for their rights to home, land, inheritance, personal and property protection and help with educating their children.

Taking control through collective action

These examples demonstrate the potential in collective action by
widows. In these and other actions, widows have on occasions shown
themselves to be in many respects more militant than married women.
The desperate need to earn a living, and freedom from conjugal control,
often drives widows to be more assertive and to adopt more
independent life styles than their married sisters. Even those women
who are illiterate have been able to take charge of their situation, fight
for their rights, control resources, and resist all attempts to subordinate
them.

It is abundantly clear that where widows are able, by custom, religion
or law, to control a resource - such as land, income, pension, livestock,
- and are able to move around without restriction, freed from the taboos
and limitations often imposed on married women, they can become
successful businesswomen, market-traders, landowners, and
decisionmakers. West Africa, Nigeria and Ghana in particular are
famous for the bargaining power and success in trading of older women,
often widows, who travel far and wide buying and selling.

In this book the focus has been on those widows who are oppressed
and made destitute, but for every thousand of them there will be a few
widows who wield considerable power in their families. These
exceptions aside, it is clear from the foregoing chapters that the reason
why widows are among the most discriminated-against of women is their
powerlessness. Because of this they often cannot benefit from new
legislation guaranteeing their human right to be free of discrimination
on the basis of sex or marital status. Their powerlessness stems from
(a) the negative image of widows worldwide, (b) their dispossession of
inheritance rights in land and other property from both their natal and
their husband's family,(c) their lack of any legal protection of person or
property, (d) the interpretation of traditional, customary and religious
practices by a male patriarchy, (e) the burdens of supporting dependants,
(f) their economic dependency due to lack of education and training.

But this can and should change. Widows must organise themselves
to address their common problems and fight to change their image from
one of defenceless dependent beings to that of women with huge
potential. Whilst laws which discriminate against widows - such as
patrilineal inheritance, land rights, pensions - need changing, law reform
alone will not make any difference to the millions of illiterate and
impoverished widows who are subject to the 'living practice' determined
by male patriarchy unless those women are empowered to know their
rights, take action, go to court, and be represented on decision-making
bodies from village councils to national parliaments.

There is so much still to know, to research, to study, to understand. If widows can organise themselves, as they already have in some countries in all sorts of innovative and highly interesting ways, they can assist in this much-needed research, acting as channels for the exchange of information between widows themselves in the villages and innercities, the policy-makers in governments, and NGOs, national and international.

Widows' groups at the local, regional and national levels within countries should be able to network with similar groups and organisations worldwide, thus improving and adding to what is already known. Policy-makers and legislators will be better served: new legislation will have come about because of the efforts of the widows themselves; and thus they will have more investment in its implementation.

Below are brief descriptions of some organisations already working to improve the status of widows.

The Self-employed Women's Association (SEWA) in India

Anyone who has worked in the women-in-development field since the early 1980s will be well aware of SEWA's success in empowering women working in the informal sector. It has organised women working as homeworkers, rolling beedis, making incense sticks, papads, garbage collecting, vegetable hawking, head-loading and tobacco-picking. It now has more than 100,000 members who are investors in the SEWA bank, can get loans and take out insurance for health care. In 1995 SEWA introduced a scheme under which SEWA members could insure against their husband's deaths.This has helped hundreds of widowed SEWA members to survive the trauma and penury of widowhood. By becoming a member of SEWA, even the poorest widow knows she will have kind friends, both in her village and in the organisation's headquarters in the city of Ahmedabad, who will see her through her worst period and help her to sustain herself and her children. SEWA can also assist her with legal advice when she has problems over inheritance and land disputes.

SEWA's success in providing women generally with training, work, markets, unions and co-operatives in the states of Gujerat, Madhya Pradesh and Rajasthan also ensures if a woman's husband gets ill, deserts her or dies. she is already economically self-supporting. This is particularly important once, as we have seen, the type of work a woman does affects directly what happens to her income after widowhood.

Whilst SEWA has not consciously focused its activities on widows, it has provided an important economic support for them. Because it is based in the community, widows find it easy to join. Emotionally vulnerable and fearful of making new social contacts, SEWA is right in their village.

Banuben, a beedi-roller, said: 'After my husband died, as is the custom, I did not leave the house for six months. But Shardaben, the SEWA organiser, came to know of my sorrow and visited me to console me, and made me a member. Then she met my neighbours and made them members and now we all work together.'

Another very young widow, who was already a SEWA member when her husband died just three days before the birth of her fourth child said: 'When Minaben, the organiser from the town, came to see me and bought clothes for the baby, I thought she was visiting to get my membership payment for the bank loan. But it wasn't for that. She came just as a sister, full of goodness and kindness and friendship. Then I knew I had real support, and people who would help me to survive and raise my children. Already my husband's family were tormenting me, but SEWA helped me to fight back.'

SEWA links up local groups with others within the same region and helps women to organise more than one group in the same village depending on the number of workers. The groups are small so everyone knows everyone else. To ensure that the banking system works smoothly, SEWA's savings mobilisers visit the urban areas and the villages once a week to collect the payments. Women have shown extraordinary aptitude for managing their savings accounts, loans and insurance schemes. Childbirth, accident, disease, natural disasters (floods, drought, earthquake), and more recently, a husband's death, can all be insured against.

One hot dry dusty March we headed out to the garment district of Ahmedabad to visit the block-printers, head-loaders and cart-pullers. Belaben and her helper were about to collect the savings payments from SEWA members. They hopped in and out of the shabby old office car, in the middle of busy streets - carts pulled by camels, women carrying rolls of cloth, small boys dashing in between the rickshaws - to greet and be greeted by the dozens of women water vendors, paper pickers, and vegetable hawkers, all busy with their work. A word here, a bit of gossip there, some jokes, and the money is fished out from under the blouse, the sari, the sandal. It all happens in a minute, for time is money for these hard-working women. It is the women who have asked for weekly collections, fearful that otherwise the savings will be spent. The women's hands dart forward with pads of folded notes; some of them are proffering as much as 100 to 150 rupees. One family of grandmother, daughter and granddaughter, all working as head-loaders, each have their own passbook so the incomes can be controlled individually.

We walk the narrow streets off the main road and Belaben calls out that she has come. The word flies around. Even the men are smiling as we walk into courtyards, wave up at windows, or find our way into the backs of the booths, or into the courtyards where members of a large extended family are working as block printers.Eventually we sit down under a tree for shade, and more women come, waving their little books and holding out their money. Someone gets some Coca-Cola, and we are offered betelnuts to chew.

Partiben is a poor widow of sixty-eight, in a tattered white sari, and her lank, wrinkled breasts are easily visible for she wears no blouse, nor a petticoat underneath. Her grey hair flies wildly all over the place, for she has not used any coconut oil since she was widowed when she was twenty-three. The others tell me that she lives all by herself in a rented room, for she only had two sons. One went away to Bombay, and one died leaving a widow and small children who do not want her around. Partiben is a paper picker, collecting paper rubbish for recycling, but even she has some coins wrapped in a ragged cloth. Not only has this old woman understood the concept of saving, and gaining interest on her deposit, but she has even persuaded a neighbour, also a widow living alone, to join the SEWA bank.

In dusty busy Ahmedabad the SEWA headquarters is awash with women coming and going with their savings books. Upstairs on the roof, some of the block-printers are working and drying out printed cloths. In a building across the road, the SEWA video unit is showing the films its members have made themselves of women working together in the villages, organising their savings and income-generating groups, childcare and family planning meetings, crèches and legal support groups.

'Now that we have child care, I can send my older daughter to school. Before, she had to care for the little ones. She is a bit behind but she is clever and will catch up.' Another widow said with a giggle, 'And we are learning how to have fewer little ones, and make some money'.

In the tobacco and vegetable fields, the women are more relaxed knowing that their children are looked after. But SEWA has made them more demanding and more critical of their situation. They laughed and shouted in agreement that in the fields where they work from 7 a.m. until 7 p.m. with one hour for lunch to feed their families, they should be paid not less but more than men. They say, 'We work as hard, we pick more, and we have children to feed.'

BRAC and Prism, in Bangladesh

BRAC (the Bangladesh Rural Advancement Committee) works with women in the villages, helping them to establish themselves in income-generating groups and co-operatives. In recent years it has set up a para-legal programme in which one woman member of the group is chosen for special training in awareness of legal rights for women, including widows. One consequence of this initiative has been that when a widow in the group is confronted with harassment by her relatives, and is at risk of violence or losing her home and property, the group together appeals to the village council for support.

Prism is another NGO in Bangladesh, which provides unattached women, divorced and widowed, with seasonal work in fishpond and duckweed projects. The widows receive not only wages and low-interest loans, but also ownership of shares in the company in return for their labour.

The mullahs and shalishahs have condemned these young development NGOS which are helping women to achieve economic and social independence. The mullahs and conservative village chiefs and headmen, the *zamindars* (landowners) and moneylenders do well when women know their place and stay at home.

TASO in Uganda

TASO (the AIDS Support Organisation of Uganda) was founded in 1987 by a remarkable Ugandan widow, Noerine Kaleeba. It was born from the tragedy of the death through AIDS of her husband Chris. He had contracted the HIV virus through a blood transfusion during an operation in Uganda before he left to study at an English university. He had desperately needed blood after his leg and foot were badly injured in a street accident. In 1983, students, friends and relations willingly donated blood; Noerine could not - which might have saved him - as she was heavily pregnant with their third child.

Noerine suffered greatly as she nursed her dying husband and witnessed his distress and pain. Afterwards she began to meet some of her husband's close friends and make contact with others infected or affected by AIDS. Soon after, this small group of sixteen people (all of whom with the exception of Noerine have since died) decided to set up a support group. TASO grew from there.[5] Its members were wives of men who were dying or dead of AIDS, and couples still battling with the illness. There are people working for TASO today who are in great pain, but they continue as long as they can.

Today TASO is a fully fledged NGO, offering counselling services, information, outpatient clinic care, and homecare for people with AIDS and HIV infection. But as well as providing comfort, care and understanding to individuals and families, it has managed to imbue the widows of men who have died of AIDS with a new strength and sense of independence. In Uganda, as in many parts of Africa where traditional practices are in direct confrontation with public health messages about AIDS, the idea of male polygamy and male promiscuity is still accepted; women have learnt to accept this, and have no power to negotiate about or discuss sexual matters. A wife cannot question her husband about where he has been, and who he has been with; if she did so she would risk being beaten or abandoned as an impossible partner. In TASO meetings women have talked frankly about the impossibility of discussing condom use; yet even the most uneducated of the widows know now that everyone may perish unless there is change, and that education must start right away with the young boys and girls.

Now the widows meet and talk about their lives openly. The TASO workers and staff have 'come out' about their HIV infection. The graceful, beautiful young women I met in the villages and in Kampala are HIV-infected, but look buoyant and bright as they help each other and others to tackle the pandemic and the problems that it causes. Education, training, income-generating projects, cooperatives, loan and credit schemes, help with food, shelter, and school fees are just some of the achievements of TASO.

Widows are coming together, fired by Noerine's leadership and her impassioned determination that Ugandan women and widows will become economically independent and socially secure. It is ironic that it should be AIDS that has made these women so strong. Family planning issues, frequent child-bearing and maternal mortality never had this effect.

Widows and Orphans Society of Kenya
This society was started in 1991, funded in part by ActionAid and in response to the huge increase in the numbers of widows caused by AIDS. It now has village-to-village widows' groups in every five villages in Kenya, with 100,000 widow members who, unless they are completely destitute, pay a modest subscriptions. Hilda Orimba, its founder director, says that half the adult female population in the country are widows struggling to cultivate their farms, educate their children, and deal with the harassment and abuse of relatives. The society offers counselling,

loans to set up income-generating projects, continuing education, advice and legal representation in disputes, and deals with complaints about sexual abuse, rape and violence.

> In Nyanza district eight co-widows of a man who had died of AIDS asked for help with raising fifty children. The society provided low-interest loans for fertiliser and seeds, provided school uniforms made by one of their projects, and trained the co-widows in a sewing project.

Hilda Orimba, a widow herself, was beaten badly by her brothers-in-law after she had suffered a 'ritual cleansing' by them. She says frankly that she did not resist this sexual contact, for 'I was lonely and distressed and I felt desire so I did not resist my husband's brothers. Many poor abandoned young widows come to me asking how they can satisfy their sexual needs when they are sero-positive. Our society is realistic, not prudish, and we give them condoms along with food rations and tell them to find a man who is like them.'

In one village the society was alerted to twenty cases of widows being robbed of their property by the District Officer; in another village widows complained that a local councillor had beaten several widows in efforts to get them to sleep with him. Another group of widows accused a village elder of threatening them with violence if they attended a local widows' meeting. Hilda, in response to this information, organised a hundrd widows to march together to avenge the beatings. The councillor was so frightened by the sight of the angry widows that he jumped through a back window and sought protection from the police! The society has now demanded that all District Officers provide them with full reports on widows' complaints. In addition to the individual help it gives to widows and their children, the society also finds accommodation for destitute homeless widows in members' households, paying rent for them and providing training, tools, food and clothing. It has also begun to rent land for groups of landless widows to cultivate, and assists them to market their crops.

Philly Lutaaya Project in Uganda[6]
Philly Lutaaya was a much admired and gifted Ugandan singer who courageously 'came out' about having AIDS at a time when such openness was rare. The project, administered under the auspices of UNICEF, provides friendship, counselling, practical help, loans, assistance for orphans and training for income-generating to AIDS sufferers and their families, and encourages widows to work together

and help each other in their local communities.

Maria was only seventeen in 1990 when she discovered she was HIV positive. Her lover had died, and she had had two children, one of whom had also died. When Maria's mother discovered she was infected she put her in a small back room and made everyone hold their nose when they visited her. Finally her father took her to Philly Lutaaya to abandon her. They took care of her and she enrolled in the UNICEF 'go public' campaign. Last year, she had earned money and was so much better that she went home for Christmas with presents for all her family, whom she forgave for their cruel treatment of her. Her mother cried for she had thought that Maria was dead.

IrishCare responded to a group of Philly Lutaaya widows who asked for loans to set up a garden cultivating medicinal herbs using their special knowledge of traditional therapies. Now this widows' sub-group has become so successful that the good quality of their herbs, and their wisdom about traditional medicine are well known throughout their region, and traditional practitioners now come to them to purchase their herbal remedies.

Uganda War Widows Association (UWW)

UWW was set up in 1989 to assist the war widows of the Luwera triangle, the region worst hit by the war in Uganda. Women who had fought with the liberators, or had fed and supported the army, or were the widows of men who had been slaughtered and had been left dislocated, starving and without resources all came to the army headquarters begging for assistance. In 1991 there were about 200,000 war widows. The demographic balance had been so upset that the sex ratio was now 2:1. More than half the population was under fifteen. The widows could not find food or pay school fees and many are HIV positive.

UWW counsels the widows, provides them with essentials such as soap, oil, and salt, and most important, tries to help them become self-supporting through income-generating activities. It also provides legal advice when widows are involved in inheritance disputes.

The Widows' Ministry - northern sector of Ghana

In the Bolga region of northern Ghana, the Widows' Ministry, a non-governmental organisation based on Christian principles, not only helps destitute widows evicted from their homes by relatives, but also sexually abused widows. Widows' organisations have been formed in other

African societies in response to the breakdown of traditional family support, and the erosion of widows' land rights. For example, in Burkina Faso a Widows' and Orphans' Society was established in 1977 to help those driven off their land by husbands' brothers.

Using the Media

An intelligent use of the media can create public awareness, and educate widows and their families and community about widows' legal rights. Sensitising the press to cover not only sensational crimes against widows, but also the new ways in which widows are organising themselves to maximise their economic contribution, and to provide community care may change local attitudes to widows, and create a more positive image of such unattached women.

Films such as the excellent Zimbabwean film Nuria (see above) can be not only good entertainment but, more seriously, effective educational tools if shown in schools and village groups. Widows' organizations might consider making up their own stories for videos, as SEWA has done in northern India so that the 'widows' story' aptly reflects local attitudes and customs.

When widows speak out

NGOs, activists, and scholars who help widows to get together so that they can collectively express their needs are well rewarded by the results. Scholar Dr Marty Chen, who, along with Dr Jean Drèze, was among the first academics to study widows in north Indian villages, helped bring together forty-nine of these widows at the Widows' Conference in Bangalore in 1994. Some of these widows had never travelled away from their villages before. Although they spoke different languages, wore different clothes, had different customs, and were of different ages, they came together in their common experience of the humiliations of widowhood. They brought a sense of down-to-earth reality to the academic content of the policy discussions. Although illiterate and unused to structured debate, they were brilliantly clear in their descriptions of their oppression, and their proposals for solutions. These were some of their demands:

'We want our own house. We do not want to stay with our in-laws or our parents. We want the government to give us housing or a loan to build. If we have no land we should be allotted fertile land to cultivate so we can be independent. There should be a law that automatically transfers our husbands' land to us when we are widowed. All rights to this land should be ours until we die. The police should protect us from violence. Education should be free for our children. We want hostels for our school age daughters. We should have the right to retain custody of our children. We want training and jobs. There should be a widow on every *panchayat*.'

These widows had become 'empowered' through coming together, and were determined, as one woman vowed, to ' start the revolution'.

Conclusion

The active participation of widows themselves in any movement to improve their status is crucial to its success. The experiences of some of the programmes and projects described above, and of others equally successful but perhaps less known, need to be shared around the world so that collective action by widows can become a common response to grave breaches of their human rights. The existence of a network of widows' organisations, both within countries and regionally as well as internationally creates an important channel for the exchange of vital information between widows themselves and governments and the NGOs.

As this book goes to press, thanks again to the generosity of the Swedish International Development Agency (SIDA), that network now has a base, a programme, and a name. Empowering Widows in Development (EWD) was set up at the suggestion of an international workshop on widows held at the NGO Forum at the time of the 1995 Fourth World Conference on Women in Beijing. EWD should become, in the near future, as powerful in its advocacy and lobbying on behalf of widows as UNICEF and Save the Children Fund are on behalf of children, Amnesty International on behalf of prisoners of conscience, and Anti-Slavery International is for those in captivity. Through EWD it is to be hoped that the voices of widows will finally be heard.

Widows may be poor, illiterate, marginalised and abused, but they are the only people who truly know what their needs are, and they deserve to be given the opportunity to work with others in achieving them. In organising themselves, widows are taking one step towards involvement in decision-making and being represented in the society that has until now abandoned them to misery and scorn.

Notes

1. Marty Chen and Jean Drèze, *Widows and Well-being in Rural North India*, Development Economics Research Programme Paper No. 40, London School

of Economics, 1992.

    2. Christine Obbo, 'Some East African Widows', in Betty Potash, ed., *Widows in African Society*, Stanford Press, 1986, p. 105.

    3. Funded by the Swedish Development Agency SIDA and made in Zimbabwe, this film is available as a video from Development through Self-Reliance, 9111 Guildford Road, Suite 100, Columbia, MD, USA.

    4. Paul Harrison, 'Living Dangerously', *People* (published by the IPPF), Vol. 18, No. 3, 1991, p. 6.

    5. Noerine Kaleeba, *We Miss You All*, TASO (PO Box 10443, Kampala, Uganda) and Women and AIDS Support Network (WASN), Zimbabwe, 1991.

    6. See Chapter 6, note 20.

Index

abortion, 2, 185; clandestine, 78, 156; criminalisation, 113
ActionAid, 203
adultery, 78
Afghanistan, 127; Family Code 1921, 132; women, 169
African Charter on the Rights and Welfare of the Child, 131
agriculture: mechanisation, 37; work, 29, 38-9, 154
AIDS/HIV, 1, 35, 73-5, 78, 86, 89, 92-3, 120, 122, 142, 145, 173-4, 185, 190, 197, 202-5; behaviour changes, 77, 110; brides, 2; changing pattern, 81; economic impact, 83; fear of, 132; female circumcision link, 82; health costs, 99; official denials, 85; orphans, 95; polygamy, 90; rape, 88; support groups, 97; transmission, 13; widows, 14, 84, 87; women's vulnerabilty, 98
Amnesty International, 207
Andhra Pradesh, 44
Anti-Slavery International, 207
Anti-Slavery Society, 20, 144
anxiety, 156
Aquino, Corazon, 185
ashrams, 161

Bangalore Widows Conference 1994, 20, 47, 61, 121, 135-6, 206
Bangladesh, 10, 20, 29, 39, 42-3, 65, 84-5, 108, 114, 127-8, 140, 145, 150, 157, 159; constitution, 182; Ministry of Women's Affairs, 158
Bangladeshi Rural Development Committee (BRAC), 121, 134, 189, 192, 202

Bantu people, 107-8
begging, 35, 40, 159, 162
Bhatt, Ila, 48
Bhutan, 150
Bible, the, 51
Bihar, India, 7, 135-6
black, wearing of, 16
Bosnia, women, 79
Botswana, 32, 55, 63, 155; census, 1; mourning rituals, 13
Brahmins, widows, 33
Brazil, 148
brick breaking, 36
brideprice, 3, 15, 53, 112, 127, 159, 190
brides: child, 140; harassment, 19
brothers-in-law, 27, 29, 59-60, 64, 119, 137, 159
Burkina Faso, Widows and Orphans Society, 206
Burundi, 166

Cairo Declaration on Population and Development, 104, 131, 180
Canada, 181; Supreme Court, 193
Caribbean, the, 155
carpet-making, 144-5
castes, Hindu, 8, 10, 18, 116, 134, 158
census surveys, 31
Chad, 74, 150
Chen, Marty, 3, 25, 31, 54, 157, 206
Chikore, Judith, 55
children: brides, 127; care facilities, 48, 118; childhood definition, 131; childlesness, 4; custody, 16, 109, 112, 130; debt bondage, 94; labour, 30; widows, 4, 14, 19, 25, 28-30, 41, 43, 53, 90, 95, 103, 108, 111, 116, 118,

children *cont.*
134, 141-4, 186
China, 148, 156; one-child-one-family
policy, 151, 153
Choto, Robert, 84
Christian missions, 162
cleansing rituals, 14, 77
Clinton, Bill, 181
co-mothers, 111
co-widows, 3, 87, 91, 138, 151
co-wives, 3, 77, 87, 91, 93, 159
cohabitation, 3
Commonwealth, the, 182
condoms, 88, 91, 204
constitutions, 182-3
contraceptives, use, 151, 185
Convention on the Elimination of
All Forms of Discrimination against
Women (CEDAW), 5, 47, 52, 54,
63, 67-8, 73, 103, 129-30, 179,
181-6, 192-3; monitoring, 191
Copenhagen Social Summit, 131
courts, traditional, 23
credit, gender bias, 48
crime, 143
Cuba, 150
cultural relativism, 180
customary law, 58, 61, 126, 140, 180, 184,
190-1; colonialism, 62; patriarchal bias,
55, 63, death, ceremonies, 9

debt bondage, 26, 30, 145
Declaration of Rights of Older Persons,
UN, 163
Defence of Children International, 127
Demographic and Health Surveys, 128
demographic change, global, 152, 162
depression, 156
diet, prohibitions, 18
dishonour (zina), 138
division of labour, gender, 23, 37
documentation, lack, 141; obstacles, 64
domestic service, 29-30, 40-2, 48, 144,
146
Dominican Republic, 154
dowries, 117, 135-6, 138, 140-1, 190, 197;

deaths, 154; harrassment, 158;
murder, 19
Drèze, Jean, 3, 30-1, 54, 64, 68, 157, 194,
206
Dukawa people, Nigeria, 111, 119
Dumdumia refugee camp, Bangladesh, 176
Dwip Unnayam Sangstha, Bangladeshi
NGO, 196-7

education, 114, 29-30, 42, 33, 136, 163,
183, 185; access, 151; cost, 95, 207;
importance, 138; lack, 132, 155; law,
186; state expenditure, 30
Empowering Widows in Development
(EWD), 164, 207

family planning, 76, 180, 185;
associations (FPAs), 73, 76
Federation of Women Lawyers Africa
(FIDA), 56, 67, 96, 98, 121, 142,
187-8, 190, 192
Felton, Monica, 124
female longevity, 156-7
female-headed households, 90, 155
Fertility and Health Surveys (FHS), 83
fish farming, 42
formal law: importance, 141;
ineffectiveness, 55-7, 61, 66, 132;
reform, 68
Forward-Looking Strategies for the
Advancement of Women (FLS), 5, 52,
99, 128, 163
Fourth World Conference on Women,
Beijing, 73, 104, 163, 178, 182, 207
France, 181
fundamentalism, religious, 14, 84, 192
funerals: expenses, 25-6; rituals, 8-9, 12,
186

Gambia, the, 125
Gandhi, Indira, 79, 185
genital mutilation, 2; health effects, 76, 82
Ghana, 74, 96, 98, 112, 153, 182, 186,
198; Akan people, 10; legislature, 187;
Supreme Court, 184, 192;
Widows' Ministry, 96, 98, 112, 205

Ghiladi, Doctor, 145
Global Plan for Action, 1995 (GPFA), 5, 52-4, 67, 104, 163, 178
Gonshashtaya kendra, Bangladesh NGO, 176
Greer, Germaine, 71, 74
grief, 24, 74
Guatemala, 145
Guinea, 128
Gujerat, India, 12, 26, 28, 30, 36, 38-9, 44, 63-4, 192, 195, 197, 199

Harrison, Paul, 151, 197
health care, 72-3, 85, 185; access, 151; appropriate, 96; expense, 145
Hindu law, 63, 66, 113, 115; Succession Act 1956, 57, 63, 67, 196
homeworking, 33-4
'honour', 73
household slavery, 29

illiteracy, 155, 192, 198
immigration policies, western, 170, 176
India, 10, 20, 29, 64-5, 114, 125, 127, 150, 154, 156-60, 184; census, 1; Communist Party, 37; National Sample Survey, 32; north, 25; proposed pension scheme, 47; widow mortality, 18
Indonesia, 148
informal sector, economy, 24, 29, 31, 33, 36, 40, 48, 143, 160, 185
inheritance, 13, 83, 102, 122; conflicts, 58; disputes, 56; 'endogamy', 68; lack of rights, 23, 63; laws, 67, 187, 197; unequal, 51-3, 56-7, 66, 75
institutionalisation, old people, 157, 162
International Criminal Tribunal, Arusha, 79
International Declaration on the Elimination of Violence against Women, 179
International Federation of Women Lawyers, 16
International Labour Organization (ILO), 34, 144

International Planned Parenthood Federation, 73
International Research and Training Institute for the Advancement of Women (INSTRAW), 31
International Research Centre on Women (IRCW), 156
International War Crimes Tribunal, The Hague, 174
International Women's Rights Action Watch (IWRAW), 129
Iran, 132
Irish Concern, 97
IrishCare, 205
Islam, 54, 139; law, 62, 65-6, 78, 113, 187; marriage, 138, 140
Ivory Coast, 120; Baule people, 107

Jamaica, 11
Jews, Orthodox, 16, 109
job inheritance, 28, 33
jurisprudence, feminist, 181

Kalaayan organisation, 42
Kaleeba, Noerine, 97, 202-3
Kapanda, Lily, 60
Karnataka, India, 43, 120
Katun, Sabia, 197
Kenya, 29, 68, 74, 84, 89, 91, 96, 110-11, 162, 172, 194; parliament, 187; Widows and Orphans Society, 96, 203
Kerala, India, 43; public food distribution, 44
Kerala refugee village, Pakistan, 168-9
Khan, Ananullah, 132
Kikuyu people, 110
Koran, the, 51, 113, 114
Korea, Republic of, 148, 150, 156

labour: child, 143-5; gender restrictions, 23, 33; statistics, 31; sweatshops, 40; unwaged, 31
lacemaking, 34
land shortage, 11, 51
Latin America, 152
Lboyo, Emily, 188

legal rights, lack, 150; uncertainty, 191
legal systems, plurality, 52
Lesotho, 63; census, 1; mourning rituals, 10, 13L
levirate custom, 15-16, 51, 54, 74, 77, 83, 86, 102, 105, 108-12, 122, 182
life expectancies, gender difference, 148-150
literacy rates, 186
London: Brick Lane area, 33-4; east, 11
loneliness, 102
Lopata, Helen, 12
Luo people, 17, 32, 106, 110-12, 119; cleansing rituals, 14

Maharastra, India, 13, 135
Malawi, 28, 39, 52, 56, 60, 63, 68, 94, 121, 133; antenatal clinic, 84; National Commission on Women and Development, 59
Malaysia, 156
Mali, 128
Manu, 134
marriage: arranged, 20; child, 129, 132, 134, 138, 190; definition, 105; disavowal, 3; forced, 183; inter-ethnic, 109; Muslim, 115; *sororate*, 53; types, 58
Marris, Peter, 11
matrifocal families, Caribbean, 112
media: use, 69, 190, 196, 206
medicine, herbal, 161
menopause, 107, 149
mental health, 156-7, 171
Mexico, 148, 150
midwives, traditional, 161
Mies, Maria, 34
migration, 11; urban, 40, 91
moneylenders, 25-6
monogamous societies, 152
Morocco, 144
Mother and Child Health Facilities (MCH), 76
Mother Teresa, 162
mothers-in-law, 62
mourning rituals, 8-10, 13, 77, 92, 186

Mozambique, 52, 170, 171; refugee widows, 175
Mysore, India, 30
Mugabe, Robert, 51
Museveni, Janet, 84, 95

Nandi people, 32
Nasir Bagh, widows' refugee camp, Pakistan, 168
neglect, intra-household, 47, 158
Nepal, 29, 150; Supreme Court, 67
Niger, 128
Nigeria, 74, 111, 198; Hausa people, 16, 20, 119; Yoruba widows, 11
Non-Governmental Organisations Forum, Beijing, 2, 8
Nuria, Zimbabwean film, 195, 206
nutrition, 28

Obbo, Christine, 194
older populations, 148, 152
older women, knowledge, 154
Orimba, Hilda, 203, 204
Orissa, India, 44
orphans, 94-6, 152, 169; orphanages, 162
Oxfam, 42, 176, 196

Pakistan, 10, 20, 65, 108, 114, 150; Afghan women refugees, 168
panchayats, 12, 45, 47, 61, 64, 122, 184, 196
Papua New Guinea, 150
patriarchy, 23, 72, 106
patrilineality, 53-4, 64, 68, 126, 198
patrilocality, 53, 68, 126
pensions, 12, 24, 43-4, 48, 55, 120, 151, 155, 161-2, 188, 196; application obstacles, 45-6
Philippines, the, 42
Philly Lutaaya project, Uganda, 90, 96, 98, 190, 204-5
polygamy, 56, 58, 106, 113, 138, 141, 151, 190, 203; AIDS risks, 90; customs, 10
positive discrimination, 182-3
Potash, Betty, 3, 31, 54, 104, 109, 112, 119
poverty, 11, 23, 27-8, 31, 48, 99, 102, 118,

poverty *cont.*
127, 135, 142-3; feminisation, 162
Principles for Older Persons, UN, 164
Prism, Bangladeshi NGO, 139, 141, 202;
    Zavir of, 115
Prodhan, Chobi, 36
'property grabbing', 59-60, 62
Proshiko organization, Bangladesh, 25
prostitution, 35, 40, 72, 84, 91-2, 95, 99,
    143; accusations of, 8, 17; child, 30,
    145
purdah, 10, 24, 33-4, 113, 134, 137, 145,
    158, 196

Radcliffe-Brown, A.R., 109
Rajasthan, 135
rape, 15, 19, 41, 71, 73, 77-8, 87, 127,
    141, 167, 171, 173-4, 180, 185, 204;
    'law', Serbian, 174; AIDS risk, 88
re-marriage, 15, 18, 102, 104, 108, 113,
    115-16, 118-20, 128, 130, 134, 139,
    183; coercive, 103, 106, 114, 191;
    patterns, 105, 107; widow opposition,
    121-2
reciprocal care arrangements, 162
Red Cross, 177
refugees, 166; Rohinga Muslim, 176;
    women, 167-8, 173
Relief Agency for Palestine Refugees in the
    Near East, 177
research, demographic and health, 104
ritual cleansing, 83, 86-7, 191
road construction, 36
Rukuba people, Nigeria, 77
Rwanda, 79, 166, 169

safe sex, unavailable, 85
Salic law, 51
Sati (ritual immolation), 18, 116, 134
Save the Children Fund, 207
Self-Employed Women's Association,
    India (SEWA), 26, 48, 121, 137, 192,
    199-201, 206
sexuality, 71-2, 75, 86; double standards,
    88, 91; fear of widows, 79; violence, 129
Shalaya, Bangladesh, 184

Sharia law, 65, 114
Shramjivi Samaj, 195, 197
Slavery Convention, 1926, 128
SM Otieno case, 110
small businesses, 38
social services, cutbacks, 154
Social Summit, Copenhagen, 163
Somalia, 171
son preference, 135
Sri Lanka, 42, 156
structural adjustment programmes, 27,
    30-1, 99, 133, 154, 190
suicide, 18-19, 79, 113, 173
Swaziland, 112; census, 1; mourning ritu-
    als, 10, 13
sweatshops, 40
Swedish International Development
    Agency (SIDA), 207

Tamil Nadu, 44
Tanzania, 107; Swahili people, 108, 119;
    Swahili widows, 114
Tenth International AIDS Conference,
    Japan, 81
Thatcher, Margaret, 185
Third World debt, 31
time allocation studies, 29
Titmuss, Richard, 47
torture, 167
Townsend, Peter, 102
traditional birth attendants, 96-7
traditional healers, 97
traditional societies, structural changes,
    11, 54, 108, 144, 167; AIDS impact, 85
trauma, 167; post stress disorder, 171

Uganda, 66, 68, 74-5, 86, 88, 96, 98,
    20-1, 152, 159, 161-2, 189, 194, 202,
    204; 1972 Succession act, 56; AIDS
    Control Programme, 83-4; Association
    of Women Lawyers, 98; Ministry of
    Womens' Affairs, 190, 197; plantations,
    37; War Widows Association, 96, 98,
    190, 205; Widows Efforts to Save
    Orphans (UWESO), 98
unequal pay, 30

United Nations, 153; Children's Fund (UNICEF), 86, 98, 129, 177, 204-5, 207; Commission on the Status of Women, 193; Convention on the Rights of the Child, 130-1, 146, 179, 192; Convention relating to the Status of Refugees, 170; Development programme, 177; High Commission for Refugees (UNHCR), 78, 166, 172-6; Human Rights Committee, 178; Social Development Commission, 163; Statistical Office (UNSTAT), 31; War Crimes Tribunal, The Hague, 79; Women's Convention, 103

United States of America, 181; USAID, 182; widows, 12

Universal Charter of Human Rights, 180

Universal Declaration of Human Rights, 185

urbanisation, 11

Uttar Pradesh, 63, 135

UWESO training programmes, Uganda, 95

Vienna Declaration of Human Rights, 73, 104, 178

Vienna International Plan on Ageing, 164

Vietnam, boat people, 170

virginity, 127, 132-3

Voluntary Service Overseas (VSO), 163

West Africa, 107; widows' independence, 32

West Bank, the, 150

West Bengal, 63

westernization, 111

White Threads (Bengali film), 17

widowers, 8-9, 103, 105-6, 149-50, 154, 189

widowhood: definition, 3; initiation, 7

widows: abusive names for, 21, 72; AIDS, 94, 99, 103, 119; child, 90, 116-18, 124-5, 129, 133; collective action,

195-201, 204, 207; constitutional guarantees, 182; data, 2; destitution, 36; elderly, 148, 151-2, 155, 157-61, 168, 176; health, 71; HIV infected, 75, 82-3; images of elderly, 153; inheritance rights, 184; Kurdish, 174; legal rights, 181, 185, 188, 190; myth of son support, 156; refugee, 78, 166-7, 169-72, 175; reproductive health, 73, 78; 'riot', 120; rituals, 16; sexual pressure, 13-14; sexuality, 89; status loss, 4; war, 132; workload, 26; young, 106

wills, 56, 65-6, 120

witchcraft, accusations of, 8, 13, 16, 57, 93, 153

Women in Law and Development Africa (WiLDAF), 69, 189

World Bank, 26, 170, 175, 180, 193

World Conference on Human Rights, 1993, 180

World Food Programme, 177

World Health Organization (WHO), 2, 81-2, 84-5, 129, 177

World Population Data Sheet, 1995, 150

Yemen, 127-8

Yugoslavia, former, 166, 169

Zaire, 169

zakat (Pakistani tax), 24

Zambia, 15, 33, 55, 62, 84, 179; 1989 Interstate Succession Act, 57, 187; census, 1; mourning rituals, 10, 13; poverty assessment study, 26

Zia, Kalida, 185

Zimbabwe, 32, 68, 84, 86, 88, 95, 111, 143, 152, 162; African Marriages Act, 56; census, 1; Food for Work Programme, 36; Harare Legal Project, 188; Harare municipal housing, 27; independence, 52; inheritance laws, 189; Law Project Office, 121; mourning rituals, 17; Women's Resource Centre, 55